HUMAN
CARTOGRAPHY

JANOS SZEGÖ

HUMAN
CARTOGRAPHY

MAPPING THE WORLD OF MAN

Swedish Council for Building Research

© Text, maps and diagrams: Janos Szegö

Translation:	Tom Miller
Cover and typography:	Arne Öström, Förlagsateljén, in cooperation with Janos Szegö
Reprography:	Sture Göthe, City Engineering Office, Gävle
Colour separation:	Magna Repro
Computer-drafted maps:	The Central Board for Real Estate Data
Typesetting:	Uppsala Fotosättning AB
Printing:	Spångbergs Tryckerier AB, Stockholm 1987

Permission for distribution of maps of Sweden granted by the security officer of the National Land Survey, 1987-06-22.

D14: 1987

ISBN 91-540-4781-1

Swedish Council for Building Research

Table of contents

Prologue: From reality to model 7

INTRODUCTION 9
A monastery in Crete, or why are computer-drafted maps so lifeless

THE MODEL: THE WORLD OF HUMAN CARTOGRAPHY 15
The crystallized flow of the past

AN INTERLUDE: The model perceived from the viewpoint of art 36

Part I: From model to map

Observations from the "north": the model viewed in the perspectives of
different sciences 39

THE MAIN TOOL OF CARTOGRAPHY: THE INDIVIDUAL MAP 41
    The components of the map 41
    The major types of maps and their means of expression 44
    The geographical elements of the map 48
    The functional elements of the map: The setting, the actors and the play 52
    Cartographic design 82
    The statistical map: characteristics, design, types 88

THE MAP IN ITS CONTEXT: MENTAL SCANNING LINES AND
SCANNING STRATEGIES 104
    The zero map and mental scanning lines (M. Nordberg) 105
    A shaft through time (C. McEvedy) 109
    Channels in time-space (C. McEvedy and R. Jones) 114
    Wanderings in time and space (M. Gilbert) 118
    An enriched cartographic language (dtv-Penguin Atlas) 127
    A new synthesis and its precursors (the Times Atlas and W. McNeill) 128
    The third element (The Atlas of the Classical World) 135
    The map in its context: a comparative summary 138

Part II: From today's map to tomorrow's. Human cartography in practical applications: Census cartography for urban and regional planning

Part II: From today's map to tomorrow's.
Human cartography in practical applications:
Census cartography for urban and regional planning 147

INTRODUCTION 149

BACKGROUND 150
  The field of activity of urban and regional planning 150
  The planner's environmental image 153
  The demands of urban and regional planning concerning planning data 157
  Organizing information 158

CENSUS CARTOGRAPHY TODAY
  Three levels — three implemented projects 160
  I.   A local atlas 161
  II. Maps for regional planning 172
  III. A census atlas on the national level 188

TOWARDS THE HUMAN CARTOGRAPHY/CENSUS CARTOGRAPHY
OF THE FUTURE 196
  Technical prerequisites — a brief outline 196

  Four steps towards the future 199
  I.   Cartographic development based on the cartographic methods and
       technology of today 199
       1. More effective information strategy 199
       2. More effective choice of maps 200
       3. More effective organization of maps 201

  II. New cartographic methods based on today's technology 202
       1. Further development of individual map types 205
          A) development of dot maps 205
          B) development of symbol maps 210
       2. Development of systems for cartographic analysis 211
          A) Calculations of influence 211
          B) An overview of cartographic information 220
          C) Mapping change 220

  III. Improving the cartographic methods of today aided by the technology
       of tomorrow 221

  IV. New cartographic methods based on the technology of tomorrow 223
       1. An enriched language of computer cartography 223
       2. Composite models — presentation, simulation 224
       3. Shifting approaches, levels of detail, modes of presentation 224
       4. Information overviews — cartographic information analysis 226
       5. Traps to avoid 226

CONCLUDING OBSERVATIONS 227

SOURCES AND BIBLIOGRAPHY 233

Prologue: From reality to model

Introduction

A monastery in Crete, or why are computer-drafted maps so lifeless.

The destruction
of a monastery

The monastery at Arcadia in western Crete was built on the edge of a precipice. It is hard to imagine this quiet, rather remote place as the scene of the turbulent events which took place here on November 9, 1866. That was the day the monastery became the last place of refuge for rebels struggling to liberate Crete from the Ottoman Empire. They had retreated there after a hard battle which was raging fiercely as the Turks pressed the defenders back along the narrow pathways leading up to the monastery. No matter how hard the defenders resisted, they could not stop the numerically superior Turks who finally succeeded in blasting open the monastery gates behind which the defenders were ensconced.

The assault
recreated

When it had become clear that the battle was lost and that all that remained was complete defeat and the vengeance of the victors — which they had cause to dread — Gabriel, the abbot of the monastery, grabbed a torch, rushed down to the cellar which was now serving as a powder store, and blew himself, the defenders and the attackers to smithereens. More than 800 people were found in the ruins.

In spite of the peaceful character of the spot, it is easy for a latter-day visitor to visualize these events. Nearby the monastery, an indoor model has been constructed which reproduces the entire course of events. The model provides an accurate, three-dimensional reproduction of the terrain, the cliff with the monastery and the paths leading up to it. Within the model, large red arrows flash in sequence to illustrate the advance of the besiegers and the retreat of the defending forces. The noise of battle pours forth from loudspeakers. The clang of clashing weapons, shots, shouts from combatants and the wounded, the detonation when the monastery gates are breached and lastly, the final explosion which blows up the walls of the monastery destroying everyone within.

Arcadia of today is a place where the memory of the past is honoured, and where people gather each year to pay homage to the fallen. It is hard, even for a visitor without any personal relation to the spot and the events which took place there, not to be moved by the force of the scene depicted by the model.

The central
problem: to
translate reality
to map

And this fact gives rise to a question which is not restricted to Arcadia and its history. The question is this: How can situations, episodes and courses of events in the history of mankind be reproduced in a way which enables

9

the viewer to recreate a mental image of the illustrated phenomena? And the same question could be posed in the following manner by a cartographically-inclined human geographer: How can we create cartographic illustrations of human activities which take place on the surface of the earth which enable the viewer/reader to reconstruct the illustrated conditions and events for himself?

The model in Arcadia is not at all remote from the cartographic mode of presentation. What we see there is a three dimensional, iconographic model of the terrain (the landscape realistically depicted in a reduced scale) with some symbolic, dynamic elements (the arrows which symbolize the advancing movements, and which by their sequential appearance create the dynamics of the model) accompanied by a reconstructed audio background. In other words: a three-dimensional, combined iconographic-symbolic, dynamic model which is audio-visual in nature.

If we were to mount a camera above the model and open its shutter every time a new arrow lit up, a series of repeated exposures would create a map of the type often used to reproduce battles, migrations, and other dynamic courses of events.

The chain is thus   reality $\rightarrow$ $\begin{array}{c}\text{iconographic}\\ \text{model}\\ \text{dynamic}\end{array}$ $\rightarrow$ map

and the relations of the three stages to one another are simple and easy to comprehend.

The question which then arises is the following. Arcadia is a special case. Can a *general* relationship be found between reality and map — a model which enables a cartographer to illustrate, as clearly as in Arcadia, not only single, dramatic events, but even those frequent activities which may be trivial in and of themselves, but which together constitute human existence?

Human Cartography: maps *about* people *for* people

How can actual events and processes in the world of man be translated into maps, and how can this translation be made comprehensible and accessible for the human brain? The aim of this project is to seek the answer to this two-sided question. And it is this two-sided orientation of the task at hand: to create maps *about* people *for* people, — in other words: conforming to human needs and capacity — which is summarized in the title of the project: *Human Cartography.*

Computer cartography makes its entry — a retrospect

Great expectations (concerning computer cartography in the 1960's)

The origins of the project are related — as are so many other things — to advances in computer technology. The entry of computers into the field of human geography in the mid-1960's — in Sweden predicted and initiated primarily by Torsten Hägerstrand — aroused great expectations. Now that great amounts of data could be analysed systematically and presented with the aid of computer-guided drafting machines, it was believed that an entirely new type of human geography would emerge along with an equally new cartographic language.

10

During the late 1960's and early 1970's there began an intensive period of development. The computer-guided ink-jet colour printer (in Sweden called the "paint sprayer") was developed, as were a number of mapping programmes for computer-controlled line plotters using ink pens as drafting tools.

The maps drafted with the new technology could reproduce a large quantity of information, but their cartographic language was not very refined or subtle. This was initially not considered a major problem. In the first place, the material presented was considered primarily to be basic input data for analyses, which could later be edited for use in presentations. Secondly, it was expected that mastery of the basic methods of computer cartography — from the creation of geocoded input data to the actual drafting of the finished map — would make it possible to devote more time to developing and refining the language of computer cartography.

... are only
partially fulfilled

These predictions have not come to pass. Although a certain amount of progress is being made in refining the modes of expression of computer cartography, by and large, the language has fastened in the forms of the early 1970's. These map types certainly have much merit: Dot maps, grid maps, isarithmic maps, hatched colour maps etc. have a great deal of flexibility and can be used to illustrate many different situations. They are, however, insufficient if they are to represent the entire vocabulary of computer cartography. The mode of expression of computer cartography needs to be renewed and enriched.

Maps should
speak (and
speak
eloquently)

There is, moreover, a further reason for renewal: Computer cartography has not evoked the response from urban and regional planners which it would appear to deserve. Neither have researchers been as enthusiastic as could have been expected. The reason can probably be found among a number of factors including a changing outlook on urban and regional planning. Attitudes towards quantitative methods in research have also changed. But beyond this, we have to consider the possibility that deficiencies in the maps themselves have contributed to the lack of interest — unimaginative cartographic design, the lack of a powerful, well-articulated cartographic language, the fact that the computer-drafted maps did not "look like" maps.

There may, moreover, be a more profound cause concealed behind the fact that the computer-drafted maps "don't look like maps". It may be that the computer-made maps only captured certain narrowly defined aspects of human existence while ignoring other, perhaps more important, phenomena. Furthermore, it might also be true that even those aspects of human activity which can be reproduced on computer-drafted maps are illustrated in such a way that the actual meaning of the maps is only imperfectly comprehended by the viewer.

A development in
the background
(world history
recreated in maps)

Another line of development which received much less notice was taking place parallel with the process described above. The publication in 1964 of a pocket atlas, dtv-Atlas zur Weltgeschichte, can be said to be a milestone in this process.

11

Atlases of world history and of the historic development of certain regions were formerly produced for use in education and research. These earlier atlases often had a richness of content and a level of technical standards which remained unexcelled until quite recently. However, dtv-Atlas zur Weltgeschichte represented a modernization and renewal of the cartographic language and mode of expression which differed substantially from previous works.

The new mode of expression seemed to be a result not only of new methods of cartographic illustration, but also of a more profound understanding of the illustrated processes. (See the colour supplement, figures 1 to 13.)

dtv-Atlas was only one of a series of historical atlases which were published at an apparently accelerating rate from the early 1960's. The periodic appearance of new historical atlases gave the impression of a steadily increasing volume of publication. An analysis done after the fact showed that, contrary to appearances, the rate of publication was quite constant. (See figure 37.)

These atlases gave evidence of an extremely varied orientation and design. Taken together they provided a rich sampling of the different ways of illustrating human activities in a time continuum.

What is concealed beneath the surface? (The artistic anatomy of human maps)

The many historical atlases which appeared in Sweden during the last 25 years, especially those which were available before 1980, comprise perhaps the most important source of data for the study at hand. These atlases have been subjected to thorough examination in order to understand the thought patterns on which their design language is based. The point of departure for this analytical work has been the hypothesis that corresponding approaches could be useful in the design of computer-drafted maps and could contribute to enriching their language.

It is thus not a question of trying to reproduce the superficial appearance of these maps, but rather an attempt to comprehend the conceptual structures on which they are based. In this sense then, the study is not concerned with the "morphology" of the maps, but rather with their intellectual "anatomy".

Applying the lessons to capture the present

Insights gained in the analysis shall primarily be applied to the field of urban and regional planning and more precisely to "census cartography", i.e. cartographic presentation of census results. The censuses attempt to capture the patterns of distribution and movement of the population within a given area at a given point in time. This is a present-day equivalent of the reproduction of historic episodes and courses of events. Furthermore, the study and presentation of demographic conditions is an essential part of all urban and regional planning — one of the fields with many applications for computer cartography. Census cartography is, therefore, considered to be an interesting component in the arsenal of urban and regional planning tools. Its prerequisites and framework correspond then to the conceptual world of urban and regional planning.

Cartographic design is an active endeavour which cannot be studied merely by observing the activities of others — especially not if one intends to contribute to its development. One of the most important reference sources for this report has, therefore, been the author's own experiences during a 20 year period as active cartographer primarily within the fields of urban and regional planning and urban geographic research. This work has taken place largely within a planning organization and in close touch with many other planning bodies. In addition to the experience gained through working in the field, this setting also made possible "participant observation" in the informal conceptual world of urban and regional planning. These experiences too shall be utilized in the work presented here.

In connection with the preparation of this report, several new methods have been developed for analysing the contents of historical atlases. These methods would appear to be useful in several other fields, in theoretical as well as practical applications.

The focus has, however, not placed on particulars, but rather on developing a global perspective. The intention is to summarize the ideas and concepts regarding the mapping of events in the past, the present and in a planned or predicted future. The work focuses on combining the cartography of research and planning, but also of literature, legends and dreams to create a comprehensive picture. The aim is to outline a theory of "human cartography" which should provide a more profound understanding of these maps, but also contribute to their more effective application and — hopefully — a refinement of their design language and mode of expression.

This book has been prepared in order to develop a *conceptual outline*. The main objective must be to capture the totality of the conceptual structure which slowly began to reveal itself piece by piece during two decades of work within the field. The work was done against the background of current Swedish and international developments in the field documented in the international scholarly literature of human geography as well as thematic cartography. The primary objective of this study is, however, the outline of a theory of human cartography — a structural framework, major features — rather than detailed theoretical discussions relating to each source.

As the term "human cartography" indicates, the project touches on several areas of the humanities, history, historical geography, but first and foremost human geography, and within the field of human geography most especially on time geography. The starting signal for the project sounded — without the author being aware of it — in the spring of 1966, at the seminar at the Geographical Institution in Lund where Torsten Hägerstrand introduced the time geography research project. Torsten Hägerstrand intended to study the present and the future, not analyses in an historical perspective. He stressed aspects of system theory, the links between the daily routines of individuals and the complex network of actions, their opportunities and limitations which together shape the limits and reality of human society. But, in the sketch with which Torsten Hägerstrand described the time-space linkage, the author could not help but see history taking form, see time and events deposited like sedimentary rock, see — in the patterns of "human geology" thus created — the spread of peoples and cultures like tissues formed from the lives and destinies of individuals. Finally, it is this view, this evasive while at the same time persistent and recurrent image which, along with the succeeding years spent studying human geography and its practical applications, forms the real basis of this work.

Almost twenty years went by before these ideas could be transformed into an actual research project. A preliminary study was implemented in early 1980 with support from the Swedish Council for Research in the Humanities and Social Sciences. During these few short months, the work's central models assumed distinct shape in the mind of the author. But the allotted time was too short to commit the concepts to paper. It was not until 1985 that the project itself was initiated with support from the Swedish Council for Building Research and the Central Board for Real Estate Data. The author wishes to express his sincere gratitude to these two government bodies for their support and their understanding attitudes during the course of the project.

Olof Nordström, assistant professor of Geography and Hans Regnéll, professor of the Theory of Science were kind enough to read the author's manuscript and offer many valuable comments. Unfortunately, it has not always been possible to follow their advice. Despite the generous support given to the project, it was still not possible to carry out the work with the thoroughness required by this comprehensive subject. It must be stressed once again that the book which is hereby delivered to the reader is a conceptual sketch which seeks a holistic view. It should in future be expanded, enriched and anchored within various fields of science. It is, however, the hope of the author that until this can occur, the work will contribute constructively to the intensive developments now underway in this broad and fascinating field of research.

Gävle, Sweden in June 1987

Janos Szegö

The model: The world of Human cartography

The crystallized flow of the past

The life path of
a young Cretan

Let us return in our imaginations to Arcadia in Crete and consider one of
the battling Cretans. We can envisage him as being 25 years old at the time
of the siege, born and raised in that very village. His life path, plotted
according to Hägerstrand's model where the horizontal plane represents a
segment of the Earth's surface and the vertical axis stands for time, would
be straight and vertical: He was born in Arcadia, spent his whole life there
and never moved or changed his place of permanent residence. This is the
case if we plot his life using a small-scale approach with a high degree of
generalization (figure 1A). If we examine his life path more thoroughly, in
more detail, a completely different pattern emerges. We see a myriad of
journeys, short and somewhat longer, of which the shortest, numerically
predominant ones are concentrated to the immediate vicinity of the home
in which he lived until the siege of the monastery. We observe somewhat
fewer but longer journeys made in connection with his daily work. We see
him making these journeys between his dwelling and the olive groves and
pastures in which he toils. We can imagine all these movements marked by
exceedingly fine lines in the time-space framework. The life path, represented by the bold vertical line in figure 1A, is formed where the density of
these fine lines is highest. Beyond the life path, the lines are so sparse that
they are not visible without special scrutiny.

Let us now select a random journey made by the then only 17-18 year-old
Cretan, and follow him for a few moments on his way home. We register his
journey in a special way by viewing it through a camera which hovers
motionlessly above the surface of the Earth. We photograph him at a point
in time t_1, again at point t_2 (a brief moment later), a third time at t_3 (with
the same interval as between t_1 and t_2) etc. (see figure 1C).

The life path is
captured in
images

We envisage the first photograph and all the successive ones as being
recorded on extremely thin sheets of film. On each of these sheets, our
Cretan is depicted by a dot which penetrates the entire thickness of the
film (figure 1D). If we now lay the sheets of film one on top of the other, all
of these dots will form a more or less contiguous line in the three-dimensional time-space framework (figure 1E). The thickness of a sheet of film
represents the space of time which elapses between the taking of two
pictures. The total thickness of all the sheets of film represents the duration
of the journey.

Observed from above, the path formed by the dots representing the ob-

15

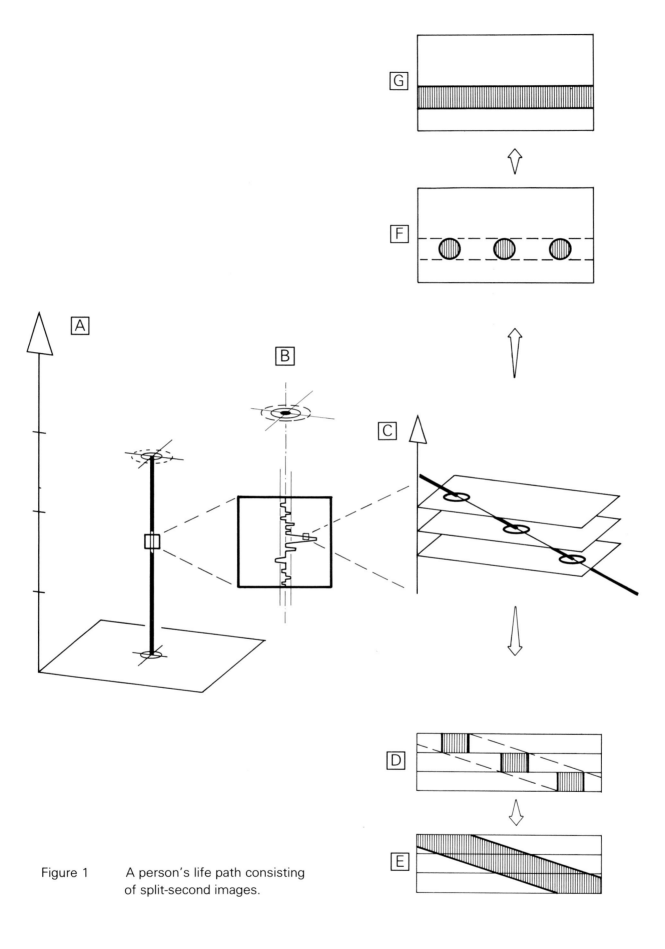

Figure 1   A person's life path consisting
of split-second images.

served positions of the Cretan at three different points in time describes our man's movement on the map (see figure 1 F-G).

The life path — the generalized life path as presented in figure 1A — is formed where the density of the dots is highest. It is surrounded by an inner zone where the individual's movements are relatively frequent, but do not occur often enough to be visible without careful scrutiny. Surrounding this is another zone where the density of the movement lines is even lower. (See the black core area surrounded by two concentric zones with fading visibility above the life path in figure 1B).

The geographical history of a family

Figure 2 presents an example of how the life path appears when observed from above and "from the side" respectively. This figure shows the life paths of some members of the young Cretan's family. The broadest line is his own. It emerges from the life path of his mother who moved to Arcadia from a nearby village, and whose path thereafter runs parallel with his father's who was a native of Arcadia. His older sister, whose life path is depicted by the broken line, got married and moved to her mother's native village. Both parents barely survived the death of their son.

If we observe the family's life paths from above (see figure 2A), their geographical aspects stand out — represented here by the movements of the two women. The chronological aspects, however, cannot be discerned. If, on the other hand, we follow the cluster of life paths "from the side" (figure 2B), the chronological aspects of the family's life history become visible — the genealogy of the family. But now the geographical aspects disappear completely. The distance between the two villages, for example, and the movements of the two women cannot be observed at all.

The photographic image which reproduces our man's journeys in figure 1C is represented by a rectangle.

This photograph could, however, be round — the camera with its circular lens makes round images, but we crop them into squares or rectangles better suited to the formats of our books and magazines.

So let us imagine our Cretan youth reproduced on a round sheet of film. He is easily discernible since he has been photographed from low altitude by our perpendicular — and as we soon shall see — very special camera. It hovers freely in time and space following only the courses determined in our minds.

And we now order it to rise straight up into the sky and to follow this upward trajectory until it enters into a geostationary orbit. And while our flying camera continues to reproduce our man image by image on the way to his home, the contents of the pictures changes minute by minute.

The perspective is broadened

First the circular surface of the photographs is filled by our observation person and the cultivated landscape through which he passes. Soon the range of the camera broadens, however: it captures the Mediterranean to the north and Mount Ida to the south. After a few more seconds, Crete

17

appears as the island that it is, surrounded by the Mediterranean Ocean — with our man as a very tiny, but fully discernible speck in the centre of the picture. Soon we can make out the north coast of Africa, the Greek archipelago, the coasts of Asia Minor, Peloponnesos. The camera continues inexorably upward, and the images with their radiant colours capture greater and greater portions of the Eurasian continent and Africa. Soon it is the curvature of the Earth which sets the limits — but our wondrous camera continues to collect visual information beyond the bounds of the Earth's curvature, and does not stop on its journey until its circular image includes the entire surface of the Earth.

Let us now forget this fantastic camera and consider its no less fantastic photographs.

We can imagine these circular, infinitely thin images approx. 5 metres in diameter, transparent yet shimmering with colour, materializing out of thin air before our feet. After a brief examination, we can distinguish their major components: the outlines of the continents where the deep blue of the oceans brightens into emerald green; the huge expanses of vegetation; the deepening early-summer greenery of the Mediterranean region melting into the lighter shade of the late-spring deciduous forests to the north; the dark green of the evergreen belt in the northern hemisphere with the slight suggestion of paler shades which mark the lacy spring crowns of deciduous trees; the ochre and reddish tinges of the great desert to the south and east bordered by savannahs turning yellow, which little by little melt into the rich, deep green of the rain forests. All this and more besides can be perceived at a brief glance standing beside the image, but if we lean closer, we can distinguish individual small dots, often forming clusters of various sizes — the record of people, individuals, captured at a single instant, spread in varying patterns across the surface of the earth.

If we refrain from purposely influencing the course of events, i.e. the presentation of the images — we must assume that it is completely within our control — a new image, identical to the previous one in size and composition, will soon appear above its predecessor. The images are extremely similar, but the latter presents the surface of the Earth captured a unit of time — let us say a minute — later. This is shown most clearly by the changes in the swarms of dots: comparisons between two successive images show that some of the individuals have moved.

And now the images appear at a steadily-accelerating rate and are collected one above the other in a slowly growing pile. We can follow the progress of a day — the sunlit parts of the image soon take on warmer, darker tones as the sun sets and is succeeded by the dark of night while other areas are lit up by the rising sun. Soon we see the seasons progress across the continents; the shift from spring to summer, autumn and winter in certain parts of the Earth, the rotation of dry and rainy seasons in others, and in still other regions, the barely discernible changes between the different phases of the year. We can accelerate the rate of change so that days and seasons hardly can be distinguished any longer. In the growing pile of images which represent increasingly long periods of time, and which slowly sink

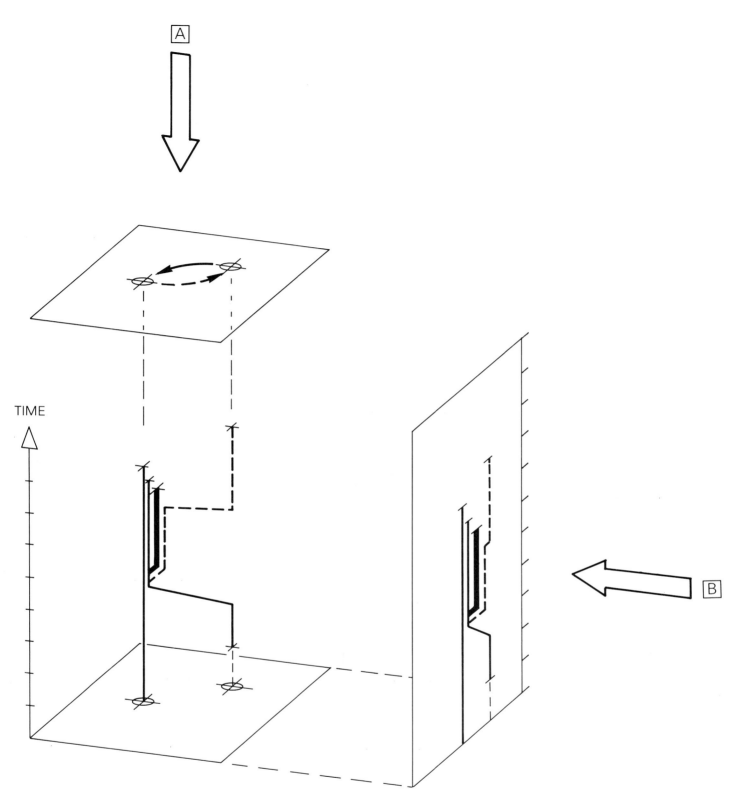

TIME

Figure 2   A cluster of life paths: the bibliography of a family
            observed from spatial (A) and from chronological (B)
            viewpoints.

down at our feet so that we can continue to observe them from above, the quickest historical changes begin to appear, shifts in the expanse of zones of vegetation, and we can even begin to perceive how the outlines of the continents slowly — slowly are transformed.

If we bend forward and observe the features of the images carefully, we can distinguish, image by image, the tiny dots and the more easily visible clusters. When the images replace one another slowly, we can discern the position of single individuals minute by minute. When the images are projected at a more rapid rate, we can catch sight of how the successive dots coalesce into 3-dimensional lines which reproduce the movement of each individual within the volume formed by the pile of images. We can distinguish them within a cylinder formed by all the round images together, and which together represent and reproduce the entire visible history of the Earth during the period under observation. We can follow the major features of its development through the variation in colours within the volume. If the outlines of the continents have been unaltered during a period, they appear as vertical, transparent columns, tinged with the shades of the vegetation, surrounded by the green and then ever-deepening blue of the oceans. If the ocean has made inroads in one area, the column will slope in towards its centre, and its surface area will be diminished. If the expanse of vegetation has been unchanged during the observation period, each vegetation zone will form a vertical column, coloured through in the characteristic shade of the predominant flora — although a more thorough examination will also reveal the rotation of the seasons.

A more complex pattern is created by the life paths formed by the coalescence of the dots which mark the occurrence of individual people at certain given points in time.

If we wish to study this pattern at some time in the distant past, we must leaf our way down through the circular, colourful column. By doing this, we lift off, make invisible, that part of the model which represents the events of later epochs. When we delve down to an era thousands of years earlier than our own, the clusters of dots on the circular surface we are viewing become small and sparse. If we now allow new images to appear, and follow the pattern formed by the life paths of individual people, we will find small bundles of paths which create rhythmically changing patterns in the shape of spirals or other periodically recurrent movements (see figure 3A). They represent the systematic wanderings of nomadic peoples which correspond to the rhythm of the seasons. These patterns of movement persist for long periods of time, and are thus homogeneous elements of a lasting nature. Intertwined, individual life paths coalesce to form the life path of the clan (the tribe, the people, the civilization), and appear in the model, when observed from a slightly greater distance, as a single, straight or slightly winding, perpendicular stem.

If we continue our journey in time and space — we let the circular, transparent images be piled one on top of the other to form the transparent, shimmering, colourful model — small, but slowly growing groups of people appear whose life paths are mainly vertical. These small, thin

The Earth's past captured

The rhythm of events

20

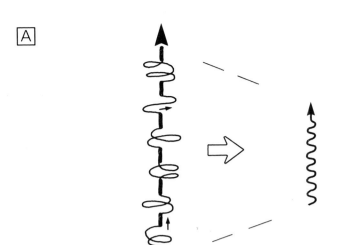

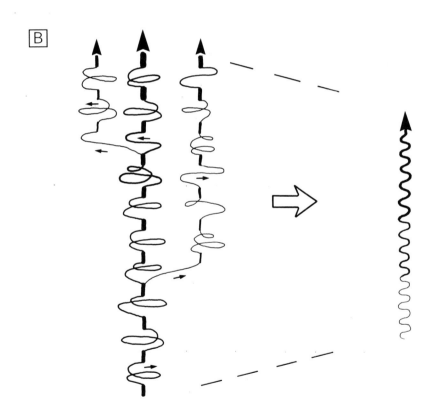

Figure 3   Periods in the existence of a group of (for example) nomadic people and their simplified representation. Life paths with even, balanced rhythms (A) and during a period of expansion (B).

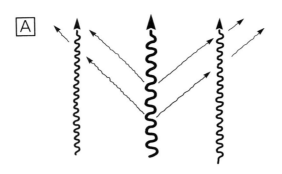

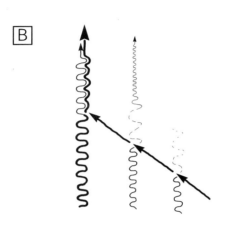

Figure 4   Oblique streams: the dissemination of information, knowledge etc. (figure A) and a migratory people who, in the course of their wanderings, destroy a tribe, weaken another and conquer a third but are absorbed by it (figure B).

bundles of perpendicular paths represent individuals in permanent settlements whose entire lives are spent in and around the same habitation, and whose journeys all focus on this point. Some of these people move and unite with other groups, others are more mobile, but the basic way of life continues.

The flow of life paths becomes more abundant — the population grows, more and more life paths are woven together into ever denser, thicker bundles — villages appear, and small then gradually larger towns develop in the heart of agricultural districts. The movements between these clusters, the connecting strands, become increasingly numerous and systematic, creating evermore complex patterns. Periods of even, balanced existence are replaced by growth, development (see figure 3B).

The fertile
tissue

From time to time, flows of individuals of a completely different type make their appearance. They are bundles of individual paths running not vertically but obliquely within the model. Viewed on individual images, these paths appear as swarms of dots in continual motion. When an obliquely-moving stream of individual paths meets a perpendicular flow, a collision may occur. The oblique stream may only pass through the vertical one, but when it has gone by, the perpendicular stream will often have become sparser, less well-organized than before. A wave of migration has washed over an urban or agricultural civilization leaving destruction in its wake (figure 4B).

At other times the oblique stream may stop near the vertically rising web of individual paths. The continual motion ceases, and the paths of the oblique stream become intertwined with the stationary one — a migrant people has conquered a highly-evolved civilization, but perhaps also been absorbed by it (see figure 4B).

An oblique flow can also break up a perpendicular one, transform it into a huge, dry river-bed and take its place as the stationary vertical element in the time-space framework: a migrant people has driven away another population group, and taken over its territory.

Moving "oblique" streams are not always so aggressive: an abundant, dense, perpendicular stream may send out a constant flow of life paths to other regions, near and far, where the oblique paths of movement once again become perpendicular: the migrations from overpopulated regions to other, less intensely-exploited ones which have taken place throughout human history (see figure 4A).

In a similar way, it is possible to identify and systematize other types of patterns formed by the life paths of individual people, interwoven into evermore complexly-organized webs in time and space. These life paths will usually adhere to one of the three basic classes of movements: the stationary, vertical life path; the rhythmically-oscillating pattern of continual motion which, when observed from a greater distance, appears as a single, perpendicular stream and, finally, the single, non-recurrent movement.

If we actually enter "into" our model and really observe the individual's life path close up, a pattern emerges which is even more complex. Around the life path of each individual, a cluster of paths appears, representing not people but other living beings or objects. Buildings, which are often unifying elements for several, often for many, human life paths, are the most obvious and easy to distinguish, not only on account of their size, but also because of their completely vertical nature. But the life path of each individual person is enveloped by flows of trajectories — life paths or existence paths — belonging to objects which often have longer life spans than man himself. Because of this, they often unite several, sometimes many, human destinies. Works of art such as jewellery often have this quality. They are kept long after their creator or previous owner has been forgotten. But most of the objects with which people surround themselves do not have this quality, instead their "life paths" are interrupted much earlier than those of their users, perhaps to appear again hundreds or thousands of years later as reconstructed archaeological objects in a museum.

Thus our model appears in its totality: the transparent, round, shimmering column radiating colour and encompassing the surfaces of the oceans and the continents throughout history, with their swarming abundance of vegetation and other visible phenomena of the surface of the Earth. This iridescent, vividly coloured cylinder is, moreover, interwoven by a growing number of increasingly intertwined bundles of life paths belonging to people and other living beings but also to objects and to buildings.

The riches of the Earth

Up to now we have observed the images while they were appearing before our eyes and piling one on top of the other in front of our feet. Now we step closer to them and wander around the cylinder formed by the combined circular images. In order to establish our position, we introduce a perpendicular pair of axes, a "north-south "N" — "S" and an "east-west" "E — W" axis (see figure 5) which are only loosely linked to geographic realities. Their main purpose is to help us to locate ourselves on the circumference of the cylinder, and has nothing to do with the civilizations which happen to exist at these points of the compass.

Shifting facets (the model observed from different sides)

When we begin our tour around the cylinder — which may conceivably rise above our eye level — we realize quite soon that it, to all appearances, has polarizing qualities. We can peer into the interior of the cylinder from all directions, but the streams of trajectories — the life paths of people, objects and other phenomena — as well as the columns formed by continents, vegetation zones and oceans which together make up the three-dimensional model, take on different appearances depending on our vantage-point along the periphery of the cylinder. It is not solely a shift of perspective which takes place, instead the various elements appear in different illumination and with varying degrees of intensity depending upon from where they are observed.

In the mirror of legends and myths

If we are close to the "South Pole" — i.e. where the "S" axis passes through the periphery of the cylinder — the streams of trajectories, life paths and the events they represent appear in a very special, shimmering light. The interwoven life paths representing the destinies of groups of people, tribes, entire nations are hidden behind iridescent veils of light, and are replaced by a small number of persons, or small groups of people in whose actions and experiences long historic periods and complicated contexts are re-created in compressed form. Situations, events, and episodes, compressed in the model, are here seen through the veils of legends, myths, poetry and emotions. This is the side of the model where we meet Odysseus drifting on his raft on "the wine-coloured sea". Here we see Theseus, the Prince of Athens, involved in a life or death struggle with the Minotaur monster in the labyrinth in Crete, and following the thread of Ariadne back out after his victory; here too we meet Sinuhe the Egyptian in the company of the dreaming pharaoh Eknathon; but we also meet the brave soldier Svejk who is searching for a way to survive in a world gone mad; and here we discover Selma Lagerlöf's Nils Holgersson riding on the back of Martin

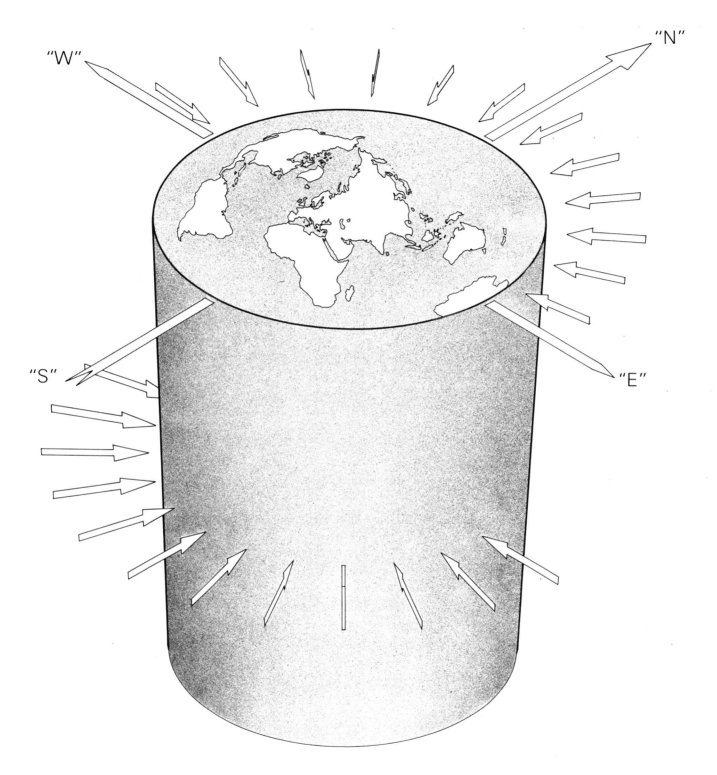

"W" "N" "S" "E"

Figure 5   "The crystallized flow of the past" — and various
perspectives for observing it.

the goose in the company of a flock of wild geese, and listening to words of wisdom from Akka of Kebenekajse whose often pungent but — sometimes — heartwarming, emotional commentaries evoke profound echoes within us.

If we continue our wanderings around the model and pass the "east" axis, the appearance of the model changes dramatically. The veils of emotions, legends, and poetry — these warm, shimmering and highly charged, but sometimes dark and spiteful veils — disappear. (There are evil legends too, malignant slander, malevolent falsifications of reality, deliberate, propagandistic misrepresentations, emotionally-charged descriptions which also belong to the southern part of the cylinder.) They are replaced by a cold light, but one in which the interior structure of the model appears clearly and sharply. The web of individual paths which make up the model appear plainly and distinctly — or just the reverse: disappear almost entirely, are reduced to traces during periods for which we lack knowledge about them. This is the model observed by science, the scrutinizing eye of the scientific method.

In a colder light (the model seen from the scientific vantage point)

We realize quite soon that although the illumination is similar along the entire periphery of the cylinder from the "east" to the "west" axis, the model appears differently from every single point along its periphery. Seen from one particular point, the life path of every single human being stands out quite sharply — except where segments become invisible or barely visible because of insufficient knowledge about them — while all other elements recede into a more diffuse background. We have observed the model from the point of view of the demographer. If we move just a short distance further away, we can see a totally different combination of elements. Organic patterns of human life paths are still major features, but they are more succinct, less detailed, and lack the complete dominance they enjoyed from the previous observation point. Instead, different kinds of "life paths" appear, trajectories of buildings and objects, but also environmental conditions which together create the prerequisites of human productivity. We observe the model of our world from the standpoint of the economist.

The changing image

If we move a few more steps, the combinations of trajectories, bundles of life paths once again change radically. Now we only see the life paths of a relatively limited number of individuals and certain groups. Instead, the existence paths of special objects stand out very distinctly. Their conjunction with individuals, groups and events can often be seen as clearly as the life paths of the people from whom the objects are derived. We study our model from the point of departure of the history and theory of art.

In this way we move step by step, and while we continue to direct our attention to the model, we see how the constellations, the assortment and combination of visible elements, change — how first one, then the other category of phenomenon gains prominence, and how the rest subordinate themselves or become totally invisible.

When we pass the "north" axis and continue on towards the "west",

26

however, a major change occurs. Now the webs of human life paths, while still visible, are relegated to a subordinate role. Instead it is the life paths of other living beings — animals and plants — which become predominant. The life paths of human beings remain only as disturbances seen from the point of view of animals and plants.

The model also contains other kinds of visual elements: a small segment of — say — a plain covered with vegetation does not have its own life path — it cannot move, it is only crossed by the life paths of mobile individuals. But just as a building has a life path, a vertical trajectory, so too does each unit of area on the surface of the Earth. The components of the trajectory are those periods during which the constitution of this surface area is unchanged. One phase may comprise a period of abundant growth of grass, another — several years later — of scrub followed by a "forest period". Within the "grass phase", dry or moist periods can be distinguished, and even the briefer rotations of spring, summer, autumn and winter.

As we thus approach the "west" axis, the latter type of trajectory becomes preponderant. We are now at that part of the cylinder's circumference from which the natural sciences study the surface of the Earth and events which take place there. Seen from this point on the circumference of the model, man is only one of the actors, and indeed, during long periods of time, not even a major one. We find ourselves on the territory of zooecology, phytoecology and other branches of the natural sciences which have the *surface* of the Earth as their field of study.

As was stressed above, when we choose to observe our model from a certain point on its periphery, we are choosing to focus on certain elements in the infinitely complex model, to make other components subordinate to these and to exclude all the rest. In this way we obtain a model which is still three-dimensional, but which has become much less dense. Nevertheless, the wealth of information is still overpowering. How can we then scan, explore its content, and especially its interior geometry?

We can start by examining two extreme approaches. We can choose to completely ignore the time dimension of the model, and to isolate, refine its spatial aspects.

In that case we are not dealing with the entire model, but rather with one single image which presents situations at one single moment in time. We then scan its surface point for point, determining the geometric position on the Earth's surface of each point — each single individual, each object but also of every other spot on the image. Indirectly this also provides the relative geometric relationship of all of these points. In order to implement this survey, we must, however, disconnect our image from the continuous flows of events among which it belongs. We gain geometric precision at the cost of knowledge about the position of the elements in a time sequence. We thus obtain an isolated, purely geometrical, if you will, *geodetic, synchronous* or — to use a relatively little-known geographical term — *chorological* record of the surface of the Earth. This approach is symbolized by the

27

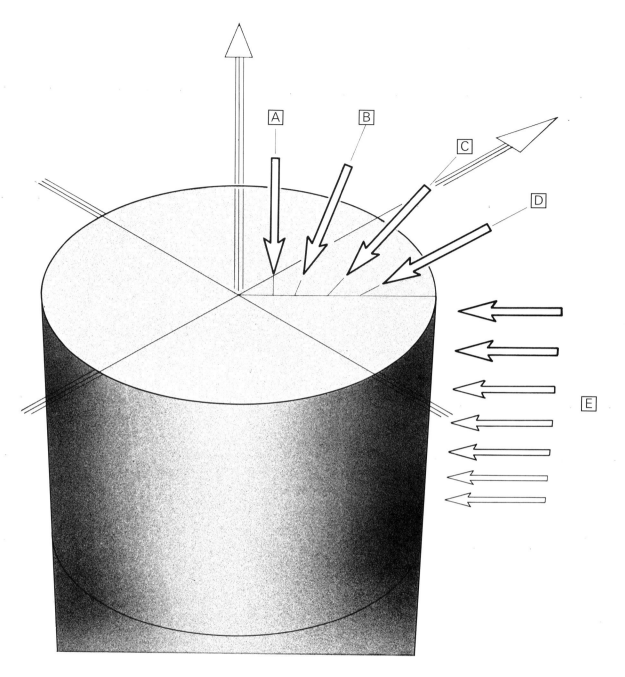

Figure 6   Observing the present and the past: geometrical (A),
             geographical (B), historical (D) and chronological (E)
             approaches.

arrow "A" in figure 6 which is aimed perpendicularly towards the picture
plane of the model. We can imagine that we scan the surface of the image
point for point using this approach. Our gaze is focused on the surface of
the image, and does not penetrate it.

We can also choose another extreme approach for studying the content of
the model. We can select a bundle of trajectories and follow their course
through time. We observe at what point in time the trajectories start and

stop (when a person is born and dies, when an object is created and ceases
to exist), which individual phases can be distinguished in their paths, and
how these trajectories are related (see figure 2B). We then study how long a
person lives in a certain locality, for example, when he gets married, when
he has children, how these children in turn get married, intertwining the
family's life path with those of other families, how they move etc. In all of
these observations, however, it is the time-related aspects which are predominant as well as the logic of the changes occurring at different times.
Where on the surface of the Earth these changes occur is of minor importance. The spatial aspects can be inferred indirectly from the time sequence, but they can also be completely concealed within the changes. We
are dealing with an extremely time-oriented approach that can be labelled
chronological or *diachronic*. The vertical row of arrows, designated "E" in
figure 6, represents this approach. The arrows suggest that the observer
has moved along the model parallel to the time axis, and is observing the
path of the trajectories in time. This type of study can, for instance, result
in a chronological table of events, a chronicle of kings, a genealogical table
containing chronological data on the lives of individual persons, a numerical time series showing a country's population growth (see figure 26 from
McEvedy-Jones) or similar tables.

Both of these extreme approaches have great merit. The former approach
allows us to capture characteristic, absolutely critical moments in a sequence of events, and to infer the relative geometric relationships of the
components of these events on the surface of the Earth or on a selected
portion of it. If we apply the *chronological* approach, we can obtain a very
clear image of chronological or logical relationships among different events
in time. But both approaches also involve considerable limitations. If we
wish to interpret the geometry of a photograph, we generally have to be
acquainted with the series of events leading up to the situation depicted in
the photograph and preferably also with developments taking place after
the photograph was taken. If, on the other hand, we trace how different
existence paths are intertwined in time, i.e. use a chronological approach
— sooner or later we must try to comprehend where these paths are
located in geometric terms — otherwise we will not be able to interpret the
observed course of events.

Let us take a concrete example. Assume that we use a perpendicular
camera to capture all the people in a town during a morning rush hour. A
map based on the photograph will show a myriad of dots — a number of
individuals — spread across different sections of the town. The image can
prove very difficult to evaluate. At worst it may appear as a confusing
cluster of specks. Assume on the other hand that we have taken a series of
photographs with, let us say, 1 or 5 minute intervals. If we lay these photographs side by side, or let them fade into one another, we are then able to
see how people leave their dwellings and journey to different sections of the
industrial districts of the town. The single photograph which was so hard
to interpret assumes its logical position in a sequence of events which ends
a moment after the photograph is taken when the majority of the recorded
individuals have reached their places of work. The photographic sequences
have retained their predominantly spatial quality. By introducing a

29

chronological aspect, we replace the *geometrical* character with, if you will, a *geographical* quality. It is this combination of a predominantly spatial approach with respect for the chronological component which is represented by arrow "B" in figure 6 with its slight deviation from the perpendicular. (The direction of the arrow indicates that we scan the surface of the photograph primarily to determine the geometry of the uppermost image, but that we also examine the layers lying directly underneath in order to investigate the time factor.)

If, on the other hand, we choose to stress the *time-related* aspects of a sequence of events, but at the same time introduce the relative spatial locations of the individual events which together constitute the sequence of events, we are using what can be called an *historical* approach instead of a purely *chronological* one. Arrow "D" with its slight slope symbolizes this approach. Examples of graphic presentations with this balance between chronological and spatial aspects are provided in the colour supplement, figure 24.

Finally, arrow "C" symbolizes a balanced situation where the spatial and time-related aspects are given equal treatment. This approach can be difficult to define, but examples can be found in certain works of human geography which stress the importance of evolution, the passage of time for the emergence of geographical patterns (for example Spencer-Thomas: Cultural Geography, 1969) or in the works of historians who use models of spatial interaction and the diffusion of innovations to define and describe the major elements in the history of human civilization (McNeill: A World History, 1967).

Focus on the future

A huge majority of the analyses which devote attention to the time factor deal with events and processes in the past. This type of analysis can, however, even be future-oriented. It can aim either at forecasting events or at intervening actively in order to guide them in the direction of predetermined goals (forecasts and plans respectively).

Figure 7 attempts to illuminate the problem. We choose a point in time in the past, and ignore events which occurred earlier. Accordingly, we cut a horizontal section through the model, and observe it from below. We define an area which we analyse, and we determine a target date in the future for which we try to forecast developments (see the circular area bounded by a broken line surrounding a square).

Planned and forecast visions of the future

We have, even in this case, various alternatives for stressing chronological or spatial aspects respectively. We can choose to view the entire forecast area as a homogeneous unit within which we do not differentiate our forecast. We can make a forecast for an entire country, for example, perhaps even an entire continent without taking into consideration its inner, geographical differentiation. We treat the flow of population as a continuous stream, and we monitor its development through time. We can label this alternative *prognostic* (arrow F in figure 7). We can also select a more geographically-oriented approach. We take into consideration the spatial distribution of the population, for example, and its consequences within

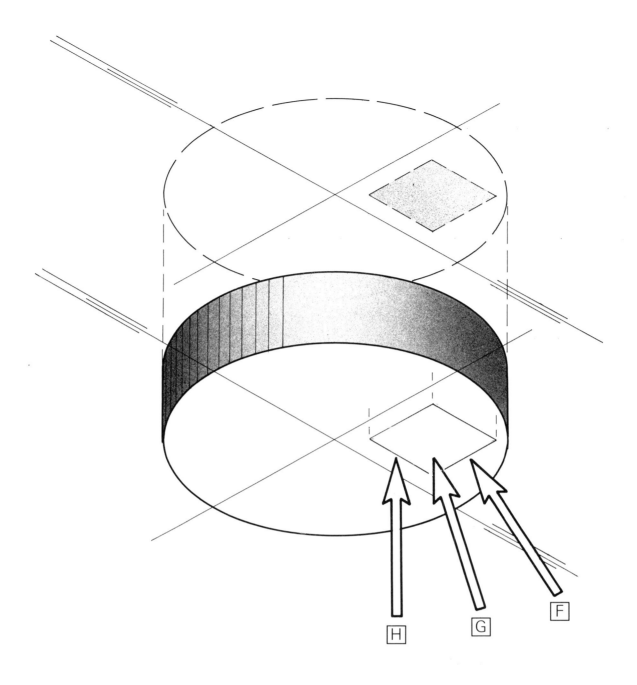

Figure 7   Viewing the future: prognostic (F) and planning-oriented
            (G) approaches respectively.

the forecast area. We attempt to forecast the effects of this distribution on population development, and perhaps, to influence the future spatial distribution. We can call this a *planning-oriented* approach (arrow G in figure 7).

The two latter terms are quite arbitrary. It is certainly conceivable to apply spatial concepts to pure forecasts. An examination of the planning literature gives the general impression, however, that spatial analyses are carried out primarily in situations where they result in concrete plans.

31

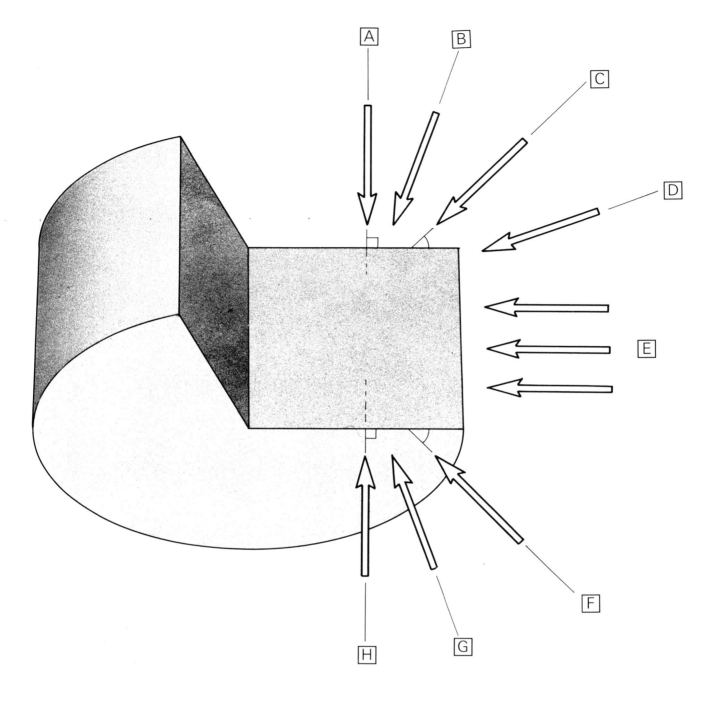

Figure 8   The entire spectrum of approaches: geometrical, geo-
            graphical, historical, chronological, prognostic and plan-
            ning-oriented.

We can exemplify this concept with the help of a section taken through the circular model (figure 8). The section represents demography's point of entry into the model. The arrow "A" then represents the determination of the geographic distribution of the population at a selected point in time. "B" represents the approach of population geography, "D" the study of population development with attention also devoted to geographical aspects ("census history"), "E" cohort studies (the study of the development through time of a selected population group without any further consideration of geographical aspects) "F" population forecasts, "G" plans for population development.

Similar series can be constructed for all other cross-sections corresponding to all branches of science which — quite consciously — have not been specified here, or all their various concerns. A trial series is outlined here for the history and theory of art. "A" represents the determination of the geographical location of objects of art, artists etc. at a point in time which has not been selected through developmental analysis ("art topography"). "B" represents geographical analyses of the spatial distribution of objects of art, styles, and techniques in which attention is also devoted to time-related aspects of this distribution — an attractive, but relatively unexplored field within the history and theory of art. "D" represents investigations in art history which also stress the importance of geographical conditions. "E" symbolizes chronological studies of art. "F" and "G" are activities which, as far as is known, are not carried out in the field of the history and theory of art, and probably never will be either.

Art's vision of the future

Within the "southern region" of literature, art and poetry, a descriptive approach is predominant focussed primarily on the past and the present. But even here there are future-oriented accounts. Belonging to this category are utopias, prophesies and other accounts describing future situations which are imagined, foreseen, desired or feared.

Each branch of science investigates the world on its own terms. In the language of the model, this means that each discipline chooses its own points of entry along the periphery of the model — which also means limiting the content of the research — and chooses a methodological approach for scanning the model. Of course each branch of science deals with a spectrum of different concerns. In the terms of the model, this means that each discipline seeks entry to the model along several points or vertical lines which, however, are usually close to one another. Since certain issues are dealt with in more than one discipline, a certain amount of overlapping must take place among the expanses of the different disciplines along the periphery of the model. It must be stressed, however, that this only applies to branches of science which deal with phenomena which are visible on the surface of the Earth.

Models of the model: changing scientific paradigms

From time to time, a new paradigm emerges within each discipline, in figure 9 symbolized by three cylinders with "points of the compass" added for the purpose of orientation. They are clustered along a path representing the entry line to the model of an unspecified discipline. The vertical position of each small model corresponds with the period during which the paradigm was predominant.

If we now inspect these "small models" individually and compare them with each other, we obtain a picture of how the paradigm, content and methodological approach of this unspecified discipline have evolved. In other words, we acquire a representation of the respective disciplines' doctrinal history.

33

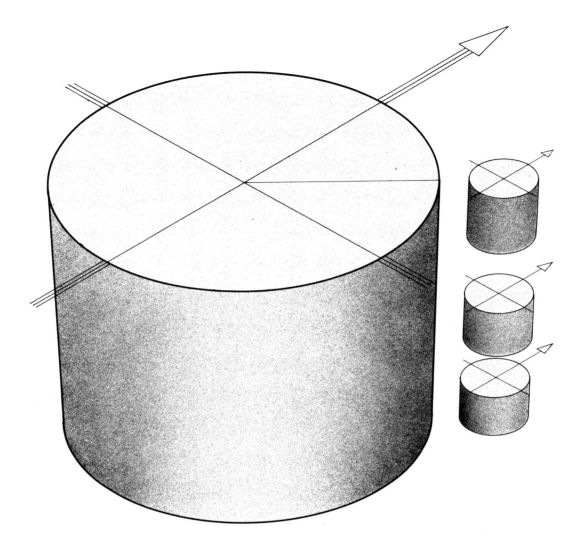

Figure 9   A fragment of "a singular planetary system": the
            "mother-model" with three small models representing a
            scientific approach towards the Earth and its inhabitants
            at three different periods of time.

Since there is a very large number of vertical entry lines on the periphery
of the main model corresponding to the paradigms of different disciplines,
we can imagine the main model as being surrounded by a "planetary
swarm" of small models. Each and every one of them represents the view
of a certain discipline concerning man's role on the surface of the Earth at
a certain juncture.

The number of branches of science has varied through time — and continues to vary — as do the approaches they represent. The planetary
swarm of small models which surround the main model are, therefore,
somewhat unevenly distributed — the swarm becomes denser towards the
present — reflecting the successive differentiation of disciplines and
changes in approach.

Thus we have a complete "planetary system" of models before us: a "mother model" — a direct photographic-physical representation of reality — and a swarm of "small models" which represent the way man comprehends and formulates the content and structure of the mother model at different periods and from different points of departure.

The swarm of models is supplemented by additional "small models" on the southern periphery of the mother model representing man's view of himself as an inhabitant of the Earth as related in myths, tales, literary works and other forms of artistic expressions.

Disposition of the continued presentation

How can the infinitely comprehensive and multi-faceted "mother-model" summarized above be translated into a comprehensible and well-organized presentation?

As an introduction and a background against which the content of the model can be reproduced, we first observe the model through the eyes of art and the artist, i.e. as the model appears when viewed from the "south". After that, the model is analysed as it reveals itself when observed from the "north" — from the vantage point of scientific analysis.

Part one: the individual map and the map in context

The specific tool used to reproduce spatial relations is the map. The structure, qualities, and limitations of the map as well as its capacity to interact with other means of expression are essential for our ability to reproduce the contents of the model. Consequently, the individual map and its most important features are studied first in a number of sections. Only then is the map placed in its context, interacting with text and illustrations. This is done through the study of a number of atlases which deal with historical periods. These volumes are chosen to illustrate special aspects of the reproduction of the structure of the time-space model. The results of analyses of individual maps and atlases then form the background for the discussion about the application of human cartography to urban and regional planning today and its development in the future based on the technology of tomorrow. This is the subject of the third part of this book.

Part two: "census cartography" for urban and regional planning

An interlude

The model perceived from the viewpoint of art

As we have seen, the contents of the model appear in fundamentally different ways depending upon whether we observe the model from the "south" or the "north".

Art as a source
of inspiration
for cartographic
interpretation

In subsequent sections, most interest is, of course, focussed on the scientific reproduction of human activities as they appear when we observe the model from the fictive "north". However, certain aspects of cartographic presentation are closely related to artistic endeavours. Let us, therefore, first observe our model from the "south", and study the way its contents are portrayed. In the present context, a study of this sort must be extremely brief and superficial, and be based more on personal reflections than on scientific analysis. Certain concepts may, however, enrich the subsequent discussion.

Artistic versus
cartographic
presentation

As a rule, literary or artistic interpretations of human actions are presented much more concretely than are scientific accounts. The former presentations usually focus on a limited number of people whose qualities and actions are chiseled out distinctly while the actions of others often are generalized. Uniform generalization such as can be found in cartographic applications is rare in the fine arts.

The concreteness is manifested in another way as well. Literary and artistic interpretations are, to a large degree, representational. They seek to portray three-dimensional reality: the verbal or visual descriptions reproduce the world of man in such a way that the reader or observer can reconstruct the situation or events in his imagination as if he himself had been an invisible participant. (Abstract art and literature are exceptions in this regards.) The account is filtered through the emotions and perspective of an artist or author while a skeleton of reality remains. In this way too, artistic interpretation contrasts with cartographic representation. The map reduces the three dimensions of reality to two, and reduces the human and physical environment to symbols. For the map to represent a living reality, the reader/observer must carry out the opposite process: he must decipher the symbols, and recreate in his own imagination the reality represented by the map.

The time
dimension of
the image

Artistic and literary interpretation use other means of expression. The primary tool of literature is the written word. The picture, the drawn and painted picture, has an enormous capacity for recreating situations and

36

events from the world of cartography. Landscape paintings often differ only slightly from deliberate topographical drawings. Representations of historical situations not only present highly tangible physical environments. They often reproduce moments within sequences of events which are absolutely central, critical. Paintings of historic battles, for example, often portray pivotal moments during which various decisive components converge as a result of a previous series of events (with which the painter assumes that the observer is acquainted). This decisive moment often carries in its logical consequence a sequel which is not reproduced in the painting, but of which the painter as well as the observer are aware. Thus the frozen moment not only contains a physical environment but also — indirectly — a time sequence. The presentation could be classified as historic with pronounced geographic aspects (or vice versa: geographic — if the description of the environment is exhaustive as in many paintings of battles, and is done from a bird's eye view — with expressly chronological aspects).

Reconstruction of events

This kind of dramatization of events can be carried even further. Sometimes historic events are reconstructed in the surroundings in which they really took place. In connection with the bicentennial celebration in the United States, important phases of complete military battles were staged in this manner before audiences. In the case of feature films with historical themes too, more or less accurate reconstructions of events are often made in the original surroundings or in similar environments. Sometimes reconstructions for this type of film are based on contemporary records such as paintings. In many cases the reconstructions are highly geographical and include large authentic portions of the landscape.

Reconstructions on the stage are of necessity more limited in their capacity to recreate geographical environments. The surroundings can be hinted at, however, and through a suitable sequence of scenes, the observer is enabled to imagine that he is participating in the events which extend over great expanses of geographic space and time.

The possibilities of computer graphics

The animated film provides great opportunities for portraying real or imagined historical episodes. Computer graphics are beginning to make possible visual interpolation. If drawings of a human figure engaged in two "border phases" of a movement are provided, the computer will reconstruct the intervening sequence in graphic form. It becomes possible, with a relatively small amount of labour, to construct long action sequences involving one or more persons. By adding suitable backdrops and other scenery, not only can one create sequences in feature films, but also reconstruct actual historical processes or simulate imagined ones, in other words scenes with actors who are mobile and active.

Advanced computer technology in the form of image processing is already opening up new opportunities for graphic designers and artists. By making it easier for people who lack extensive specialized training to use these graphic means of expression, this technology provides major new opportunities even in the field of cartography.

The map is a relatively rare occurrence in the "southern sphere". Literary works which are set in expansive geographical areas sometimes contain maps for orientation, but this is more the exception than the rule.

The literature of sagas and fantasy belongs to a special category. Works of this type sometimes contain maps. They may be strictly correct in appearance and resemble simple, hand-drawn maps. Their special character derives from the fact that they are portraying non-existent worlds in this correct manner (see Le Guinn 1975).

Saga maps and the landscape of pictorial maps

The pictorial map is more common. It is a map in which oblique illustrations are inserted which blend in with the rest of the map. Mountain chains, for instance, appear on the map in a birds-eye view and in their correct topographical locations. Pictorial maps are sometimes supplemented by completely "correct" maps, sometimes by entire "atlases" illustrating sequences of events (e.g. Strachey 1981). The predominant feature of pictorial maps seems to be that the illustration and the map blend together. The maps often cover large territories which a person could only experience by extensive travel or by observing them from an aeroplane or satellite. In contrast, direct, personal perception of the landscape occurs when one can behold smaller, more limited portions of the landscape. The pictorial map seems to construct cartographic illustrations by fitting together these small, fictive segments of the landscape to form cohesive geographical spaces. The world of pictorial maps is therefore easy to experience. They retain a certain geographic quality, but the landscape becomes in some way miniaturized. Their manner of portraying a fictive reality is in certain respects not very different from that of the medieval map (See also Harvey: The History of Topographical Maps 1980, ch. 5).

The cinematic language as a source of inspiration

Feature films made during the Second World War especially, often contained many fascinating visual effects. The war was fought across a huge geographical theatre, with distinct chronological periods. Portrayals of the events — not least in feature films — often depicted the geographic locations in very interesting ways. For instance, we accompany a person on a long journey. We see him mounting the ramp to an aeroplane, the plane takes off, we see him sitting there looking out of the cabin window. Simultaneously, through double-exposure, we see a map passing by in the background on which the shadow of the plane indicates its route. With the aid of similar, increasingly effective and often visually innovative new methods in cinematic technology, film-makers succeeded in combining the concreteness of these individual events with a correct depiction of the geographical context. This type of presentation made it possible to experience events in time and space in a more tangible way than had been possible with any previous method.

Part I:
From model to map

Observations from the "north":
the model viewed in the perspectives
of different sciences

The main tool of cartography: The individual map

The components of the map

The model presented above consists of split-second images which blend together to form a three-dimensional model. It contains the streams of the ages — the life paths of individuals, but also "life paths" of objects and of surface elements. How can we reconstitute — portions of — this model and its contents back into maps, i.e. two-dimensional images?
There are two fundamentally different solutions to the problem.

1) By making *one* horizontal section through the model, and performing the necessary reduction — demarcating a portion of the surface of the image and "thinning out" its contents — we can translate the contents into graphic symbols. In this way we obtain a split-second image in the form of a map.

2) By making *two* horizontal sections, we define and then lift out a part of the model, i.e. all processes which take place between two chosen points in time. We then carry out the same reduction as in 1) — we demarcate a geographic territory, select certain portions of the contents of the model, and then summarize and reproduce the results of the demarcation in cartographic form.

Elements of the map

Let us take the storming of the monastery in Arcadia as an example. We can choose to observe a sector of the circular photograph taken at a moment in the heat of the battle. Our enlarged picture shows the landscape with an infinite wealth of detail. In the midst of the landscape the combatants are reproduced "frozen" in the positions they had assumed in the instant in which the picture was taken. If we choose to reproduce the contents of the image in the form of a map, we must portray:

1) The landscape where the battle takes place.
2) The combatants and their deployment in the landscape.

Or in more general terms:

1) The setting (or scene)
2) The positions of the actors on the set.

We can choose to observe a whole sequence of images. If, for example, we were to superimpose the first image on the last, we could then trace the movements of each actor during the intervening period of time. We could then superimpose image 2 on image 3 in the same way, then image 3 on image 4 etc. It would soon become impossible to keep track of all of these observations: we would be forced to gather the separate individuals into

41

groups which act jointly, and to let their common movements be represented by symbols. We obtain the third element of our map:

3) The play

i.e. the scenario which reproduces the movements of the actors and other activities on the set. In order for a map to fulfill its function as a medium of communication, it must often be furnished with additional elements of information. These are the links, i.e. cartographic elements which unite the different parts of the map with one another and with the surface of the Earth. They are:

4) Links between the surface of the Earth and the setting.
5) Links between the setting and the actors.
6) Links between the setting and the play and between the actors and the play.
7) Explanations of the symbolic language employed (the legend)
8) Reference elements ("pointers").

The particular design and contents of the map determine which of these mutually complementary elements must be present for the map to be comprehensible.

4) Links between the surface of the Earth and the setting.

These cartographic elements answer two types of questions.

A) *Where* on the surface of the Earth is the setting located? This information must be provided if the setting comprises such a small portion of the Earth's surface that its relationship to well-known geographical features is not evident from the map. In regions that are unfamiliar to the reader, such areas may be quite large. This type of information is often provided in the form of *orientation maps* or *orientation sketches* which indicate the location of the map in question within the framework of the more familiar map of the world. This type of orientation sketch or orientation map may show the location of a relatively obscure country on a continent, but also the location of a map-sheet in a municipality.

Geographical names are other elements whose usefulness in locating settings is often overlooked.

B) What is the relationship of the surface area of the setting to the surface of the Earth? This question arises primarily in regards to maps dealing with portions of the Earth's surface which are so large that the curvature of the globe must be suggested in order for the contents of the map to be interpreted. Reproducing the global network of parallels and meridians on the map in question not only fixes its location on the surface of the Earth, but also illustrates the distortion of the Earth's surface which occurs when it is transferred to the plane surface of a map. Interpretation of the map — its relationships of distance and direction and the size of the illustrated area — is hereby facilitated.

5) Links between the setting and the actors

When *situations* are portrayed, the map reproduces the location of the actors at a specific instant. This immediate manner of representation does not require any additional explanation. When the actors are presented in a more generalized fashion, however, it may become necessary to describe their geographic locations more precisely. Assume for example, that the actors comprise the entire populations of different countries each re-presented by a symbol such as a graduated circle. The boundaries of the different countries must then be shown on the map. They then serve as links between the setting and the actors.

6) Links between the setting and the play and between the actors and the play

As mentioned above, the play is often a direct representation of a course of events in which the relationship between the setting and the play is usually quite evident. The arrow which represents a migration route often requires some explanation: exactly how broad was the migration flow; when did the migrating group reach different points etc. It is often necessary, however, to make much of this information inherent in the design of the symbol itself (the arrow). Special elements are seldom necessary for linking the play to the setting. When the map reproduces complex events with a large cast, it may, however, be necessary to point out in which element of the play the different actors participate.

7) Legend

The simplest kinds of maps employ such an elementary cartographic language that there is rarely need for any special explanations. Most thematic maps, however, are much too complex to be deciphered without a legend.

The visual organization of the legend should be such that the logic of the design of the symbols is immediately apparent. It will then be easier for the reader to reduce composite symbols to simpler patterns which can be compared with similar patterns on the map. This facilitates a systematic visual review of the elaborate contents of the map.

The legend may be supplemented by more exhaustive discourses dealing with the significance and design of the symbols, and offering suggestions for further reading. The latter may be necessary for new and especially-complex types of maps.

8) Reference elements (pointers)

It is often necessary to indicate a location, a line or an area on a map. Parallels and meridians are seldom suitable for this purpose — especially on small-scale maps where the graticule often becomes transformed in ways which make the map difficult to comprehend. It may often be much easier to deal with a gridiron pattern where letters and numerals designate the two direction.

Thematic maps often require another type of reference system. When analysing the geographic pattern of a special-purpose map, one will often stand in front of the map, and use a pointer or a pen to indicate various points, lines or patterns which are subsequently analysed and placed in context. It is quite unusual to find explicit "pointers" with corresponding functions on printed maps. One of the few maps of this type — in which the "fertile crescent" is accentuated by use of a shadowing technique — is reproduced in the colour supplement (Atlas of World History — dtv Atlas zur Weltgeschishte, see figure 3 in the supplement). Many maps emphasize particular features in a more indirect, integrated way: the graphic accentuation of the features making them stand out from the map as a whole. More explicit kinds of pointers can sometimes be seen on TV screens where arrows, circles or shadows help make contexts and patterns comprehensible by accentuating first one element then another. The increasing use of the computer screen, video technology and electronic image formation in cartographic design offers tremendous opportunities for the development of thematic cartography.

The major types of maps and their means of expressions

The components of the map, its functional elements, will be dealt with in subsequent sections. However, it can be noted already in this overview that different combinations of elements create a variety of map types which can be classified according to their contents and their relationship to our reference model.

Maps of situations and events, processes and changes
(The dimensions of time and action in maps)

While discussing the cartographic reproduction of the storming of the monastery of Arcadia, we dealt with the depiction of

A) *situations*, i.e. the reproduction of split-second images
B) *events*, when split-second images are linked together (superimposed) in order to reproduce the sequence of situations which constitutes a coherent event.

We may choose to illustrate the course of events in another way. We can present the initial position of the attackers before the start of the attack as well as the positions then held by the defenders. We can then present the positions of both groups about an hour later at the peak of the battle when the defenders are attempting to stop the Turks from breaking into the monastery. Finally, we can show, for example, the deployment of both forces immediately before the collapse of the defenses. We can illustrate the location of the front on the battle scene, i.e. on the map of the terrain, at these three points in time.

We have then captured three characteristic phases in the unfolding of events, three periods of uniform activity in this process in which occurrences repeat themselves for varying lengths of time. We are thus illustrating a — more or less long-lived

C) *phase* in a course of events

Figure 3 illustrates the principle for defining this type of situation in the context of time and space. Figure A may be interpreted as the movements of a person in the vicinity of his dwelling during a period of six days. It might be meant to signify "the movements of a group of nomads during the winter quarter for a period of six years". It could, however, also represent six stages in the course of battle where the line represents the attempts by a combatant or group of combatants to resist the attackers (the vertical lines) succeeded by a period of retreat which is replaced by one of advance. The advance is halted, the defenders are forced back, press forward again, hold their ground for awhile etc. The example is artificial, of course, but hopefully it illustrates the principle: a period of time in a sequence of events in which the occurrences are repeated time and time again. A phase of this sort can be reproduced by drawing the line along which it occurs, for example, or the area within which it takes place. In the case of Arcadia, the events are symbolized by the fronts which become stabilized during the storming — if only for short periods.

In certain cases several phases can be presented on one and the same map. When we can follow the succession and development of different phases, we obtain a

D) *map of change*

By describing certain characteristic phases of a course of events — for example, by pointing out the location of the front during the storming of Arcadia on a map of the battlefield, and then adding the positions of the front at other points in time — we make it possible to trace the progression from one situation to another, i.e. to see *changes* in the course of events.

In practice, it is often difficult to distinguish between "event" and "change". As a guideline, we can choose the term "event" for a chain of individual *situations*. "Change" is a chain of processes in which each process is characterized by the repetition of certain events.

In summary

The basic cartographic elements

> the setting
> the actors
> the play

can be employed to reproduce on a map

a situation	(a split-second image)
an event	(the transition between two situations)
a phase	(a rhythmic repetition of certain events)
a change	(the transition between two phases)

The relationship between these terms can be summarized as follows

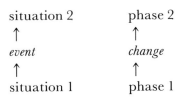

The zero map, the setting map, the play map
(Main categories for the design of maps)

How can we design the maps suggested above?

Geographical
processes
reproduced
verbally

The method which is technically simplest but perhaps most demanding for the author is to present the map *verbally.* The author describes the setting verbally so that the reader can imagine it in its entirety with all important details located as precisely as possible. Then — still using words — he populates the setting with actors and lets them get on with the play so that the reader is able to picture the map and the events which appear one by one against this background. We have before us what can be called a *zero map* — a map which appears in the reader's imagination without any map being drawn on paper. The example of Arcadia is perhaps not especially suitable for illustrating the zero map since the events took place within such a limited area that the reader can directly imagine the events taking place in their real, physical context without having to translate them into a map.

A better example would be the gradual expansion of the Ottoman Empire. The author first describes the setting: Asia Minor, the Balkan Peninsula, the Carpathian Basin with the aid of verbal references to well-known geographical features. He assumes that the reader, aided by these references, can develop a mental image of the setting. He then populates the setting with actors, i.e. the people who inhabit these regions. Finally he lets the play begin: describes the repeated military campaigns of the Ottoman Empire and the progressive conquering of the entire region. By skillfully employing this technique, he provides the reader with an equally lively though perhaps not as (geographically) detailed presentation of the course of events as could be supplied by a map.

It is easy to forget that just a few decades ago it was difficult and expensive to produce illustrations in print. It was much simpler to paint with words, and many authors developed great skill in the art of reproducing geographic processes solely by verbal means.

Events depicted
against a setting
map

Another solution to the problem of describing a course of events is the use of a *setting map*. The author creates a map of the terrain where the events take place — of Arcadia or of the geographic region where the expansion of the Ottoman Empire took place. Geographic locations which are important from the standpoint of the course of events are emphasized carto-

46

graphically, and important place names are specified on the map. Then follows a verbal description of the process which led to the expansion of the Ottoman Empire. The events are depicted verbally above the graphic image of the setting. Since a detailed description of the setting exists on paper, the reader's memory can be utilized primarily to reconstruct the course of events more exhaustively and with a greater amount of detail than had been possible if the setting as well as the positions of the actors and the play had only been described in words.

The maps found in most bibles are examples of a very widely-circulated type of setting map. These maps made it possible for the reader to follow the events which took place long ago, often in little-known places in a distant land.

The play can be described more thoroughly and in even greater detail if the positions of the actors on the set during some key situation are also specified, for example at the start of the historical process being described.

The illustration broadens the frames of reference

The graphic image of the setting can be supplemented by a description of events — for example arrows which depict the advances of the besiegers in Arcadia or the drives of the Ottoman armies via the Balkan Peninsula and in towards Hungary. Different phases of the armies' progress at Arcadia or across the Balkan Peninsula can be illustrated at selected points of time (a map of change). As a rule it takes more than a single map to present complex processes. These composite presentation methods — series of maps, single maps combined with text and statistics, even illustrations etc. — are dealt with in connection with atlas cartography.

The individual map can thus consist of

    a) words (zero map)
    b) a cartographic illustration + words (setting map + verbal description of events)
    c) a cartographic illustration of a situation
                    an event
                    a phase
                    a change

A complement to the map which must be mentioned here is the *illustration*.

A map of a part of the Earth's surface is a two-dimensional parallel projection of a three-dimensional terrain. It depicts a portion of the Earth's surface as if observed from an infinitely distant place. It is assumed that the reader, with the aid of the map, his knowledge of how to interpret this type of image and supported by previous experience, can reconstruct the terrain depicted on the map in his imagination. However, maps often depict environments which may be unfamiliar to the reader. It may be a question of far-away or exotic geographic environments, or surroundings which do not exist anymore — for example natural landscapes which have disappeared or man-made environments which have been destroyed. In

47

such cases, illustrations can contribute greatly towards supplementing and clarifying the informational content of the maps. Not least, illustrations can help make the mental image constructed with the aid of the map more similar to the real terrain, and less an analogy extracted from the reader's previous world of experience. In addition to the terrain (the setting), illustrations can also help visualize events, critical moments in historical processes, etc.

The geographical elements of the map

Occupied space, movements, fields of motion Physical extent and zones of influence

Peter Hagget's elements

Figure 10 is borrowed from Hagget (1965), and shows "stages in the analysis of regional systems. A. Movements B. Networks C. Nodes D. Hierarchies E. Surfaces" "...shows the build up of such a system; viz., the study of *movements* (...) leads on to a consideration of the channels along which movement occurs, the *network* (...), to the *nodes* on that network and their organization as a *hierarchy* (...), with a final integration of the interstitial zones viewed as *surfaces*."

The expression "such a system" refers to his term "open system" as opposed to a "closed system". "Closed systems have definable boundaries across which no exchange of energy occurs".

Hagget's concepts and outline refer to the elements in a complex civilized landscape where the "channels" consist as a rule of roads, railways, etc., and the "nodes" and the "hierarchy" consist of villages or towns, but the figure can also be given a more general interpretation. The outline can be said to illustrate the main geographic elements of the time-space model.

With the aid of these elements, it is possible to describe major features of technologically-advanced as well as less-sophisticated societies.

The relationship between Hagget's elements and Hägerstrand's life paths

Figure 11 shows in outline form how the movements of individuals in time space can be translated into Hagget's "movements" (figure 10A). Figure 11B shows the daily movements of two people between their dwellings (in the two small settlements) and their places of work (in the largest urbanized area) along "channels" which link the "nodes" that together comprise (a small part of) a "hierarchy".

The array of elements shown by Hagget can, however, well be complemented and further elaborated.

The only point elements dealt with by Hagget are the nodes at the intersection of two links. The points can also be defined in another way. The space occupied by an individual or a group can be defined by a point. The space may be occupied temporarily — a point one passes or where one makes a

48

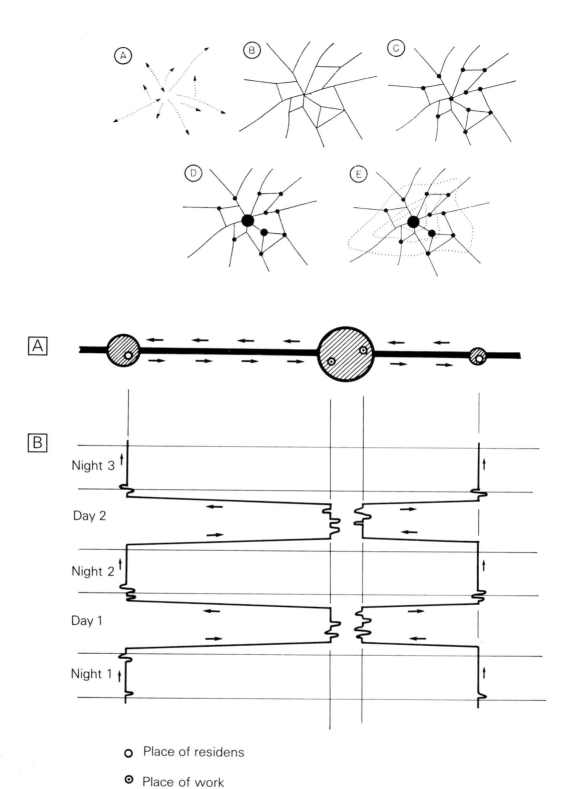

Night 3

Day 2

Night 2

Day 1

Night 1

o Place of residens

⊙ Place of work

Figure 10–11   The relation between Hagget's and Häggerstrand's models. Example: the commuting journeys of two people
during 2 1/2 days (= movements in a channel between
nodes and movements in time-space respectively).

short stop — but it may also be a location to which one returns again and again (station; Hägerstrand 1962). Points can also come into being where two movements intersect — a meeting point, but not infrequently also a conflict point.

"Movement" may be a single discrete movement which is considered unique. It may also be a recurrent movement along channels in one or both directions i.e. a route. (Channel is mentioned by Hagget but not singled out as a separate element).

The areal concept is referred to in Hagget's work only as a graduated surface adjoining hierarchically-structured nodes. Areas can, however, be defined from other points of departure and on the basis of other attributes.

Discrete elements and sources of influence

Areas can be *discrete* or *gradually fading*. By a *discrete* area is meant a territory whose boundaries can be defined in distinct geometric terms — the surface area of a nation or of some other administrative unit, for example a county, of a piece of landed property or of some other type of territory at the disposal of a person or an organization. This type of discrete territory is defined with the aid of its boundaries, i.e. the geometric extension of the boundaries in the physical landscape.

Zones that gradually fade out can come into being around the activities of individual people or groups. Such a — temporary — zone can be formed around the space occupied by the person or the group. We can imagine such a temporary territory around the camp of a group of nomads. The "territory" would then consist of the area which the members of the group can keep under observation and over which they hold sway. The "territory" is temporary and its boundaries are difficult to define precisely. The territory comprises the area influenced by the group. Since its influence diminishes with distance, the boundaries of the area constitute a zone instead of a line.

The individual or the group may be mobile. If movement occurs within a limited area, a central zone is formed encompassing the actual movement. Outside this core can be found a zone of influence which as in the previous case diminishes, fades towards the periphery.

This diminishing influence may have a more intricate structure. The movements may be concentrated to a smaller central zone. Outside of this there might be a zone which is seldom visited by the person or the group. Beyond this, though, extends still another zone which can still be kept under observation by the actors, and which is affected by their influence in other ways as well. This zone may have varying depth, and can be assumed to fade towards the periphery.

We can imagine several groups with contiguous areas and spheres of influence. If the groups are similar, a unified, joint territory may emerge. It may be a functional area — the groups influence one another or co-operate with one another — but it may also be largely an abstraction — many years later a scientist may observe several groups of individuals, find

50

common traits among the groups, believe that they share a common culture, and illustrate their joint territory as a single geographic area on the map. This is assumed to be a homogenous population. If there are dominant groups within this culture, the hierarchical areal structure suggested by Hagget in figure 10E can easily come into being.

Zones of influence

A similar zone can evolve alongside individual movements of individuals or groups. A large group may move along a rather narrow line. Other members of the group may, however, be sparsely distributed along a broader channel. Their temporary deviation from the common route may cover an even wider belt beyond which at least news of their presence makes itself felt. From this outer zone, one can also reach members of the group. Thus the influence of the mobile group diminishes progressively along the line of motion. The phenomenon may be made more tangible by imagining a tribe in rapid motion.

Thus we obtain the following sequence of geographic elements

Geographical elements — a summary

1)	Space occupied by	— an individual
		— a group
2)	Movements of	— an individual
		— a group
3)	Channel (route)	
4)	Intersection between	— movements (meeting points)
		— channels = nodes
5)	Zones around	— spaces occupied by individuals spaces occupied by groups
		— movement of individuals movement of groups
		— channels
6)	Discrete territories	
7)	Hierarchies	— of occupied spaces of movements of channels of nodes of areas

Cartographic design of discrete elements and sources of influence respectively

"Discrete territories" is the only one of these concepts for which the definition of the phenomenon is predetermined. All the other phenomena can be looked upon either as "discrete" elements or as sources of influence. When we consider them to be discrete, we define their geographical extent as corresponding to the physical presence of the actors — the space they occupy at rest or in motion. It may be a question of physical entities — roads, buildings or the like.

If, on the other hand, we define their geographical extent from the viewpoint of the influence which they exert on their surroundings, we specify their physical presence together with the range and measure of their influence. This can be done in precise terms — the suggested elevation contours in figure 10E in Hagget's book demonstrate this type of presentation. This can, however, also be illustrated with other methods in which the influence is implied but not precisely defined.

Phenomena are often illustrated with symbols which give the impression that the phenomenon is discrete although that may not be the case. This usually occurs without any particular deliberation. One of the prerequisites for improved thematic cartography is that this unconsidered use of cartographic symbols is replaced by a systematic analysis of the relationship between a cartographic symbol and the geographic reality represented by the symbol.

There are two relationships which must be stressed in connection with this argument.

1) The concepts presented above are suitable for portraying individual events or lasting situations. Pictures of change can then be synthesized from these situational illustrations. How these pictures of change can be developed, or alternatively: how individual illustrations of conditions in a certain region can be linked into sequences of images which together illustrate a process of change, shall be studied in connection with an analysis of the structure of different atlases.

2) The examples chosen often depict fictive nomadic societies or peoples with similar types of cultures. However, the principles can very well be applied to urbanized industrial society. A point with a well-defined centre and diminishing fields of influence can represent a person in his dwelling. A traffic artery can serve as example of a linear source of influence. In similar terms one could describe a factory as an areal source of influence. The person, the road and the factory are considered as individual phenomena unrelated to their surroundings — they are, of course, integrated into regional systems with hierarchical structures, a fact which should be made clear by the cartographic presentation.

Sources of
influence:
Examples from
modern societies

The functional elements of the map: The setting, the actors and the play

The setting

Requirements
for a map which
describes the
setting

The setting usually comprises the physical landscape. As a rule, a map presenting this information — and which has as its main purpose the portrayal of the physical landscape — has a high level of informational density. If we add additional elements to a map of this kind such as the positions of the actors or their actions, it becomes overloaded and hard to read. The amount of detail in the reproduction of the physical landscape is, therefore, limited in such a way that the major theme of the map — the positions or the actions of the actors — remains the dominant element of the map. The identity of the actors is determined by our vantage point when we observe our circular model. They may be human beings, groups of individuals, objects, but also parts of the physical landscape such as towns or roads. Depending on who these actors are, we select components of the physical landscape which would constitute a suitable background for them.

The functional requirements for the contents and disposition of the setting map can be summarized in three points.

1) The contents of the setting map must be relevant.
2) The informational density of the setting map must be high enough to locate the actors and their actions on the setting with the necessary precision.
3) The setting map must be subordinate to the cartographic elements which present the actors and their actions.

The major components of the setting map are

1) Hydrographic elements
2) Political boundaries
3) Elevation data and the shape of the terrain
4) The characteristics of the vegetal covering
5) The man-made elements of the civilized landscape — buildings, and clusters of buildings such as towns and villages, roads, railways, man-made waterways, cables for the transmission of electricity and information

The components of the setting map

1) *Hydrographic elements* are the most commonly-employed elements for describing the setting. The coastlines of the continents, major lakes, rivers and waterways — in this order — are among the most commonly-reproduced landscape elements.

2) *Political boundaries* are not really a part of the physical landscape. They are abstractions and expressions of forces and processes around human actors and their plays. The locations of these boundaries are, however, often well-known — at least with regard to their present positions. They are also easy to reproduce by simple technical methods without becoming too dominant. These factors make political boundaries among the most commonly-used elements for describing settings. The borders of countries, but also sub-national boundaries (such as county boundaries) and even municipal boundaries are recurrent elements in setting maps. The choice of which boundaries to use on a map depends on the size of the mapped area, the scale of the map and the degree of detail. Since political/admini-strative boundaries are found on most topographic maps, they often comprise a link between thematic and topographic map elements.

3) *The terrain*, its elevation and shape. Elevation data and landforms are probably also among the most commonly-employed elements on setting maps. It is, however, difficult to produce good elevation maps and even more difficult to subordinate this information to the thematic content of the maps. The shape of the terrain is only presented on the most advanced thematic maps, and then often in colour — and in these cases the information is often extremely valuable for the reader (see the

colour supplement). Simplified reproductions of the terrain are more often found on separate maps of the setting where the reader is expected to memorize the contents of the setting map, and to place it mentally over the thematic map or a large portion of it (see McNeill's and McEvedy's maps, figure 34 and figure 40 in the colour supplement).

4) The composition of the *vegetal covering* is an important component for evaluating many human activities. However, vegetation maps with full surface coverage create a background which may make it difficult to draw attention to cartographic information about the actors and their actions. Vegetation maps are, therefore, often produced as separate setting maps. Very often, though, a portion of a vegetation map may by inserted in a map showing the actors and their interaction. The areas illustrated here are usually vegetal areas which form obstacles for human activity: deserts, large uninterrupted wetlands, tundra and the like. These segments of the terrain often affect the behaviour of the actors in a negative way — constitute obstacles for them, force them to change their choice of routes etc. Consequently, there are no visual collisions between the symbols for this type of area and the representation of the actors and their actions on the map.

Combined topographic and vegetation maps in colour are found only in the most sophisticated atlases. As a rule they are produced in colour and usually contain elements of actors and play. Among them can be found some of the most advanced cartographic products with regard to wealth of information and sophistication of design (see examples from the Times Atlas in the colour supplement, figures 20-26).

5) *The man-made elements* of the civilized landscape are present in great numbers in the inhabited parts of the Earth's surface. They are easy to illustrate graphically, and the names and often the locations of many of them — especially the largest such as towns, major communications arteries etc. — are well-known. These elements — together with hydrographic phenomena and political boundaries — are often employed to describe the setting. This can cause problems as well: it is easy for the setting map and the illustration of actors/events to flow together. This can make the maps hard to read.

6) *Links between the setting* and the Earth's surface. The elements which determine the geographic location of the setting, i.e. its location on the Earth's surface, are also a part of the setting map. They include the network of parallels and meridians and place names. The graticule helps determine the location of a setting when familiar geographic features are lacking. The global grid also makes it possible, in the absence of other geographic features on the setting map, to determine the location of actors and their actions. In addition the latitudinal and longitudinal network provides information about how large an area of the Earth's surface corresponds to a unit of surface area on the different parts of the map. A rather important piece of information on maps which cover entire continents.

Place names have a corresponding function. Assume that we are confronted with a map which contains a number of point symbols and lines connecting them. They are surrounded by a dotted line symbol which we understand to represent a political boundary. We do not recognize this configuration of points and lines, even if we suspect that they deal with towns and roads. Assume then that the same map is provided with place names which establish that at least one of the towns is well-known — and which also specify the names of the other lesser-known towns. At this instant the map becomes "pinned" to a map of the continent in question — or alternatively: to the globe — and is placed in a context which can be interpreted. The place name of a single town has served as locational information for the entire map. If other better-known towns are identified by name on the map, this even gives an approximate scale and orientation to the map. The place names thus serve as an irregular geographic system of co-ordinates — in their function not unlike the global network of lines of latitude and longitude.

The actors

The actors on the set are human beings. The play consists of the movements they make on the set or other actions they might undertake without moving. An actor may influence his fellow actors and the audience by means of speech or without it, with the help of gestures or purely through the force of charisma.

Man with his life path also appeared as protagonist, the dominant actor, in the play within the cylindrical model — at least when the model was observed from certain directions. However, his life path was intertwined with other kinds of life paths: those of objects, of other living beings etc. As we shall see, other, more ephemeral phenomena sometimes free themselves from these tissues of life paths and start to live their own lives, behaving like independent actors in the world of cartography — or at least presenting themselves as candidates for such roles.

The individual, an infrequent actor on maps

The most important and most prolific actor in the world of human cartography is Man himself. Strangely enough he very seldom — only in exceptional cases — appears as a discernible individual. One of these rare cases can be found in van Heyden and Scullard: Atlas of the Classical World. Ten legionnaires of the Roman Empire who lived around the start of the Christian Era are identified by name with place of birth and death and with the highly-simplified life path which is created by linking these two points. The map is based on gravestone inscriptions, and does not provide details of events between these two points in time.

A common type of map on which the activities of specific individuals are recorded is the kind which traces the routes of the great explorers. Although these maps appear to illustrate the movements of individuals, what they usually reproduce is in fact the activities of an entire group: the crew of a ship, an expedition or some other group formed for a special task. The group is identified by the name of its leader, but he as an individual is seldom the protagonist.

Groups and organizations as actors

Groups of a more permanent nature are often portrayed as actors in atlases. The above-mentioned work by van Heyden and Scullard depicts the movements of four Roman legions "...from their formation until the 2nd century AD" (page 46). The protagonist is the legion, the organized unit, with its members who are constantly being replaced. Descriptions of the activities of this type of group — a military unit — can often be found in atlases of the history of mankind. One of the reasons for this may be the importance attached to military affairs in the writing of history. Another explanation is that these groups are well-defined, and that their activities have been registered rather systematically, making them highly suitable as objects of cartographic reproduction.

"Major actors": peoples and nations

In the majority of maps in the field of human cartography, mankind collectively, the human population, is the protagonist. The way this population is presented varies according to the availability of information and the orientation of the atlas. McEvedy, in his atlases of the history of Africa and the modern world (see McEvedy 1980 and The Penguin Atlas of Modern History respectively) presents population maps that are very general in nature. He reproduces the approximate geographic distribution of the population in the form of a dot map where each dot represents one million persons. The point symbols have schematic human form. In spite of the simplified placement of these symbols, we get a fairly clear picture of the approximate location in the setting of the different population groups during various historical periods referred to on the map.

In the New Cambridge Modern History Atlas (pages 88 and 91), H.C. Darby and H. Fullard illustrate the distribution of the population in Central and Western Europe in 1870 and 1914 using a completely different technique — and with an entirely different level of precision. The maps show population density in the scale of 1:15 million, and it appears that geographical precision has been carried far.

The examples have been chosen arbitrarily — a wide variety of similar types of maps can be found in a large number of atlases.

Comprehensive vs. focussed presentation of ethnic groups

Maps where groups of people are presented as actors can be divided into two categories. To the first belong maps which present the *entire* human population within the defined area divided into different groups. Maps belonging to the second category draw attention to and identify one, two or a few groups while the rest of the human population is merely implied or is ignored. A transitional form between these two extremes is the type of map which presents the entire human population within an area, and identifies one or a few groups as a part of the total population.

An example of the first category is McEvedy: The Penguin Atlas of Medieval History, where the author divides the surface of the map into distinctly-demarcated, non-overlapping fields which together cover the

56

entire mapped area, i.e. the inhabited part. The unique shading pattern of each field identifies the ethnic group occupying the area (see the colour supplement, figures 16-17).

The actors are presented — an example

The author demonstrates here, incidentally, an unusually distinct example of separation of the setting, the actors on the set and certain elements of the play (the flow of goods) (see the colour supplement, figures 14-19). The setting map shows only the major physical features of the mapped area. The actors — the various ethnic groups represented on the other maps by shaded surfaces or by distinctly-demarcated areas of expansion covering the entire surface of the map — are represented on this introductory map solely by circular areas. These circles are placed on the map with their centres at the approximate midpoint of the expansion of an ethnic group, and are shaded with the pattern subsequently used to identify each group. The circles are positioned so as to emphasize the genetic relationship between the groups. Since circular areas are presented rather than the exact geographic extent of the groups, interest is focussed on the identity and developmental relationships of the groups — an extremely clear way of introducing the setting and the actors.

States as actors

Perhaps the most common protagonist on human maps, especially historic maps, is the state defined by its boundaries and name. States are in fact actors, which cannot be said of constructs such as ethnic groups, language groups or other groups of people whose identity, interrelationships, spheres of influence and ability to carry out joint action are questionable. Sources are available which describe the territorial extent of states, their actions etc. They are also objects of scientific investigation by researchers and latter-day successors. An additional factor is that the boundaries of states are easy to reproduce cartographically.

Focussed presentations

The other extreme — groups of people singled out from among an un-specified total population — is illustrated by a couple of examples in figure 8 in the colour supplement. The examples are borrowed from The Penguin Atlas of World History, page 50. They show the expansion of the Greek and Phoenician civilizations and the confrontations between them. The actors are the two civilizations whose expansion, strength and, to a certain degree, inner structure are implied against the background of surroundings which are not elaborated upon.

On page 32 of the same atlas, the expansion of the Indo-european peoples is illustrated (see figure 7 in the colour supplement). The map draws attention to elements of the play (the expansion), but it also suggests the distribution of the actors on the set at the start of the expansion. The tribes are specified by name only, but the names — in combination with arrows which show the direction of expansion, and together with the well-ba-lanced, plastic reproduction of the physical landscape — specify the approximate positions of these tribes at the start of the expansion. The other ethnic groups are not accounted for. In both examples, the group being studied is singled out from the context of an unspecified population.

A transitional form between these two extremes — mapping the entire population on the one hand and focussing on one, two or a few groups on the other — can be found, for example, in H.C. Danley and H. Fullard: The New Cambridge Modern History Atlas, pages 214-215. On opposite pages are shown first the total population density of the USA, and second the coloured population's proportional share reproduced in different shades of colour. It is very difficult to develop one well-defined absolute map from two relative ones in one's mind, but the reader still gets a certain impression of the distribution of the coloured population seen in the context of the total population.

A map which is unusual in many respects, and which is related to these examples can be found on page 110 of The Penguin Atlas of World History, vol. 1 (see figure 12 in the colour supplement). The map gives an impression of the complicated ethnic situation which arose in Central Europe, especially in the Carpathian Basin and its surroundings around the year 900. Several ethnic groups mixed with each other here, in part "horizontally" — note the way the expansion zones of the Bulgars and the Avars overlap one another — in part "vertically" — Hungarians, who after their entry into the area remained as a population group "above" the Avars who already inhabited the area.

With effective and skillful use of air-brush techniques, they have been able to suggest the patterns of expansion of the individual groups — more pronounced concentration in the centre which diminishes progressively towards the periphery — and of the different ethnic mixes mentioned above. These techniques have even made it possible to communicate the impression that knowledge about these groups and their expansion is neither exhaustive nor precise. The map can serve as an example of the use of sophisticated technology to make a well-informed presentation of the geographic interrelationships of a few ethnic groups against the background of a population described in its totality.

Buildings, trade routes, etc.

Buildings often serve as "actors" on maps. On page 121 of the Times Atlas of World History are two maps which illustrate the spread of buildings in the Black Forest and north-east France respectively by showing individual settlements which came into being before and after the 12th century (see figures 22-23 in the colour supplement). Grosser historischer Weltatlas, part 2, Mittelalter has on page 78 a map of towns with fortifications, palaces, castles and different categories of ecclesiastical buildings along with the time of their founding. These towns are then the map's "actors" even if only as proxies. They act as indicators of a feudal structure which can be discerned in the point symbols of the map. In the same atlas, on page 124, we find a section dealing with Europe's commerce and industry, the place of origin or manufacture of different raw materials and products, the network which distributes these products, nodes which evolve at the intersection of these links connecting links — a heterogeneous collection of "actors".

I.D. and R. Whithouse's Archeological Atlas of the World presents "The Phoenicians Abroad" on page 104. The "actors" are the settlements — towns and the like — founded by the Phoenician colonizers.

Trade routes are a category of physical element which serve as actors. They can often be looked upon as expressions of the flow of goods — related most closely, therefore, to the category "play". However, the maps of the progressive expansion of the railway network — illustrations of the size of the network at different points in time — ought rather to be assigned to the actor category. The "play" is then the expansion of the network. It becomes increasingly difficult to separate actor and play.

Commodities often appear as "actors". Maps specifying the names of the areas of origin of such commodities along with their distribution routes are quite common (see the supplement, McEvedy's route map).

Cultivated plants and domesticated animals along with their areas of origin and expansion zones are frequent themes in historical atlases. A special example can be found in van Heyden and Scullard (1959) presenting the place of origin of animals which participated in the ancient Roman circuses and gladiator games — "actors" in the original as well as the applied sense of the word.

The word "actor" was placed within quotation marks when used to denote buildings, railways etc. since these objects are created as the result and expression of activities performed by other, real actors — human ones. They can serve as actors on the maps, since the observer's eye is focussed on them.

In some cases the works of Man appear to free themselves from him, making themselves independent of individual people, and then to almost live a life of their own — not least since the life span of some objects is substantially longer than that of a human being.

Objects as actors

Buildings belong to this class. The spread of buildings constructed in a certain style can be cited as an example of the presence of this type of actor in a setting. Westerman: Atlas zur Weltgeschichte illustrates the spread of Baroque architecture on page 108. Buildings constructed in this style can be looked upon as actors. The map shows areas with buildings erected in this style and their gradual spread — the actors and the play. The maps reflect the wanderings of the real actors — the builders — who are hardly discernible in the maps.

Certain objects, not least works of art, can appear as actors with lives of their own. It ought to be possible, for example, to draft a map of the "life path" of the four horses which today stand above the dome of the Cathedral of San Marco in Venice. These statues wandered a long and winding path after their creation in the Byzantine Empire.

Maps belonging to this category are uncommon. An unusual example is the outline map showing the wanderings of the so-called shroud of Christ, a long draping of the type which was used to wrap the dead around the start of the Christian era in the Eastern Mediterranean region. On the shroud can be seen the bodily outline and facial features of a crucified man. The Catholic Church considers the shroud to be a holy relic, and keeps it in the Cathedral of Turin. A few years ago the shroud was made the object of a scientific conference. At the time of the conference an established magazine (though not a professional journal) published an outline map which reproduced the wanderings of this object in the Mediterranean countries over the course of the centuries. It is possible to produce corresponding outline maps of many works of art as long as there is adequate knowledge of their histories. Preparatory studies for maps of this type — integrated, of course, with other art-historical analyses — should provide profound insights into art history.

Invisible actors made visible

Special types of knowledge can appear as "actors" which free themselves from the human society in which they are created. The spread of knowledge about the manufacture of paper is often presented on maps. The "actor" is then the know-how itself, the skills. In the same way we can trace the spread of the ability to write, knowledge about the various forms of calligraphy (see for example McEvedy: The Penguin Atlas of Ancient History).

Tall tales can be cited as an example of a cultural phenomenon which lives its own life. They come into being at some time and place which is hard to determine, and begin to wander in time and space. Mapping them — in the original sense of the word — must be a tempting task.

A related example of a cultural phenomenon which lives its own life is the human language itself. Examples of linguistic phenomena presented as actors can be found in atlases showing the geographic spread of languages and linguistic elements. Cartography with a linguistic content appears to be a field with considerable vitality with regard to theoretical development as well as cartographic production (see Besch et. al.).

The dissemination of ideas is another example of abstract phenomena living their own lives. Many maps can be found showing the spread of the revolution of 1848 across Europe. Capitals where the revolution gained a foothold are portrayed as centres from which concentric circles emanate like rings on water. The maps present a highly dynamic picture which is largely "play"-dominated, but the concept of freedom is an "actor" with a very tangible presence.

The play

It can be said that the play being performed on the theatre stage is composed of three main elements.

1) The actor is present on the stage but not moving, (he is engaged in activities on the stage which are area-bound).
2) The actor moves about on the surface of the stage.
3) The actor sends signals — verbal ones (spoken lines) or pantomime (motions, gestures) or the like.

The same division can be applied to the actors on the geographical set illustrated with cartographic means of expression (figure 12).

60

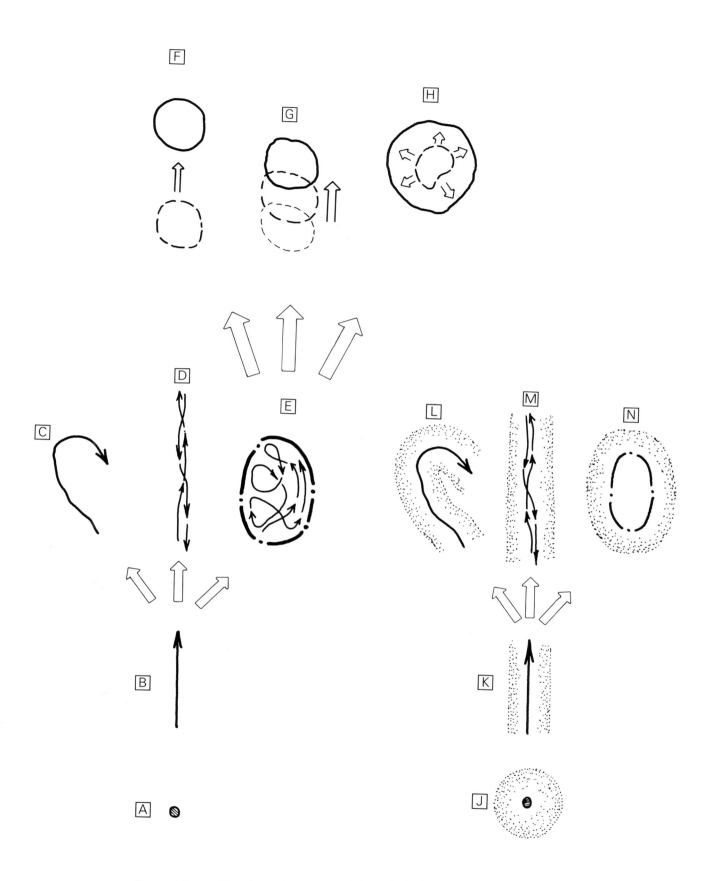

Figure 12   Simple and compound theatrical elements. Discrete
             actors and actors as sources of influence respectively.

The actor engaged in area-bound activities

All maps which show the distribution of actors at a certain point in time or during a given period while the actors are stationary, indirectly describe the type of activity being performed. For example, a map of the location of Bishops' residences during the High Middle Ages shows not only the location of the residences, but also the setting of the activities associated with Bishops' residences, that is elements of the play. This manner of presentation is hard to distinguish from descriptions of actors.

The sense of the play is more pronounced when the actors are mobile but come to a temporary standstill in the middle of a movement. Battles are frequently-recurring play elements represented by points (when reproduced on small-scale maps). We can often trace the movements of the parties concerned which culminate in battle. At other times — especially on very small-scale maps — the symbols for battles appear in isolation, lacking any description of the movements preceding them.

A considerably more peaceful example of an area-bound play element is presented by N.A. Bringeus (1968) in his map of the incidence of religious celebration of the harvest in Sweden. In contrast to the previous example, the symbols do not describe the actors, how many are involved, what effects are produced — they communicate only that a certain type of event takes place and where it occurs.

Actors in motion

The actor in motion is perhaps the most common play element on maps describing human activities (see the arrow in figures 12 B-C). We can picture the actor portrayed in the same way as in figure 1C. (We photograph the actor in motion at regular intervals and from far above. The images are superimposed on one another. The points on the individual images flow together to form a line which we complement with an arrowpoint to indicate the direction of the movement.) The movement's chronology can be indicated by notations along the arrow — notations which account for the actor's position at different times in the course of the movement. McEvedy uses this technique to present the roaming of the Visigoths within the boundaries of the Roman Empire (McEvedy 1961, map A.D. 420, figure 17 in colour). Figure 21 in the colour supplement portrays the massing of the Turkish army against Vienna and the advance of the relief forces towards that city, while also specifying the positions of the armies at different points in time.

Figure 12 C-E shows the three basic types of movement which can be distinguished in the geographic setting: the unique movement (figure C); the movement which follows some visible or invisible channel (figure D). If the channel is invisible, we infer its existence from the fact that the movement follows the same course time after time. Figure E represents the area-bound, spatially-defined or space-defining movement. We recognize it from the fact that all movements undertaken during a period of time keep within a definable, demarcatable area. The boundaries of this area are not necessarily sharp — on the contrary, the frequency of the movement can, for example, diminish from the centre of the area towards its peripheral zones.

The unique movement, (figure C) is one of the most commonly-mapped play elements in human cartography. Migrations, nomadic wanderings, deployment of armies, voyages of exploration are examples of themes which are often portrayed as unique movements. The colour supplement provides several examples of this type of map.

Figure 1 in the colour supplement, borrowed from the Penguin Atlas of World History is a schematic illustration of the attack by equestrian tribes on the territories of the higher civilizations. On page 24 in the same atlas (figure 5 in the colour supplement) are presented similar campaigns by "the sea people" as well as the campaigns of Pharaoh Thutmose III along the eastern shore of the Mediterranean and on towards Mesopotamia.

Another, extremely dramatic example of cartographic portrayal of unique movements can be found in figure 26 in the colour supplement, borrowed from The Times Atlas of World History. The map not only shows the main direction of the migrations, but also reflects the mood of dread, which historians feel they can detect, among the European population of the era at the appearance of the migratory tribes.

The channel-bound movement can be exemplified by the pattern of trade routes in 528 and 737 AD, reproduced by McEvedy in The Penguin Atlas of Medieval History (see figures 18 — 19 in the colour supplement). The design of the symbols suggests the volume of the flow of commodities along different segments of the channel network.

Examples of *spatially-defined or space-defining* movement can be found in McEvedy (1961). On pages 15 and 17 (figures 16 and 17 in the colour supplement) he presents the boundaries of the Roman Empire in the years 362 and 420 AD, as well as the distribution of the different ethnic groups outside of it. The map shows distinct territories, but by comparing the two maps, a displacement can be inferred in the positions of the different ethnic groups outside the Roman Empire indicating that the groups are in motion. The map symbols must, therefore, be interpreted to mean that the tribes limited their movements to the illustrated areas during the period accounted for.

There are several factors concerning the movements of the actors which need to be pointed out.

1) The actors can vary from an individual person to the extremely-complex organization of a politically-sophisticated state. Consequently, the pattern of movement defining the area can vary from the irregular movements of an individual which are suggested in figure 12 E to a complex, regular pattern of movement in a highly-complex network of communications where the actors include a large number of individuals, transfers, etc.
2) The difference between a "unique movement" and the regular, recurrent pattern of movement outlined above is often a matter of

63

definition. If we observe the Germanic and Slavic migrations (see figure 26 in the colour supplement), they appear to be clear-cut examples of "unique movements". However, if we were to observe this region during a period of 2-3,000 years, these individual movements would appear as elements in a pattern which repeats itself time and time again: a recurrent eruption, a periodic outflow of tribes from the midst of the Eurasian land mass towards its periphery.0 K0

The actor sends out signals

Figures 12 J-N attempt to reproduce an additional component of the play in the context of human cartography: the actor as a source of signals and other influences. In figure J the actor is a point symbol, and — in conformity with the other basic categories — he sends out equally strong signals in all directions. These signals are assumed to diminish in strength with increased distance from the source until they fade away entirely. The circle represents the outer boundary of the actor's perceptible influence. The specific pattern according to which the influence diminishes with increasing distance is not accounted for here. It is also important to point out that the graphic images employed here for movements and influences are sketchy. They are looked upon more as suggestions of cartographic means of expression than as a finished design.

Figures 12 K-M show a *zone* of influence around an individual movement and along a channel respectively. In the case of an actor in motion (figure L), we can picture an actor moving along a line and the circular field of influence which moves along with him. This circle sweeps across the entire demarcated zone, but at each instant it covers only a circular area.

A zone with a more evenly-distributed level of influence evolves along a channel (see figure 12 M) which is regularly trafficked by actors each possessing his own circular field of influence.

The field of influence around an *area* can be assumed to develop in connection with the movements of the actors similar to the way influence zones come into being around a unique movement or along a channel. If the actor is an individual human being, we can picture him as the mobile midpoint of his field of influence. The area which he physically passes and where he stops between movements is subjected to the greatest force of his influence — most heavily-affected being the portion he visits most frequently while his influence fades in the areas he seldom passes.

The actions of an actor may give rise to a uniform spread of influence, but the force of influence may also spread out asymmetrically. Figure 5 in the colour supplement (The Penguin Atlas of World History, page 24) shows, for example, the diplomatic relationships of the Egyptian New Empire with surrounding states.In figures 10 and 11 in the colour supplement from the same source, we find two maps which illustrate the system of alliances in Europe — an even more sophisticated illustration of reciprocal, directed signals among actors.

COLOUR SUPPLEMENT

SOURCES:

Figures 1 –13: The Penguin Atlas of World History Vol. 1–2
dtv-Atlas zur Weltgeschichte Vol. 1–2

Figures 14–19: The Penguin Atlas of Medieval History by
C. McEvedy
Reproduced by permission of Penguin Books
Ltd

Figures 20–26: The Time Atlas of World History
Reproduced by permission of Times Books
Ltd

Figures 27–33: A Census Atlas of Sweden

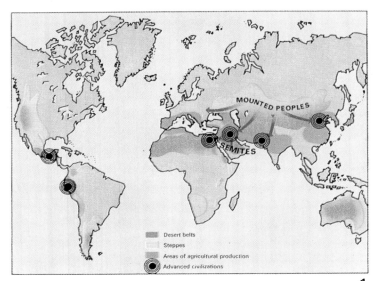

Centres of advanced civilization 1

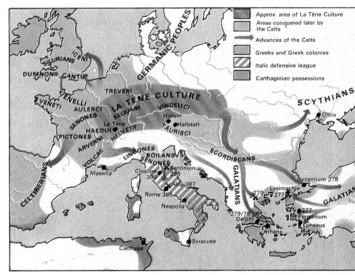

Trajan's conquests in the east

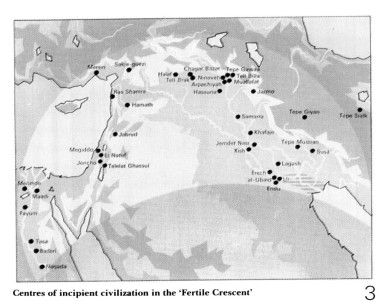

Centres of incipient civilization in the 'Fertile Crescent' 3

The Expansion of the Celts

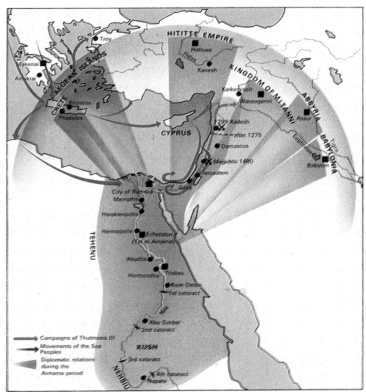

The Empire (New Kingdom) 5

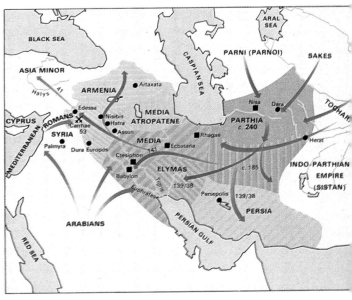

The Parthian Kingdom

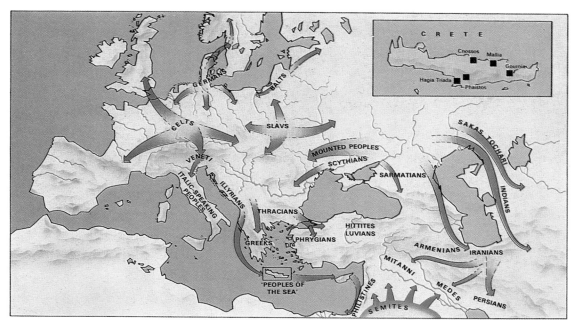

7

Expansions of the Indo-Europeans, Crete

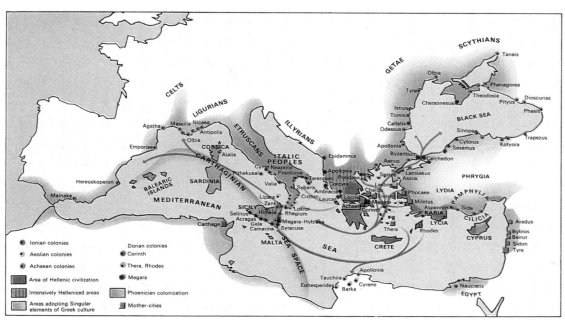

8

Greek colonization, 750–550 B.C.

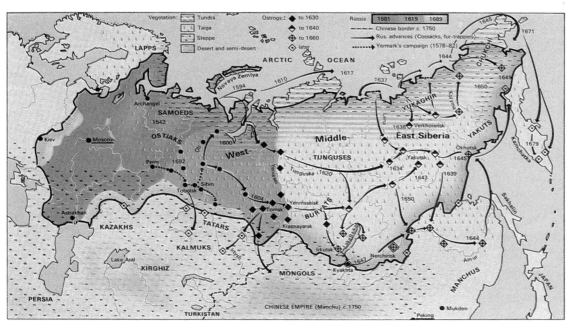

9

The development of Siberia in the 17th cent.

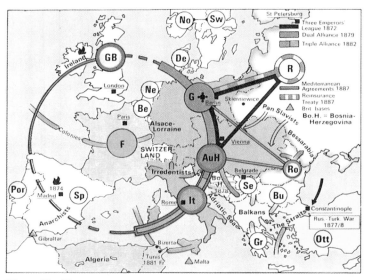

Bismarck's alliance system

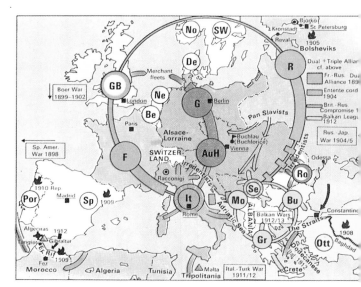

The European alliance system before the First World War

The expansion of the slavs

The Inter-War Period/Europe VI (1918–39). East European zone of unrest

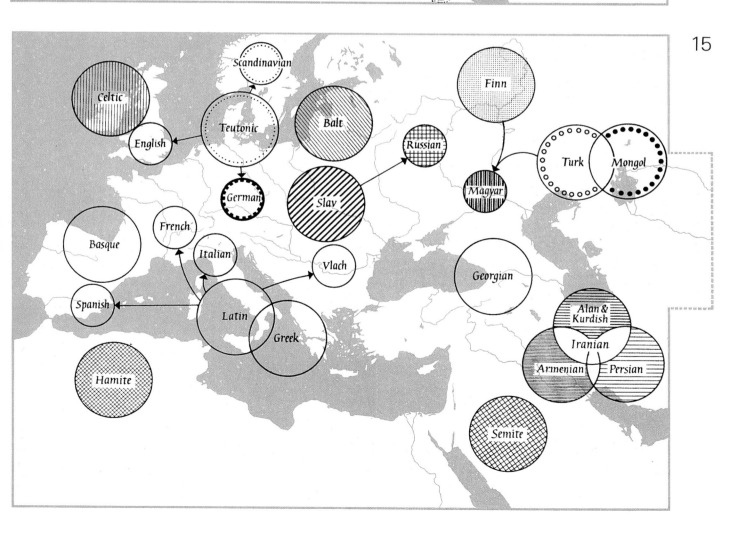

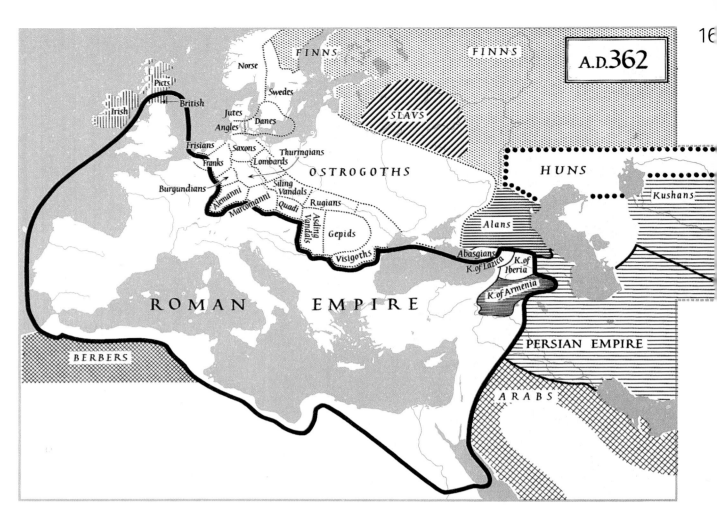

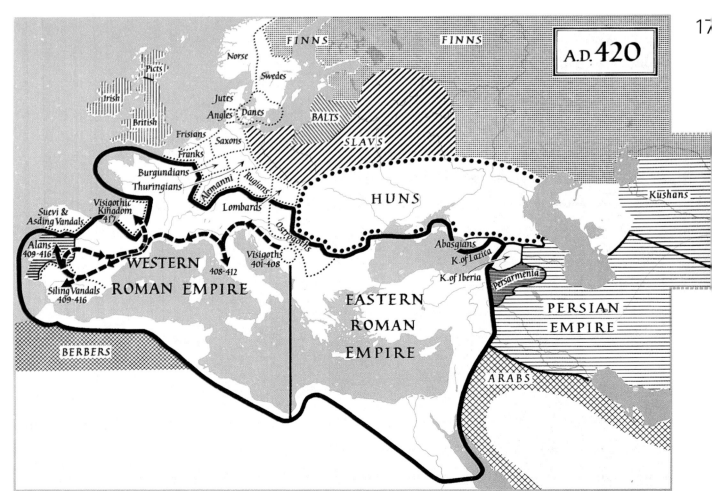

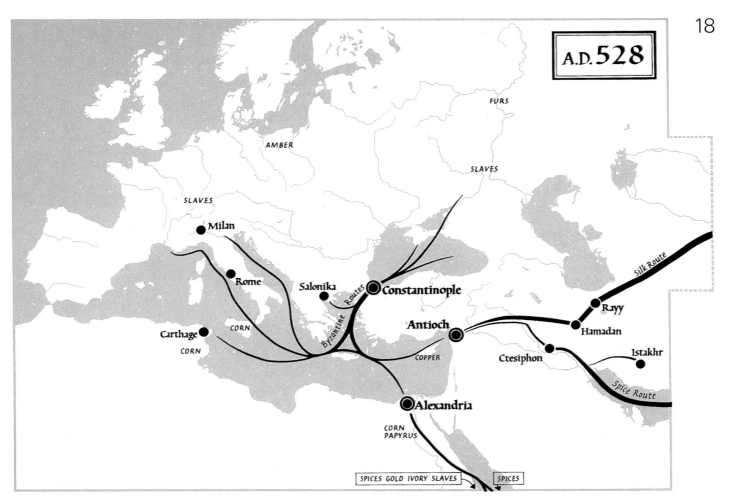

18

A.D. 528

AMBER

FURS

SLAVES

SLAVES

Milan

Rome

Salonika

Constantinople

Byzantine Routes

Silk Route

Rayy

Hamadan

Antioch

Istakhr

Carthage

CORN

COPPER

Ctesiphon

CORN

Spice Route

Alexandria

CORN
PAPYRUS

SPICES GOLD IVORY SLAVES → | SPICES →

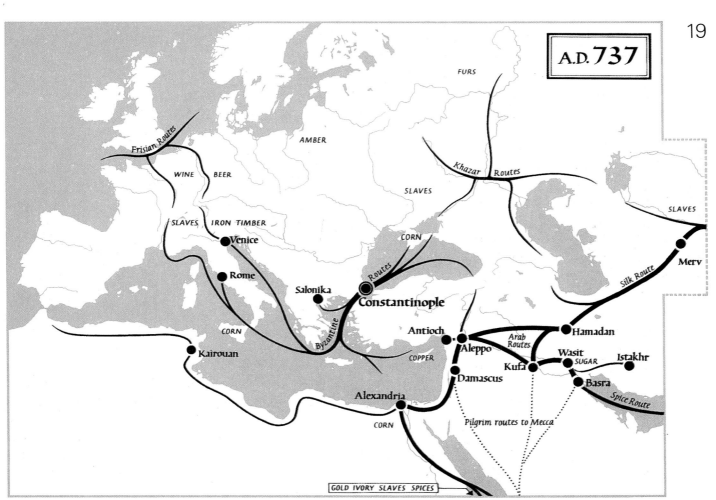

A.D. 737

FURS

Frisian Routes

AMBER

WINE   BEER

Khazar Routes

SLAVES

SLAVES   IRON TIMBER

Venice

CORN

SLAVES

Merv

Rome

Salonika

Routes

Constantinople

Byzantine

Silk Route

Antioch

Hamadan

Kairouan

CORN

Arab Routes

Aleppo

Wasit   SUGAR

Istakhr

COPPER

Kufa

Damascus

Basra

Alexandria

Spice Route

CORN

Pilgrim routes to Mecca

GOLD IVORY SLAVES SPICES →

Hunters colonise the world

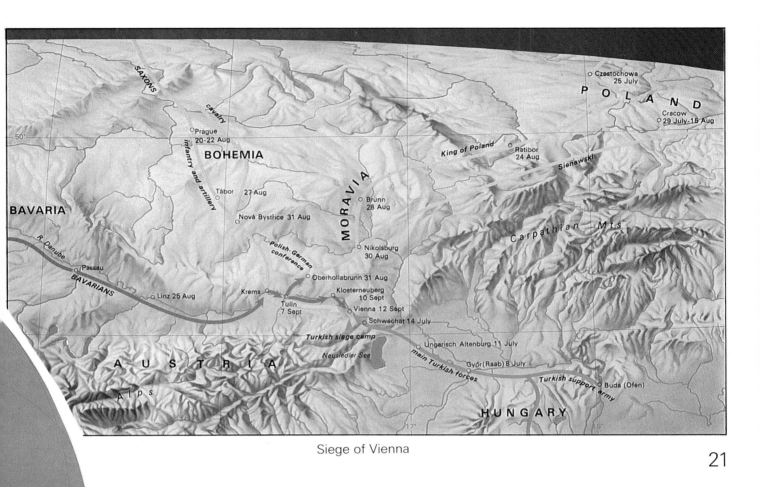

Siege of Vienna

21

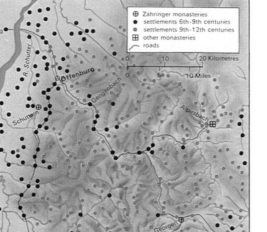

The colonisation of the
Black Forest

22

Zähringer monasteries
settlements 6th-9th centuries
settlements 9th-12th centuries
other monasteries
roads

0   10   20 Kilometres
0   5   10 Miles

Strassburg

R. Schutter

R. Rhine

Offenburg

Gengenbach

Schuttern

Alpirsbach

St. Georgen

Waldkirch

Villingen

Breisach

Freiburg

St. Peter   St. Margen

R. Breg

R. Brigach

Solden
St. Ulrich

Friedenweiler

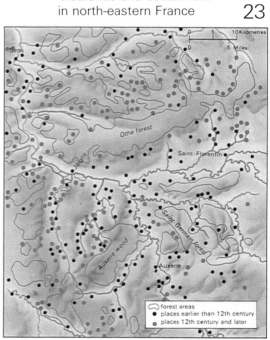

Clearance and settlement
in north-eastern France

23

0   5   10 Kilometres
0   5 Miles

Sens

Othe forest

Saint-Florentin

Joigny

Auxerre wood

Saint Germain forest

Auxerre

forest areas
places earlier than 12th century
places 12th century and later

| 1000s of years BC | 8 | 7 | 6 | 5 | 4 | 3 | 2 | 1 | 0 | 1 | 2 |
| 1000s of years before present | 10 | 9 | 8 | 7 | 6 | 5 | 4 | 3 | 2 | 1 | 0 |

TUNDRA — COLONISATION OF THE ARCTIC *Eskimo technology*

BOREAL REGION (CONIFEROUS FOREST) — INTENSIFIED HUNTING, FISHING AND GATHERING — REINDEER HERDING

TEMPERATE REGION (DECIDUOUS FOREST) — CULTIVATION — *plough agriculture mixed farming* — URBAN LIFE

STEPPE REGIONS — *colonisation* — PASTORAL NOMADS *Domestication of horse, onager, camel*

SUBTROPICAL REGIONS (INCLUDING MEDITERRANEAN) — *CEREAL COLLECTING* — *CEREAL CULTIVATION Sheep and cattle domestication* — *Irrigation Draught animals Tree crops* — URBAN LIFE

TROPICAL SE ASIA — CULTIVATION *Root crops in Africa and SE Asia*

PACIFIC ISLANDS — CULTIVATION *Colonisation of the Pacific*

24

The cumulative consequences of the agricultural revolution

25

The colonisation of Europe

Impressed ware cultures

Hunters and pastoralists

Mediterranean Se[a]

R. Loire

St Michel-du-Touch

R. Garonne

Pyrenees

O Grotte d'Escoural

O Coveta de l'or

Hen[...]

B[...]

main routes of agrarian expansion

dates of agricultural settlement (based on tree-ring corrected radio carbon dating):

7000-6000 BC
6000-5000 BC
5000-4000 BC
4000-3000 BC
3000-2000 BC

Bowl cultures — archaeological names of colonising groups

O Hembury — sites of excavated early farming villages

30°   20°

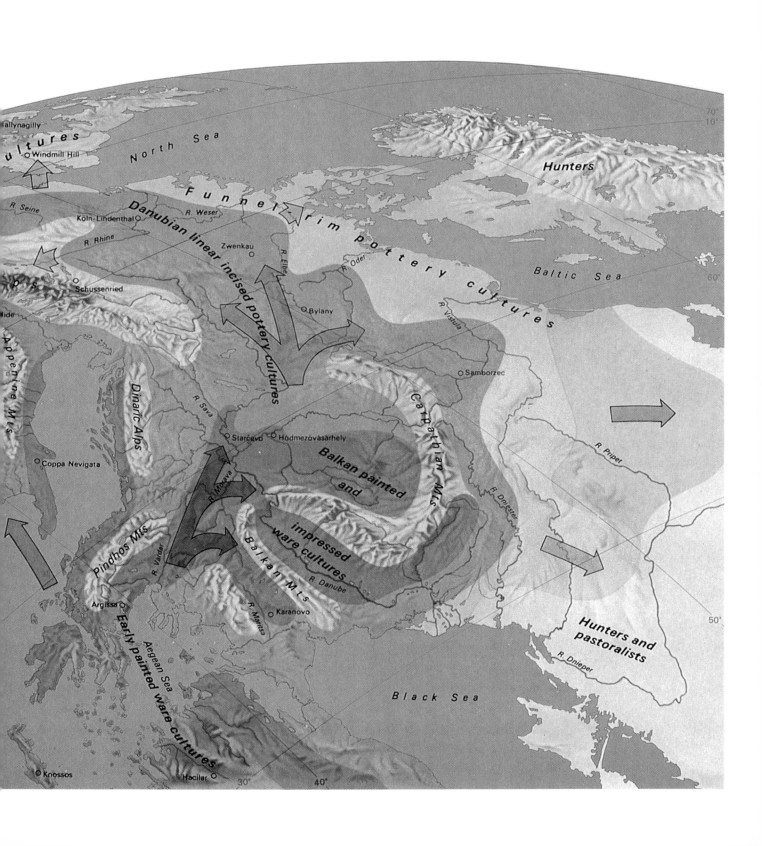

...llynagilly

Windmill Hill

North Sea

Hunters

...ultures

R. Seine

Köln-Lindenthal

R. Weser

Danubian linear incised pottery cultures

R. Rhine

Zwenkau

R. Elbe

R. Oder

Baltic Sea

70°
10°

60°

Funnel-rim pottery cultures

Schussenried

Bylany

R. Vistula

...ide

Samborzec

Appenine Mts

Dinaric Alps

R. Sava

Carpathian Mts

Coppa Nevigata

Starčevo

Hódmezövásárhely

Balkan painted

R. Pripet

R. Morava

and

R. Dniester

Pindhos Mts

R. Vardar

**impressed
ware cultures**

R. Danube

Balkan Mts

Argissa

R. Maritsa

Karanovo

Early painted ware cultures

Aegean Sea

Hunters and
pastoralists

R. Dnieper

50°

Knossos

Hacilar

30°

40°

Black Sea

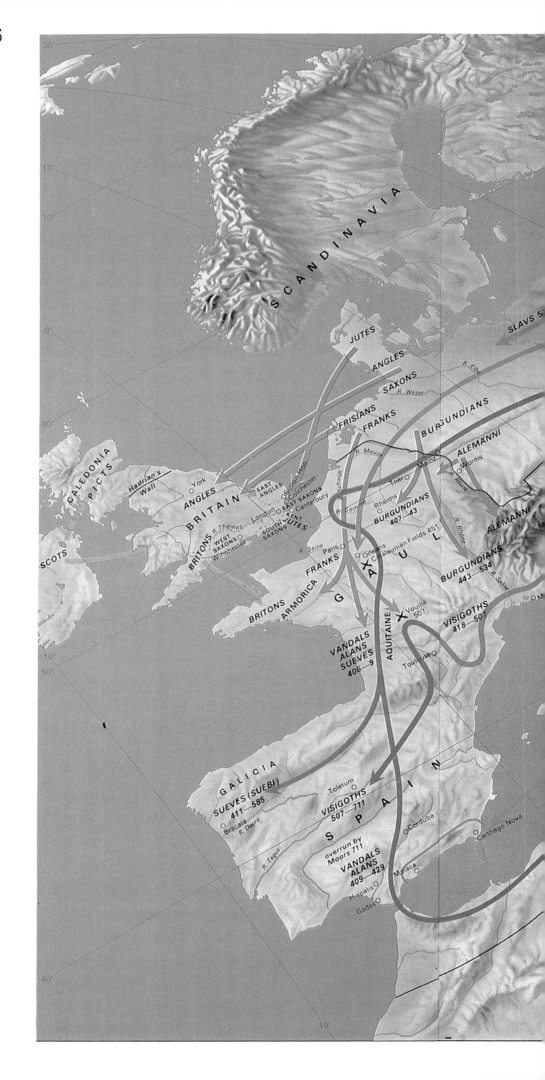

26

SCANDINAVIA

SLAVS

JUTES

ANGLES

SAXONS

R. Elbe

FRISIANS

FRANKS

BURGUNDIANS

R. Weser

R. Meuse

ALEMANNI

Mainz

Worms

CALEDONIA

PICTS

Hadrian's Wall

York

ANGLES

BRITAIN

EAST ANGLES

Sutton Hoo

Colchester

EAST SAXONS

Canterbury

KENT

SOUTH SAXONS

JUTES

London

R. Thames

BRITONS

WEST SAXONS

Winchester

R. Somme

Rheims

Trier

R. Scheldt

R. Rhine

BURGUNDIANS

407—43

BURGUNDIANS

443—534

ALEMANNI

R. Rhône

SCOTS

G A U L

Orleans

Catalaunian Fields 451

FRANKS

R. Seine

Paris

BRITONS

ARMORICA

VANDALS

ALANS

SUEVES

406—9

AQUITAINE

Vouillé

507

VISIGOTHS

418—507

Toulouse

GALICIA

SUEVES (SUEBI)

411—585

Bracara

R. Douro

Toletum

VISIGOTHS

507—711

S P A I N

Corduba

Carthago Nova

R. Tagus

overrun by
Moors 711

VANDALS

ALANS

409—429

Malaca

Hispalis

Gades

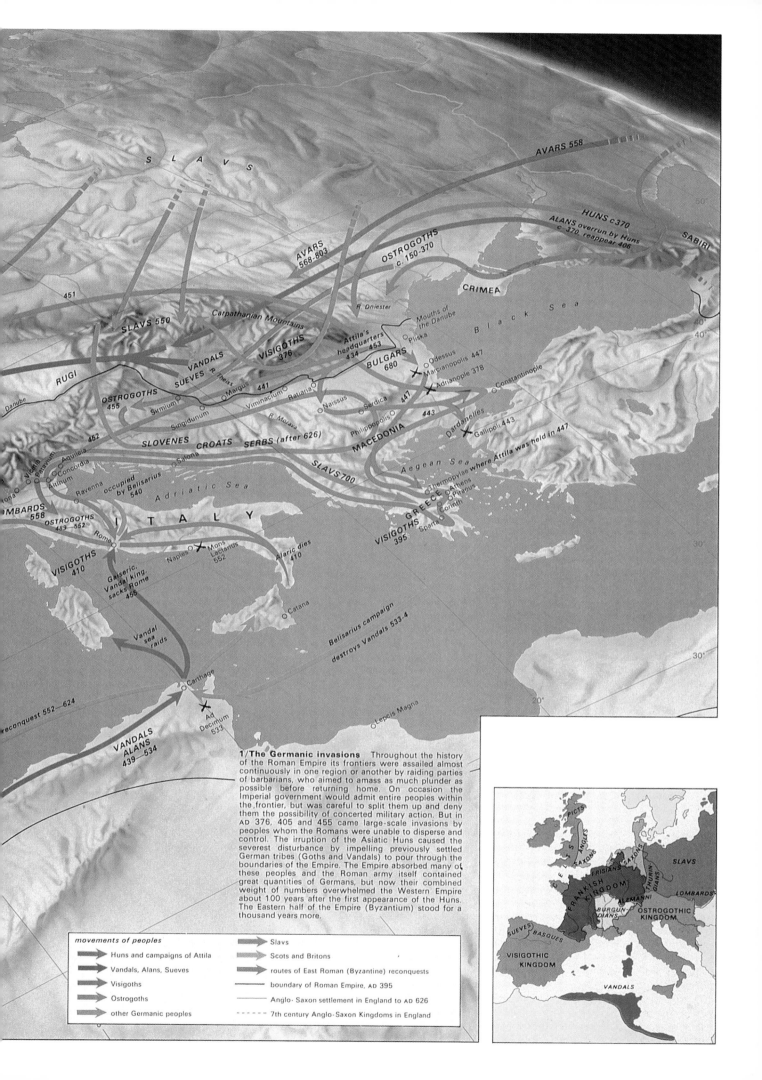

AVARS 558

SABIRI

HUNS c370

ALANS overrun by Huns
c. 370, reappear 406

SABIRI

S L A V S

451

AVARS
568-803

OSTROGOTHS
c. 150-370

CRIMEA

SLAVS 550

Carpathanian Mountains

R. Dniester

Mouths of
the Danube

Black Sea

Pliska

RUGI

VISIGOTHS
376

Attila's
headquarters
434-453

BULGARS
680

Odessus

Marcianopolis 447

VANDALS

R. Theiss

441

SUEVES

OSTROGOTHS
455

Sirmium

Margus

Viminacium

Ratiaria

Danube

Singidunum

R. Morava

Naissus

Serdica

Adrianople 378

Constantinople

452

SLOVENES

CROATS

SERBS (after 626)

Philippopolis

447

MACEDONIA

443

Dardanelles

Gallipoli 443

Aquileia

Salona

SLAVS 700

Thermopylae where Attila was held in 447

Vicelia

Patavium

Concordia

Altinum

Ravenna

occupied
by Belisarius
540

Adriatic Sea

Aegean Sea

GREECE

Athens

MBARDS
558

OSTROGOTHS
489—552

ITALY

Rome

Piraeus

VISIGOTHS
395

Sparta

Corinth

VISIGOTHS
410

Gaiseric,
Vandal king,
sacks Rome
455

Naples

Mons
Lactarius
552

Alaric dies
410

Vandal
sea
raids

Catana

Belisarius campaign
destroys Vandals 533-4

Carthage

reconquest 552—624

Ad
Decimum
533

VANDALS
ALANS
439—534

Lepcis Magna

1/The Germanic invasions Throughout the history
of the Roman Empire its frontiers were assailed almost
continuously in one region or another by raiding parties
of barbarians, who aimed to amass as much plunder as
possible before returning home. On occasion the
Imperial government would admit entire peoples within
the frontier, but was careful to split them up and deny
them the possibility of concerted military action. But in
AD 376, 405 and 455 came large-scale invasions by
peoples whom the Romans were unable to disperse and
control. The irruption of the Asiatic Huns caused the
severest disturbance by impelling previously settled
German tribes (Goths and Vandals) to pour through the
boundaries of the Empire. The Empire absorbed many of
these peoples and the Roman army itself contained
great quantities of Germans, but now their combined
weight of numbers overwhelmed the Western Empire
about 100 years after the first appearance of the Huns.
The Eastern half of the Empire (Byzantium) stood for a
thousand years more.

movements of peoples

→ Huns and campaigns of Attila

→ Vandals, Alans, Sueves

→ Visigoths

→ Ostrogoths

→ other Germanic peoples

→ Slavs

→ Scots and Britons

→ routes of East Roman (Byzantine) reconquests

— boundary of Roman Empire, AD 395

— Anglo-Saxon settlement in England to AD 626

--- 7th century Anglo-Saxon Kingdoms in England

PICTS

ANGLES

SCOTS

SAXONS

FRISIANS

SAXONS

SLAVS

FRANKISH
KINGDOM

THURIN-
GIANS

LOMBARDS

ALEMANNI

BURGUN-
DIANS

OSTROGOTHIC
KINGDOM

SUEVES

BASQUES

VISIGOTHIC
KINGDOM

VANDALS

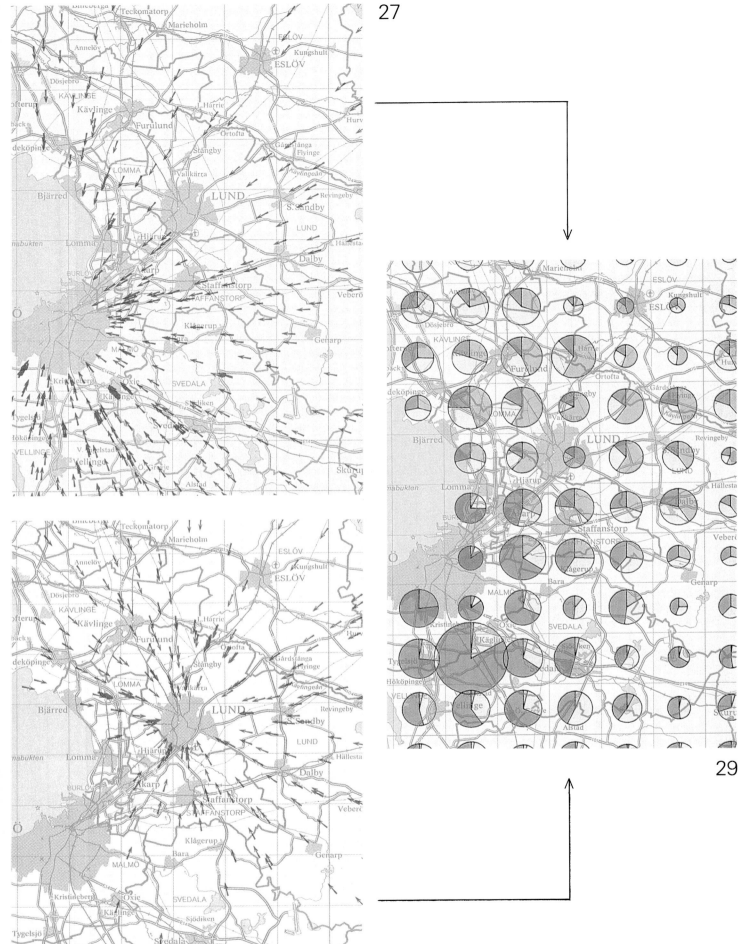

27

28

29

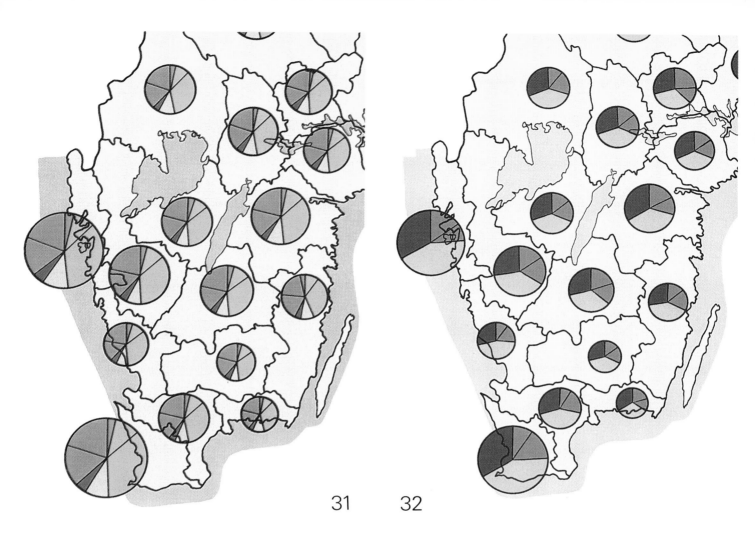

31 32

33

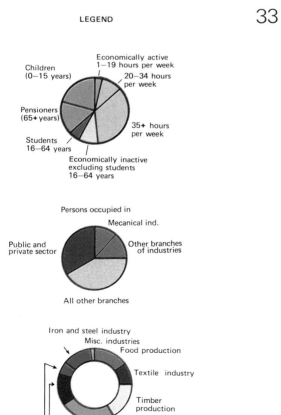

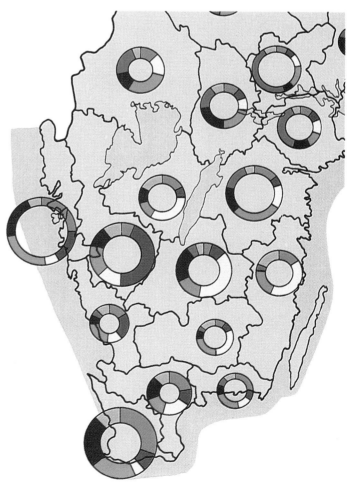

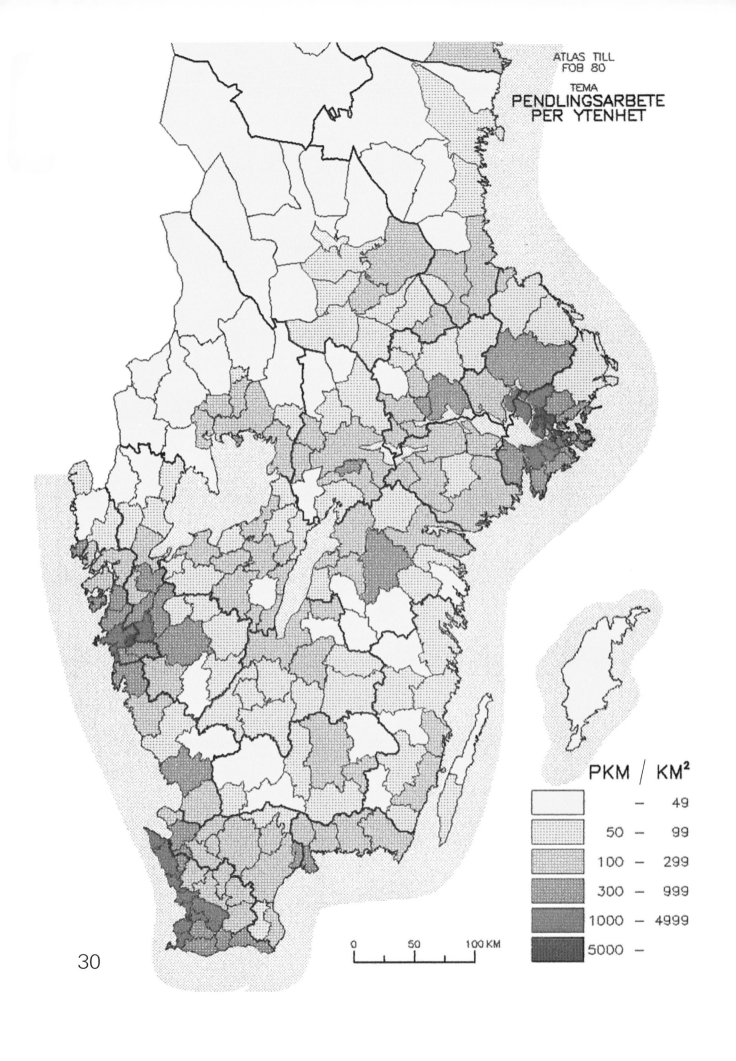

PKM / KM²

	—	49
	50 —	99
	100 —	299
	300 —	999
	1000 —	4999
	5000 —	

0   50   100 KM

30

Composite elements of the play

Most complex play situations can be synthesized from the three basic play elements presented above — area-bound activity, movement, sending signals. There are, however, some composite play sequences which recur so often that it is worth giving them special mention.

All three are based on area-bound movement, i.e. the area, the territory, defined by the pattern of motion.

Movement

The first is a matter of the territory being moved (figure 12 F). The implication is that the area-bound movement ceases, is succeeded by a phase of directed motion (see the arrow) after which an area-bound pattern of movement is again resumed.

Dislocation

The second is the progressive dislocation of the area — a continuous motion resulting in the gradual displacement of the territory defined by the movement without any well-defined movement-phase (see figure 12 G).

Expansion

The third, frequently-observed, composite play sequence is the expansion of the territory, the field of movement. It can occur in all directions as suggested by 12 H, it can also be limited to one or two directions.

An example of the first type of territorial movement is the expansion of the Huns (see the colour supplement, figures 16 — 17).

The second type of movement cannot be found in explicit form among the examples in the colour supplement. However, the arrows which illustrate the movements of population groups on several maps of mass migrations seem to have this significance — at least during some phases of the movements represented by the arrows.

The third type of movement — territorial expansion — is among the most common play sequences on historical maps.

The expansion of the Celts (figure 6 in the colour supplement) shows all three components of territorial expansion: the core, the major movements leading to expansion and the expanded territory.

An even more highly-detailed illustration of this process can be found on page 272 in the same atlas (figure 9 in the colour supplement) which shows the development of Siberia during the 17th century. The three eras of Russian expansion are illustrated on a rather highly-detailed setting map. The image of this territorial expansion is supplemented by the routes of expeditions etc. which preceded and made possible the territorial expansion.

Colour supplement
Figure 30
Commuting between urbanized areas expressed in passenger kilometres per unit of area (= passenger-kilometres per km² and day). The map indicates the impact of commuting operations on the environments of the municipalities. For additional explanation see A Census Atlas of Sweden.

It is clearly difficult in some cases to distinguish actors from certain accentuated elements of the setting map. It can sometimes be equally difficult to assign a map element to one of the categories "actor" or "play". In these cases it may be simpler to think in terms of

setting map   = background illustration or base map
and
theme   = element of the setting and/or actors and/or play
                 which is stressed against the background of a setting
                 map.

This semantic usage also forges a link between human cartography and the terms used here (setting/actor/play) on the one hand, and the established, but inadequately defined term "thematic cartography" on the other.

Cartographic design of the individual map

Graphic elements, visual planes, hierarchies

A map of human activities is composed of a description of the setting often supplemented by a presentation of the deployment of the actors and a description of the play being performed there. If the map designer wishes to communicate his conception to a prospective reader, he must first reshape it into a cartographic presentation with the aid of graphic symbols. These symbols are

points
lines
areas
alphanumeric symbols

These graphic symbols can be combined with one another

either   to illustrate a hypothetical situation or course of events in a
         direct manner. In this case the illustration is done in such a
         way as to call to mind the visual impression this situation or
         course of events would make on an observer located a great
         but finite distance away. In other words, the map contains
         pictorial elements
or   to reproduce the same situation or course of events projected
         on a plane surface, observed from an infinitely distance
         place. The map is in other words a pure, two-dimensional,
         graphic image.

Figure 20 in the colour supplement from the Times Atlas of World History can exemplify the first type of cartographic representation. The map creates the illusion that we are observing the Earth's surface from a great altitude, and seeing its topography appear very distinctly. Against this backdrop, various migration flows are depicted in the simplified form of sharply-delineated arrows. The image is thus a simplified illustration of a setting (with its landforms vertically exaggerated) and a depiction of the play taking place there, also in a simplified version. It is important to establish that in spite of this illusion, the map is constructed in a particular projection with the combination of trueness to scale and distortion which characterizes that particular type of map projection.

The other alternative, a phase in a course of events observed from an infinitely distant point, is presented in figures 14 -17 in the colour supplement (McEvedy: The Penguin Atlas of Medieval History). The setting (hydrographic features) as well as the actors (the different ethnic groups) and the play elements reproduced (such as the migratory movements of the Visigoths) have been illustrated as flat, two-dimensional images.

Contrast, visual plane, structuring

The elements of the map — lines, points, areas, letters and numerals — are perceptible thanks to their contrast with the background. With varying degrees of intensity, the symbols' size, shape, colour and even direction and texture, etc. stand out from the visual background. The stronger the contrast, the more distinctly the symbol stands out against the white, grey or coloured surface of the paper, and the closer it appears to the observer.

A narrow, black line appears close to the background, far from the reader; a wider one gives the impression of being closer to the observer. A small point symbol seems to be located in the vicinity of the visual background; a large one seems to come to the fore, to approach the observer. A point symbol which has a small surface but a more "aggressive" shape and/or more intense colour will stand out more sharply from the background, and appear closer to the observer than a symbol with less-accentuated shape and colour. The same approach can be applied with regard to surface symbols and area symbols.

The three-dimensional graphic space

The implication of this argument is that the two-dimensional graphic field is in fact a three-dimensional graphic space where the X and Y co-ordinates specify the positions and dimensions of the symbols, while the third Z co-ordinate shows the distance of a graphic element from the background surface of the image. The stronger a graphic element stands out from the background, the closer it appears to the observer.

Different graphic elements — points, lines, areas, letters or numerals — having approximately the same degree of contrast with the common background, will appear to be the same distance from the visual background, and consequently, to lie on the same visual plane. This concept has been systematized within the theory of design, and especially with regard to graphic design, and has been discussed by Scott (1951) and Graves (1951) among others, who probably refine the ideas of the Bauhaus school in Germany. Psychologists' investigations of the figure — ground phenomenon would seem to have been influential precursors. The concept has been discussed in the cartographic literature by Robinson, Sale and Morrison (1978) among others.

Intellectual and graphic stratification

To collect on one *visual* plane, all graphic elements which represent the map elements belonging to one *conceptual* level — that is one of the most urgent tasks for cartographic design. Combining these elements in independent visual planes located at specific, contextually-determined distances from one another, fulfills one of the most important criteria of good cartographic design. The process could be called graphic stratification. To "overstratify" means that the visual distance between the different graphic planes has been made too large so that the map disintegrates into its various components among which the contrast is too great. The opposite is to "understratify", i.e. to provide insufficient distance between visual planes with the consequence that non-related elements become intermingled. A cartographic illustration is well-structured when the different graphic planes are easily-distinguishable, i.e. the distance between them is sufficiently great so that the uppermost graphic plane appears clearly above the one below, but with the distance between them still sufficiently small for them to form a visual whole.

When the graphic structure so constructed is congruent with the mental concept of the map designer, there is reason to say that some of the most essential criteria of sound cartographic design have been fulfilled.

Hierarchies

The three basic cartographic elements — the setting, the actors and the play — can be combined in a map in different ways. A map can be composed of one or two such elements, for example of the setting alone or the setting with the actors. It is also possible to combine all three elements in such a way as to create the same visual distance between the actors and the play as between the setting and the actors. This presents two difficulties, however: the actors and their play are often more intimately connected than the setting and the actors. In addition, the total range of contrast of the map — the visual distance between the setting and the play — becomes so great that the map disintegrates.

Actor + play constitute their own level in the hierarchy

To avoid this, a hierarchic structure is often chosen. The first step in the hierarchy is often to separate the setting on the one hand from the actors and the play on the other. The distance between these two main components is often rather great.

In the next step, the plane of the actors is separated from that of the play. The distance between these latter two components is, however, not as great as the distance between the setting and the actors (see figure 13). The composition of the map thus reflects the fundamental conceptual structure: the setting as backdrop for the actors and their play, where the latter two are separated but still close together.

84

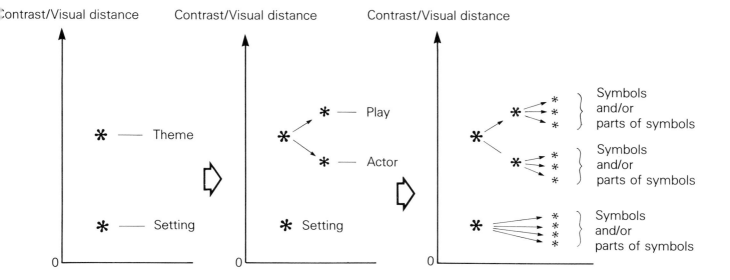

Contrast/Visual distance   Contrast/Visual distance   Contrast/Visual distance

Figure 13   Contrast/visual distance between the various elements of the map.

Hierarchic
design of
symbols

The hierarchic structure can also apply to the design of symbols. All the components of a symbol such as a graduated circle: the outlining and shading of its different parts — can, of course, lie in one and the same visual plane. If we choose, on the other hand, to draw attention to the outlines of the diagram rather than to the shading, its basic structure appears more distinctly.

Sophisticated
solutions

Grouping the graphic elements in visual planes can also be done in a more sophisticated way than that described above. In certain cases the visual planes of the setting and play elements change places. The New Cambridge Modern History Atlas provides some examples of maps in which the dominant role is assumed by the setting plane which, with its name and elements, describes the landscape. *Behind* this — in very light shading — are shown the areas where certain designated events take place. The visual plane of the play is thus placed behind the one containing the setting.

Even when the ordinary solution is employed — the plane of the play is in front of the setting, it can be implemented in unconventional ways. As a rule, the setting map is shaded in lighter tones than the plane of the actors and the play to thereby appear more distant. A more unconventional solution is to cover the entire surface of the setting map with dark, over-saturated shades. The actors and the play are then represented by symbols in bright, clear, sharp colours. This solution draws attention, with the aid of greater strength of colour, to the actors' plane, while the setting map with its over-saturated colours descends into the background.

Symbols in
front of and
behind the
plane of the play

One can also imagine the visual base plane of a map placed relatively far from the zero plane, i.e. the (usually) white surface of the paper. The base plane of the map can be a light-grey surface and plane no. 2, for example, can be placed *behind* this surface. The symbols then become white, i.e. cut-outs, "holes" in the grey surface. Plane no. 3 is placed *in front of* the

85

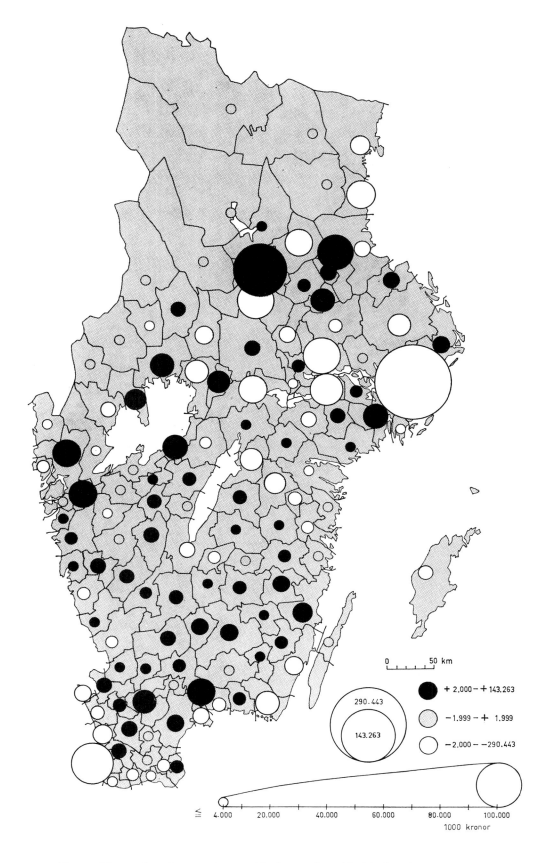

Figure 14   An element located in front of and behind an intermediate visual plane. Source: Törnquist.

base plane of the map, shaded in black or dark-grey tones. The distance between planes no. 2 and 3 thereby becomes greater, and the link between them which was discussed above — for example between actor and play — cannot be established. This type of sophisticated presentation is used, among other things, for recording changes, where, for example, white circular surfaces indicate a decrease while black ones represent an increase (see figure 14).

Symbols of dynamic and overlapping phenomena

The correspondence of concept and visual/graphic structure is a requirement which not only concerns the basic structure of a map, i.e. the arrangement of different conceptual and visual planes. The same requirement applies to the design of the individual symbols.

Cartographic representation always means simplification: the limited space available on the map requires that a good number of geographic elements be excluded from the map, and that those remaining be presented in a simplified manner. Sound cartographic design implies that the process of exclusion be done in such a manner that the remaining elements presented on the map form a logically-coherent whole, that this totality is arranged in such a way that its structure is clearly discernible (see the previous section) but also that, as far as possible, the individual symbols reflect the nature of the phenomena being illustrated.

Design of geographical elements with discrete or with fading character

Considerable portions of maps for human geography consist of discrete elements — buildings, roads, coastlines, boundaries between different territories etc. It is these discrete elements which are easiest to illustrate on a map. It is easiest to reproduce precise geometric configurations by using point, line and area symbols. Such symbols are often employed to represent phenomena which are not spatially discrete. This may be necessary when the scale of the map is so small that it does not permit the use of symbols with a fading character. It is, however, desirable that the scale and degree of generalization of the map are chosen so as to fairly represent the character of the illustrated geographic phenomena — whether or not their boundaries are distinct, whether or not their influence diminishes gradually and within which space this occurs.

Overlapping territories

It is quite common in maps of historic or other chronological occurrences for several actors to appear simultaneously within one and the same space, and for their activities to be superimposed upon one another. It is even more common for the peripheral areas of the territories of several actors to overlap. To find a cartographic design which can describe interplay of this kind in a comprehensible way is as demanding and difficult as it is important. Figure 12 in the colour supplement (page 110 from the Penguin Atlas of World History) demonstrates a convincing solution of associated problems.

87

The above-mentioned map, along with several other maps in the this section and borrowed from the samt source, provides a good example of the design of dynamic chans of events. In figure 7 (colour) the progressively-heavier shading of the arrows suggests the actual movement as well as the diffuse demarcation of the core area. In a similar way, we get a strong impression of how the territory of the Celtic tribes expanded, and of the large population movements which took place there as part of the territorial expansion (figure 4).

An even more refined example can be found in figure 20 in the colour supplement from the Times Atlas of World History). The shape of the arrows together with the boundaries of the expansion of the hunter population suggest the spread of these peoples across the surface of the Earth.

The air brush
— a tool and its
influence

These and other similar examples demonstrate more clearly than theoretical discourses the need for, but also the opportunities for, effective cartographic design of complex and/or dynamic phenomena and events. A common denominator in these examples is the utilization of a tool, namely the air brush. With this instrument progressive colour transition can be drawn, which in turn makes possible the graphic representation of the transition between different phenomena, the fading away of effects with increasing distance or the dynamics of events in a way that is directly perceivable. A large part of the recent development of the cartographic language within the field of human cartography can be directly attributed to the innovative use of this tool.

The statistical map: Characteristics, design, types

The previous section dealt with the design of maps which, in a direct manner, *illustrate* the setting, the presence of the actors or their play. These maps can be thought of as graphic minutes of the appearance of the setting or of the events taking place there. Statistical maps can be conceived of as indirect depictions of these conditions. In the design of statistical maps, one or a few components are chosen representing the setting, the actors, the play or its results. The components are then treated as an abstract volume of data, homogeneous or more composite in nature. The map aims at reproducing the geographical distribution of the data and its composition as well.

The geographical distribution of the statistical mass can be represented by points, lines or areas. The *points* either indicate the geographical position of an individual object or constitute a common reference point for several objects.

If the population of an entire town, for example, is presented in the form of a graduated circle centred on the midpoint of the town, this is then an *object point*. (See figures 15 and 17.) If, on the other hand, we base the

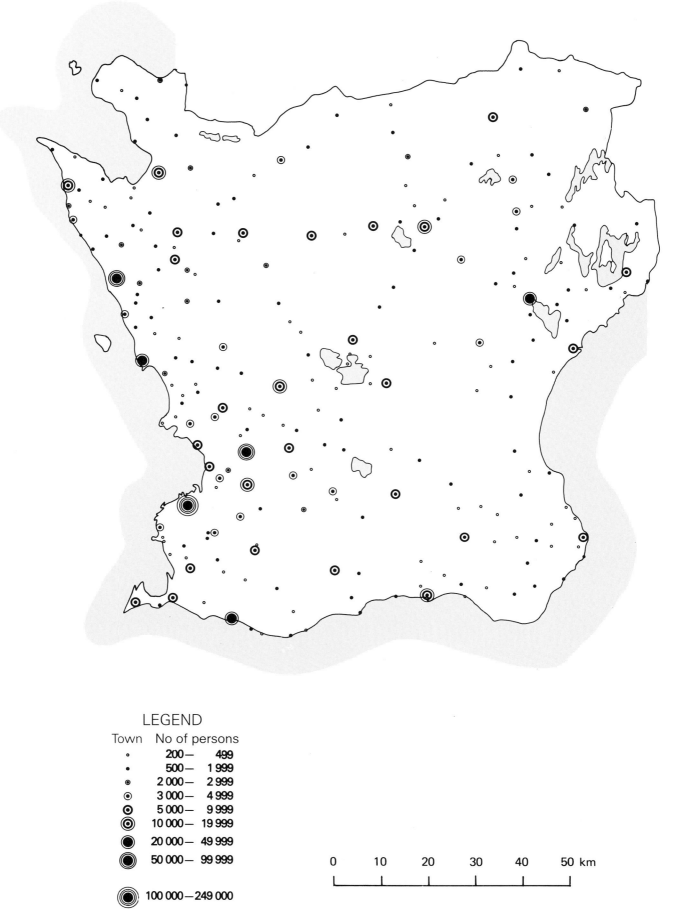

LEGEND

Town	No of persons
∘	200 — 499
•	500 — 1 999
⊙	2 000 — 2 999
⊙	3 000 — 4 999
◉	5 000 — 9 999
◎	10 000 — 19 999
●	20 000 — 49 999
◉	50 000 — 99 999
◉	100 000 — 249 000

0   10   20   30   40   50 km

Figure 15 Urbanized areas in Skåne (Scania), the southernmost part of Sweden, according to population size. (From *A Census Atlas of Sweden*)

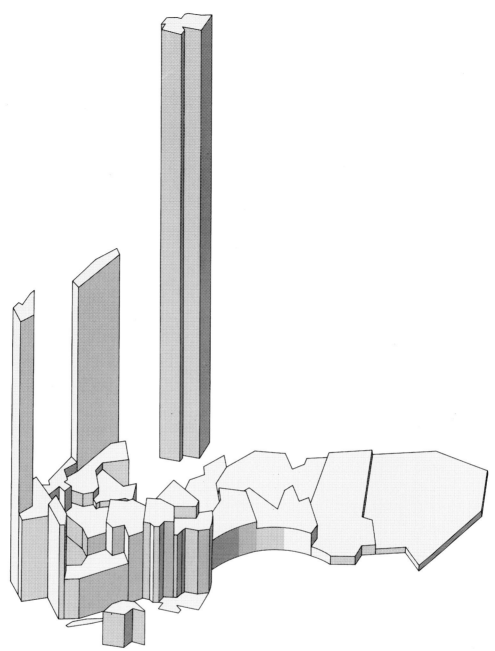

Figure 16 The variation of populations density within Sweden 1980 (Max.
density = 235 persons/km² Min. density = 3 persons/km²).
(From *A Census Atlas of Sweden*)

presentation on the populations of individual properties, and approximate
the centres of gravity of each nth individual (such as the 100th, 500th,
1000th etc.), we are employing *reference points* for several individuals/objects.
(See figure 57.)

**3-dimensional
models of the
statistical mass**

Maps which present the volume of flow along channels use *lines* as geographic references. The presentation of the volume of automobile traffic on
highways, the frequency of service and volume of traffic on railways, the
number of airline flights and the volume of air-passengers and air-freight,
the volume of shipping on different routes are some examples of statistical
maps presented with lines as geographic reference.

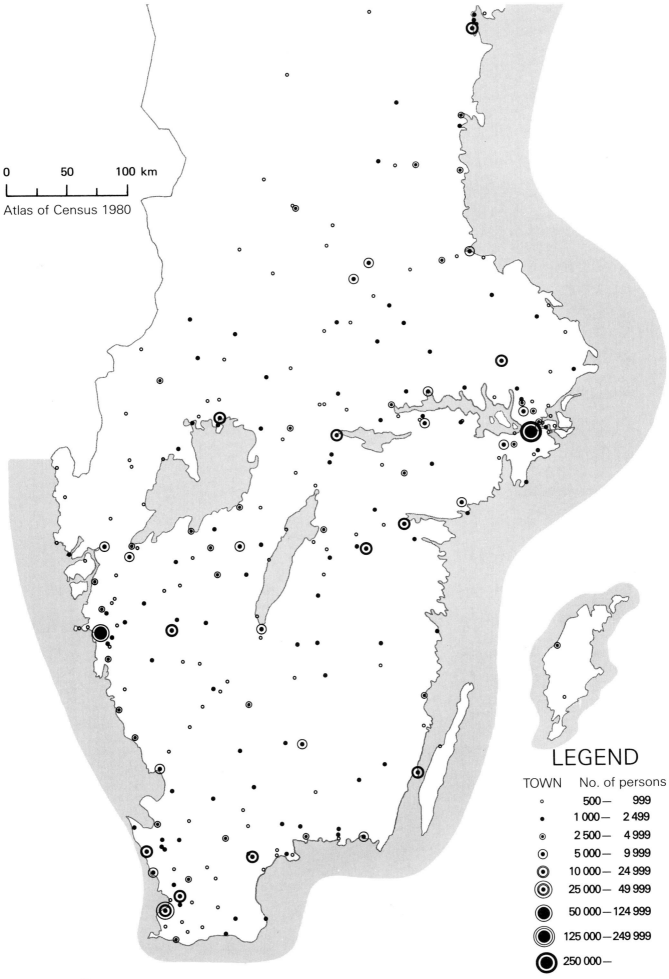

LEGEND

TOWN	No. of persons
o	500 — 999
•	1 000 — 2 499
⊙	2 500 — 4 999
⊙	5 000 — 9 999
⊙	10 000 — 24 999
◎	25 000 — 49 999
●	50 000 — 124 999
●	125 000 — 249 999
◉	250 000 —

Figure 17 Urbanized areas in southern Sweden according to the number of incoming commuters. (From *A Census Atlas of Sweden*)

Figure 18   Commuting from rural areas in southernmost
Sweden to four urbanized areas in November 1980.

Maps which present the mass of data on an *area basis* are based on the assumption that the illustrated data are spread continuously across an entire geographic space. This continuity may imply that the mass is *evenly* distributed throughout the unit or units of area covered by the survey. (See figure 16.) The continuity may on the other hand, signify continuous, uninterrupted diversity just as gently undulating terrain alternates between hills and valleys. This approach characterizes all statistical maps of the isarithmic type, i.e. maps where the distribution of the statistical mass is depicted by height contours (figure 58).

The relationship between the geographical distribution of the data mass and the way it is presented geographically is not always straight-forward. Flows, for example — which by rights should be illustrated along channels — are often represented instead by positional (point) symbols. Maps showing the number of commuters to towns and other urbanized areas in a region, present nodes in a network of journeys (see figure 17). This type of map illustrates only the nodes and the total number of journeys to these points — not the journeys, the channel-bound movements, themselves.

Other positional presentations may be more complex. Diagrams presenting commuting patterns in a region — the number of commuters to and from towns and urbanized areas and the number of people living and working in the same area (see figure 20) — provide large amounts of information indirectly about the volume of the flows, their origins and destinations within the mapped area — but not about their precise locations along the routes.

Two-point positional symbols are a transitional phenomenon between positional and linear ones (see the black and white arrow map in figure 18 and figures 27 and 28 in the colour supplement). An example is given here in which all the individual journeys are directed towards the same point (commuting to a town). The origins of all journeys are presented, and since the destinations of the journeys are approximated, it is possible to suggest the route followed by each unit (here 10 persons).

Volumetric data are often illustrated by area symbols (see figure 30 in the colour supplement). In these cases the same shading is applied to all subareas where the height of the statistical volume lies within a certain interval.

Many similar examples could be provided.

Graphic representation of the statistical mass

From a technical point of view, the easiest way to make statistical maps is to use only numerals to illustrate their contents. The numerals are placed at the relevant reference points, and printed in the same type and size, irrespective of the value represented. The locational elements may be points, lines or areas with irregular or regular positioning. Figure 19 is an

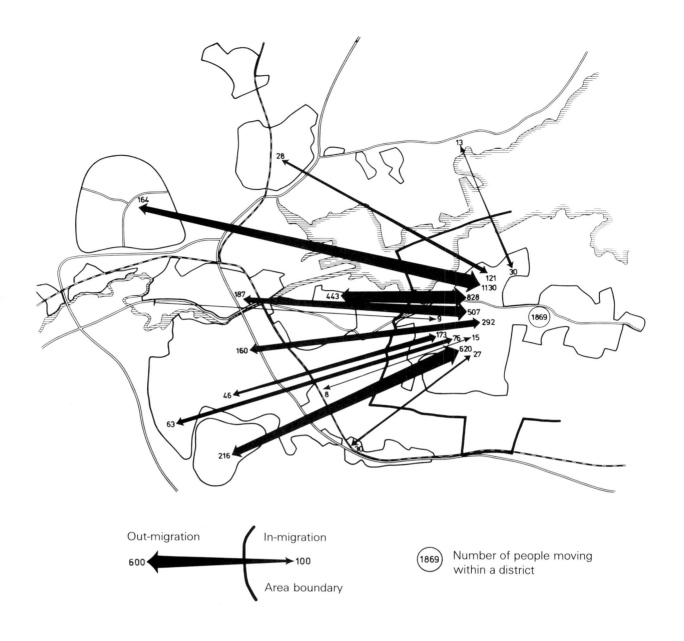

Figure 18A   Two-way migration within the town of Gävle in mid-
              Sweden, Borgegård 1984.

example of irregularly-positioned reference points (the midpoints of the Swedish counties). A hexagonal latticework with numerals is an example of numerals placed within a regular pattern of points (this type of print-out is used in choosing isarithmic levels), while the grid map in figure 58 shows numerals within uniform areas. These kinds of maps are useful as *geographic denotations*.

The limitations
of the numerical
map — and the
brain

The numerals indicate values, statistical amounts, linked to certain geographical positions, but for the magnitude of the values to be comprehensible for the reader, they need to be deciphered, to be analysed intellectually. Since this process is more time-consuming than the direct perception of graphic variables, map reading becomes a very slow process, and it becomes very difficult to grasp the contents of the map in its entirety. This phenomenon is reinforced by the extremely limited capacity of the human brain to deal with more than a few facts simultaneously, see Head (1984). Numerically-skilled and trained individuals can probably extract essential information from this type of numerical presentation, but the document can hardly serve as a "real" map.

Graphic symbols

The true statistical map employs graphic symbols to present the geographical distribution and/or composition of the mass of data. The graphic symbols consist then of point symbols — simple or composite — line symbols, area symbols of different types, volume symbols as well as alphanumeric symbols (where not only the intellectual signification but even the size, colour etc. are varied to indicate the relative size of the specified value).

The character of the symbols may be

nominal	— show whether or not a phenomenon is present in a geographic space
ordinal	— show a phenomenon ranked according to size in different geographic locations
interval or ratio	— show the variations of a phenomenon in different geographic locations along a continuous scale.

Robinson, Sale and Morrison present in matrix form combinations of these levels of scaling and of representational symbols (point, line, area) for presenting statistical values (Robinson, Sale and Morrison 1969, page 96 and 98-101).

Subdivisions bind symbols to the landscape

The graphic symbols which represent the statistical mass are — usually — presented against the background of a map of the landscape within which this mass is assumed to be distributed. The part of the landscape represented by a graphic symbol is indicated on many maps by a special subdivision. These subdivisions are the connecting links between the symbols which present the mass of data and the landscape where the data are distributed. (See figures 43-46.)

Graphic design of the hierarchy of statistical subdivisions

Statistical data are usually acquired from administrative areas. Since, as a rule, these areas belong to subdivisional hierarchies — for example the area of a country is divided into counties which in turn are divided into municipalities and further into parishes — statistical data are usually presented in hierarchic order. Even those subdivisions which are created especially for statistical purposes are usually hierarchically structured since this provides major advantages for the presentation and use of the statistics. Among other things, it is easier to familiarize oneself with statistical data when they are structured hierarchically. It is also easier to find a particular area on a map if the subdivision is hierarchically structured. Consequently, the hierarchic nature of the subdivision is stressed on maps showing subdivisions. Since it is often difficult to present in a satisfactory way the landscape comprising the background of a statistical map, the subdivision itself is often the only map element useful for locating a statisti-

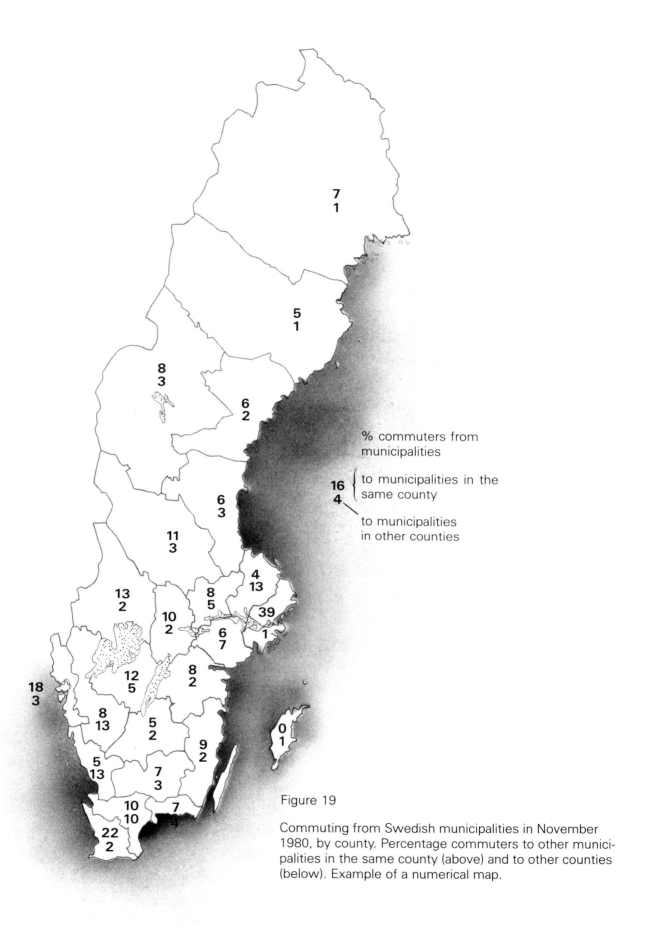

% commuters from
municipalities

16
4
} to municipalities in the
same county

to municipalities
in other counties

Figure 19

Commuting from Swedish municipalities in November
1980, by county. Percentage commuters to other municipalities in the same county (above) and to other counties
(below). Example of a numerical map.

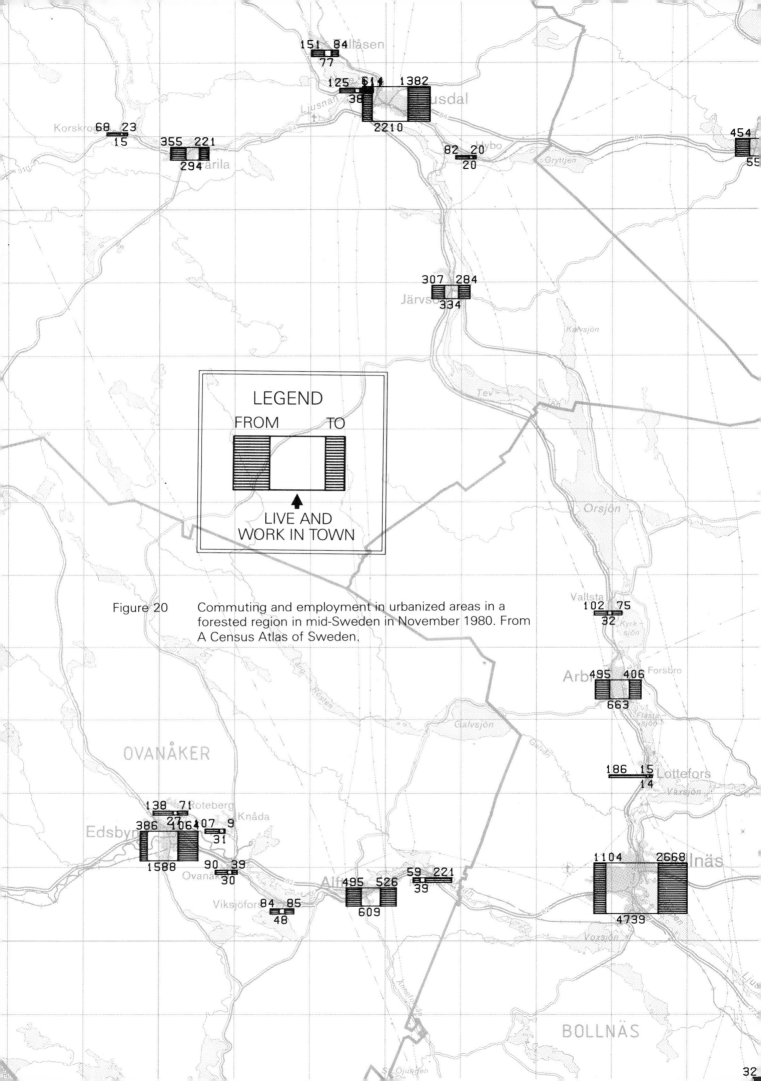

Figure 20   Commuting and employment in urbanized areas in a forested region in mid-Sweden in November 1980. From A Census Atlas of Sweden.

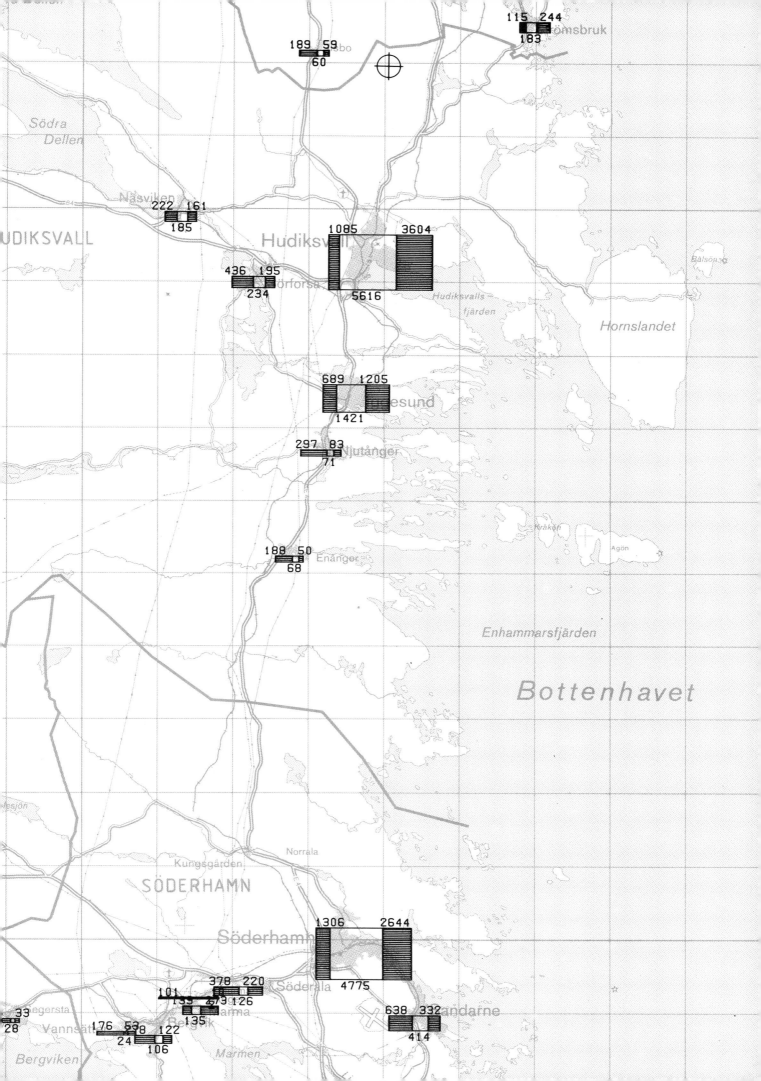

Södra
Dellen

Näsviken

HUDIKSVALL

Hudiksvall

222 · 161
185

436 · 195
234

örforsa

1085 · 3604
5616

Hudiksvalls-
fjärden

Hornslandet

Bålsön

115 · 244
183

ömsbruk

189 · 59
60

bo

689 · 1205
1421

esund

Kråkön

Agön

297 · 83
71

Njutånger

188 · 50
68

Enånger

Enhammarsfjärden

Bottenhavet

esjön

Kungsgärden

Norrala

SÖDERHAMN

Söderhamn

1306 · 2644
4775

Söderala

378 · 220
279 · 126
101
133

eger sta

33
28

176 · 53
24

38 · 122
106

arma

135

Vannsät

Be

Marmen

638 · 332
414

andarne

Södra
Bergviken

cal symbol. In this case the map designer either assumes that the reader recognizes certain parts of this subdivision — for example municipal boundaries and county boundaries in a section of a country — and that, aided by his familiarity with the landscape, he can then mentally fill in all the details not presented by the map designer. Or else he counts on the map reader having access to reference maps of the landscape on which the subdivision in question — for example municipal and county boundaries — is included. The reader can then obtain the facts about the contents of the landscape which the map designer has not presented on his statistical map.

If such a reference map is not available, the designer of a statistical map or map series can prepare one himself, and present the subdivision employed in the statistical maps as an overlay upon the physical landscape. The same subdivision is copied on the individual maps, preferably using an identical graphic design. This subdivision then serves as the link between the presentation of the data mass (in the form of graphic symbols) and the physical landscape.

Designing the statistical map

"A picture is worth more than a thousand words." This overworked figure of speech implies that the human brain has the capacity for handling large amounts of information (within a short period) if this information is supplied visually. What the figure of speech does not say is that not all visual information is available so directly. It is enough to glance at an overloaded, poorly-designed map to realize that some images do not supply any information at all without the expenditure of very large amounts of effort on the part of the reader (and vice versa: that well-prepared verbal information can evoke sequences of images using a minimum of words).

The study of cartographic communication — the chain which leads from the cartographer/the sender via the channel/the map to the map user i.e. the recipient and the processes which take place along this chain — is one of the fields of cartography where research has been most active in recent decades. Research in this field has been inspired largely by psychological investigations — especially perceptual psychology — and to a certain degree also by linguistic research, and it has been characterized by a striving for precision. Evaluations of the value of the research findings are quite varied, however: some scholars are of the opinion that theoretically-interesting results have been achieved, but that they have not yet contributed to the design of better maps, and that the field may have exhausted its developmental potential.

Head (1984) represents a more positive opinion when he observes that within a relatively short time, and partly on an intuitive basis, agreement on some basic issues has developed among a group of scholars including Bertin, Olson, etc., and he suggests that this unanimity could serve as the basis for forming a common perspective on cartographic communications. Some fundamental — and in this context essential — concepts presented in the article can be summarized in the following way

- map reading, like the reading of texts, is done linearly; the eye scans the map's surface point for point along lines
- the brain cannot retain more than $7 +/- 2$ memory units in its short-term memory (STM). Head considers this to be one of the most well-documented background factors concerning map perception
- with the aid of its long-term memory (LTM), the brain identifies the objects thus observed, and using this knowledge, synthesizes the visual impressions into structures often called "chunks" in the North American literature and "supersigns" in the European. These units, which can be looked upon as "words", can be synthesized further into "sentences" and then into "trains of thought". The visual impressions received through map reading are thus passed through a hierarchic accumulation process into complex but well-organized mental images of the landscape represented by the map.

The conclusions which ought to be drawn on the basis of the incomplete excerpt referred to above are

- that a well-designed statistical map facilitates the scanning of its contents by linear eye movements,
- that the map elements thus observed can easily be assembled into visual patterns (supersigns or chunks) and
- that these in turn can be introduced, with a minimum of intellectual effort, into an even more comprehensive pattern covering the entire landscape.

Good (thematic) cartography creates perceptible patterns

An effective design of a statistical map results, therefore, in a pattern which is easily perceptible. It should be possible to interpret with as little intellectual effort as possible.

More tangibly, this implies the following demands:

- that the statistical map elements which are bearers of information appear distinctly against the background of the physical setting
- that it is easy to comprehend the significance of the statistical symbols
- that it is easy to compare the statistical symbols with one another and
- that it is easy to see the statistical symbols and to interpret them as discrete elements in a cohesive pattern.

Here too, good map design implies effective visual order in the sense of suitable balance between the different visual planes — i.e. adequate distance but also sufficient cohesiveness *between* the visual planes — as well as good organization *within* the visual plane which contains information about the statistical mass.

101

With regard to the symbols used to present the statistical mass, it is necessary to weigh the geographical distribution of the statistical mass on the one hand, against its organization, composition, and structure on the other. A detailed geographical presentation can usually only be made for one factor at a time. A detailed dot map or isarithmic map cannot ordinarily be prepared for other than a one-component population (see for example figures 57 and 58). Such a map can present the geographical distribution of the population or of grain production in a region or similar data. If one wishes to present the main features of the age structure for the same region or the break-down of grain production in its main components, one must, as a rule, choose a lower level of geographical detail (see for example figures 30-32 in the colour supplement).

If one wishes to make an even more detailed presentation of population structure, it is necessary to accept an even lower level of geographical detail, until finally one is left with a complex diagram which lacks any geographic elements other than the name of a — usually large — region, for example an entire country, since the cartographic background has become more or less unnecessary. It is true that one or more such diagrams can be presented against the background of a map. A map of this type is so demanding to read, however, that the various diagrams have to be studied one by one. It is then hardly possible to make the rapid comparisons of location and content of the individual map symbols which enable one to link together cartographic elements into a cohesive cartographic image.

It appears that the readability even of overloaded maps can be improved by good graphic order, reading instructions and, not least, strong motivation on the part of the reader. A basic prerequisite for good design is, however, not to expose the reader to larger amounts of information than it is possible for him to absorb without great amounts of effort. It is, therefore, necessary at an early stage for the map designer to weigh the importance of great amounts of geographical detail against a high level of detail in the composition and structure of the statistical mass.

Analytical, complex and denotative statistical maps

It was argued above that the basic requirement for a statistical map is to illustrate as clearly as possible the geographical distribution of a mass of data and possibly the geographical variations of one or a few of its attributes. This requirement is valid with regard to the *analytical* statistical map. When it comes to the *complex map*, however, other requirements are assigned high priority. A complex map must first and foremost portray interrelationships, the interaction between two or more interdependent conditions. This means that a larger amount of data are compressed into one and the same map leading to reduced clarity and readability. It is assumed, however, that this reduced legibility is counteracted by the capacity of the human eye and brain to distinguish between patterns and extract information via graphic symbols even in visually-complex images. The map does not then primarily provide the type of overview supplied by

(margin note) Geographical detail must be balanced against thematic detail

(margin note) Limit the informational content of the map

(margin note) Balancing: legibility versus wealth of detail

the analytical map, but rather provides information for more limited segments *within* a map. In other words, the complex map assigns top priority to the thematic structure of the map rather than to the geographic pattern itself. E. Spiess (1986) points out the advantages of the complex map: it reduces the information flow and the reader's uncertainty about which analytical maps to combine with one another.

Spiess uses a map of the basic pattern of commuting journeys as an example of the complex map (Spiess, 1986). The gainfully-employed daytime and nighttime populations in urbanized areas, the place of residence of commuters and the major commuting flows they create are shown on one and the same map instead of being divided between several separate ones.

Spiess emphasizes, however, that it is even necessary to limit to a minimum the contents of the synthetic map, and refers to Imhof. "Complex maps are a temptation to design a product as it has been characterized by Imhof as '... a battlefield of line fragments, symbol splinters and letter corpses, everything thoroughly mingled and drowned in endless floods of colour".

Even in the *denotative* map, top priority is assigned to wealth of detail and to precision of location and content rather than to the readability of the map. As the most common example of denotative maps can be mentioned place-name maps of the classical type — for instance the Times Atlas of the World — with its high density of names, exact location of places but also rather complex design. This class of maps includes maps with numerical, textual or iconographic notations of various factors directly on the map. The statistical map (see figures 19 and 58, below) is only one type of denotative map.

Spiess/Imhoff argue for the synthetic map

When high informational density is most important

103

The map in its context: Mental scanning lines and scanning strategies

The history of mankind was depicted in the introduction as innumerable, more-or-less perpendicular, upward flows where the vertical "upwards" direction points towards the future. New events are constantly taking place in this swarm of streams, events which are mutually interactive, directly or indirectly, immediately or belatedly. This network of phenomena we are attempting to describe can be called a multilinear flow-structure. "Multilinear" in the sense that many lines of events take place simultaneously with a web of "connecting lines" of influence developing among them.

However, when we wish to describe this type of sequence of events, we have only unilinear means of expression with which to work. The linear nature of the written word is apparent (cf. Teleman 1982). Laboratory studies of eye movements have clearly shown that the eye also traces a linear pattern when scanning the contents of maps and pictures. When this "high-speed scanning" is repeated sufficiently often, the pattern of the studied image becomes familiar enough for the reader to be able to reduce it — i.e. the map's contents — to a single conceptual unit (see Head 1984). This conceptual unit then becomes an element in a linear chain of thought.

The same procedure is presumed to take place when examining entire series of maps or combined descriptive matter comprising map/maps and text.

Man's conceptual tool thus appears to be *unilinear* in nature. How then is this mental tool used to capture the contents of the *multilinear* model?

In the following few sections, we will try to find an answer to this question by studying maps in context, primarily from atlases in which the maps jointly depict sequences from the history of mankind. The main aim of this analysis is to study different strategies for laying out the course of these mental scanning lines. The study intends to show in what order, according to what strategy, different writers or groups of writers scan the content of the cylindrical time-space model, and what means they then apply to give form to their findings. Naturally the main emphasis will be placed on the map as a means of expression, but text and supplementary illustrations will also be examined in this context as organically-related elements in the reproduction of the results of linearly-organized scanning.

To illustrate different ways of focussing on and presenting the contents of the time-geographical reference model, fifteen-odd examples of atlases and quasi-atlases presenting historical events are dealt with in the following sections.

The zero map and mental scanning lines
Example: The History of Asia until 1914 by Michael Nordberg

Verbal presentation clarifies the time-space issue

Michael Nordberg's book is not an atlas. It is an example of a presentation which comes close to the zero map. Of the book's 405 pages, around 20 consist of maps with 35 schematic sketches of the spread of Asian empires during different epochs. The reason this book has been chosen for examination is that it presents with unusual clarity the central issue of all descriptions of events taking place simultaneously in time and space — perhaps precisely because of its almost complete lack of cartographic apparatus. Since these processes are basic not only to the design of all atlases with historical themes, but also to maps in general, it is appropriate to start the contextual study of maps with an analysis of this book.

Life paths of "geographical complexes"

The book's text deals with the political and cultural events within a huge area and during a time span which in some cases stretches beyond 10000 B.C. (India). The systematic treatment of historical events begins around 1500 B.C. If we examine the book's basic structure with the aid of these outline maps, we find six — what might be called — geographic complexes: the Chinese (1) and Indian (2) complexes, the Steppe complex (3) with its offshoots in various directions and with varying territorial extent during different epochs; the Persian (4) the Islamic (5) and finally the Ottoman complex (6). The analysis covers about the first 100 pages of the book.

A central position in this book is occupied by issues such as territorial control, the geographical spheres of interest and strategies of states and ethnic groups, their struggle to conquer and retain control of territories and to organize them in geographical terms. Discussions of this theme alternate, naturally enough, with sections having cultural, social or legal themes, in which the geographical aspects recede totally into the background.

The book begins in "the Chinese complex" (A — D in figures 23 and 24), and traces its development until around the year 220 A.D. The presentation then swings over to the "Steppe complex" (E) at the time of the expansion of the Hun Empire around 210-174 B.C. The author then continues to the "Indian complex" (F). Here developments are examined starting from a glossed-over, obscure past around 10000 B.C. through the historical development of the Harappa civilization (3000-1500 B.C. see G) up until Alexander the Great (around 300 B.C., H) and to the events which followed in his wake (I).

The presentation of "unrest on the Steppes" completes this part of the history of the Indian peninsula (J). Between 150 B.C. and the first centuries A.D., a series of confrontations erupted between the nomadic peoples of the Steppe area north-west of China, giving rise to a chain reaction of events. The turbulent events on the Steppes resulted in the invasion of the Indian peninsula through the pass between Afghanistan and the Himalayas, and the settlement of new ethnic groups in the Indian peninsula (see arrow from J).

Nordberg organizes his presentation around the "life paths" of the different regional complexes.

The spiral of the mental scanning line encircling the life path of the ethnic groups

We can visualize his method in the following manner. We can view all the chains of events occurring in China during this period (1450 B.C. — 220 A.D.) as a powerful river of events, a river which "flows" upwards in time-space, and consists of innumerable smaller flow elements. The author's mental scanning lines "revolve" around this river and follow it in a spiral-shaped movement through time and space. He studies one period more in depth, and then perhaps leaps forward to follow events to the next period etc. With gross simplification his train of thought could be described as a spiral (see figures 21 and 22) which rises up around the crystallized stream of events represented by the wavy lines. The spiral is, of course, a highly-simplified image: the author's thought process is not so even in time or space. He dwells at length on some familiar events and moves considerably faster past others. He looks back and seeks connections with the past. Events always flow upwards — time does not run backwards — but the questioning human mind can move both forwards and backwards. This spiral-shaped conceptual image of the thought process is, therefore, highly simplified but broadly correct.

After a brief stop on the Steppes (this first "mental visit" is not depicted in spiral no. 3 in figures 21 and 22), Nordberg continues to the Indian peninsula, and traces its history until around 3000 B.C. This history is scanned largely in the same manner as previously: a mental movement which ascends systematically in time-space, and approaches the same chronological level as in the case of the "Chinese complex" — the first centuries after the start of recorded time (spiral no. 2 in figures 21 and 22).

The meeting of the life paths of ethnic groups; the key point in the presentation

Now follows the third stage which ties together the first two: a brief treatment of events in the world of the Steppes. This has its background in developments in the Chinese complex, the consequences of which were felt on the Steppes, and which finally also affected the Indian complex (no. 3).

It is this fundamental conceptual structure which is illustrated in figures 21 and 22: the life paths of three geographically-distinguishable regional complexes and the mental scanning lines encircling each of them. In figure 22 the life paths have been removed, and the remaining spiral-shaped picture of mental movements is connected by means of broken lines. These indicate the mental leaps made by the author between different geographical regions. In this way the presentations of historical developments taking place simultaneously in three regions are joined into a single, linearly-structured verbal account.

Perspective illustrations are relatively difficult. A description which is

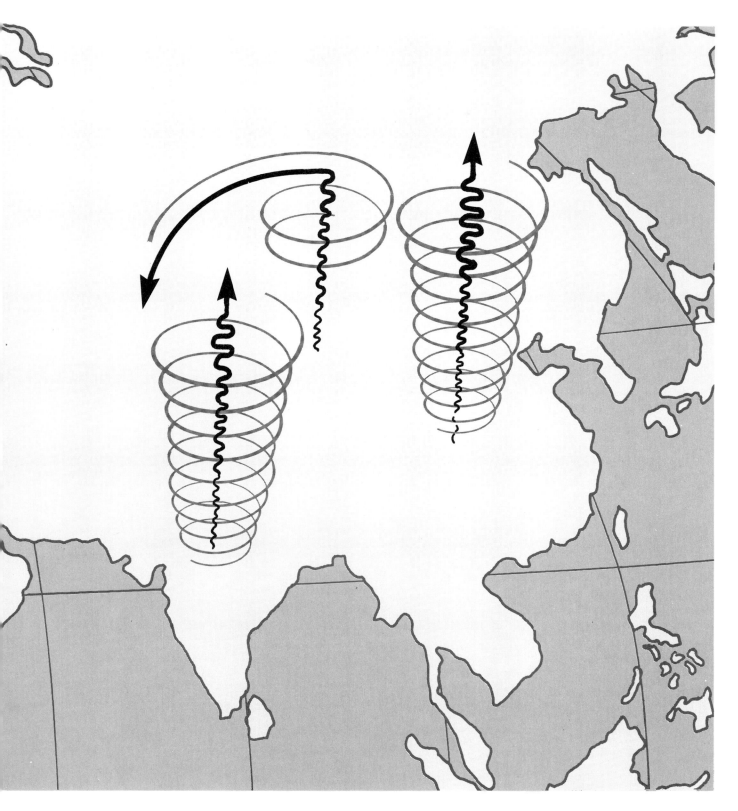

Figure 21   "Life paths" of three regional complexes and the mental scanning lines which follow their courses.

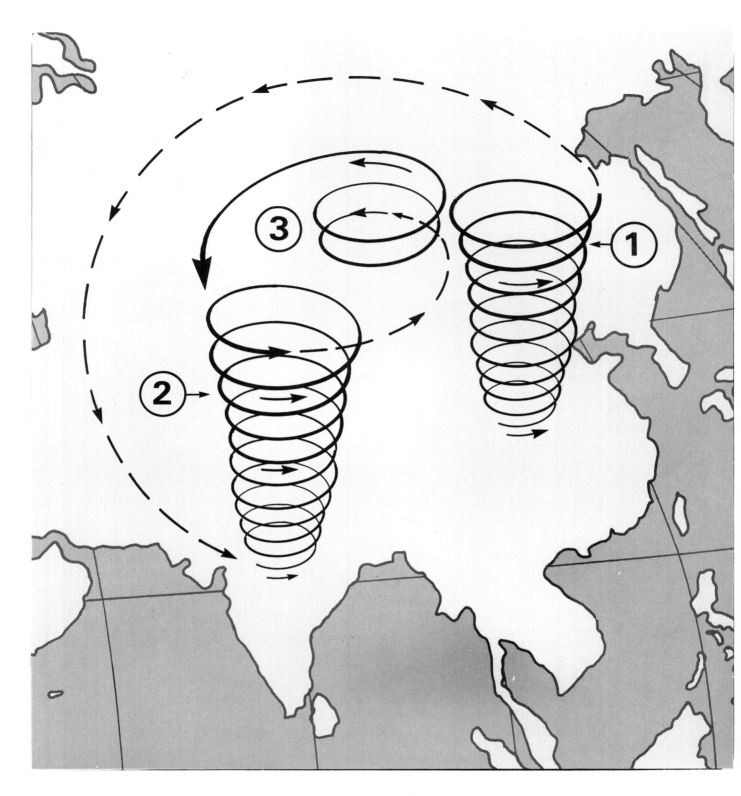

Figure 22   The scanning lines around the life paths of three regional
complexes unite to form a single mental scanning line.

graphically simpler but more detailed as far as contents are concerned is presented in figures 23 and 24 where the illustrated spirals are "pressed down" onto the map's surface by being drawn in spiral form, and where an important element of the lost third dimension — the spiral's height — is compensated by detailed chronological records as well as by references to page numbers in the book. The cartographic account of the path of the mental scanning line thus becomes a means of analysing how the book is built up.

The contents of the book are presented in compressed form in figure 25. Here the book's train of thought or thought path, is traced solely in respect to its oscillations between different geographic complexes or important parts of these complexes. In symbol no. 1 in figure 25 are summarized the periods designated by A,B,C and D which were dealt with individually within the Chinese complex in the previous figures, elements F,G,H and I are summarized in symbol no. 2. The episodes on the Steppes are omitted. The degree of detail is, therefore, considerably less than in the previous figures. The contents of the picture focus on the major features of the book.

The book's
mental scanning
line on the map

It should be emphasized that the method presented above is by no means limited to this particular book. It should be possible to apply this method to all literary or scientific presentations where the events portrayed have pronounced and simultaneous time-related and spatial elements. The core of the method should correspond to the steps presented here, namely

1) "life paths", the major flows of events, are defined
2) the path of the thought processes which scan these flows is studied and mapped out
3) the mental scanning line is depicted in cartographic terms
4) the pattern of the mental scanning line thus represented is described

A shaft through time

McEvedy's atlases of prehistoric and medieval Europe and of the modern world.

"The book is, I hope, sufficiently well-ordered to be useful as a work of reference, but its primary purpose is to present as a coherent story the origin and evolution of the historic cultures of Europe and the Near East ..." writes McEvedy in his introduction to "The Penguin Atlas of Ancient History" (McEvedy 1967). "... the atlas might be said to have the expansion and differentiation of the Indo-Europeans as its theme" (page 8). The text gives "the coherent sequence of events" within the portrayed region from around 50000 BC until 362 AD.

The next volume proceeds with an account of the course of history within the same region until 1478 (McEvedy: The Penguin Atlas of Medieval History, 1961).

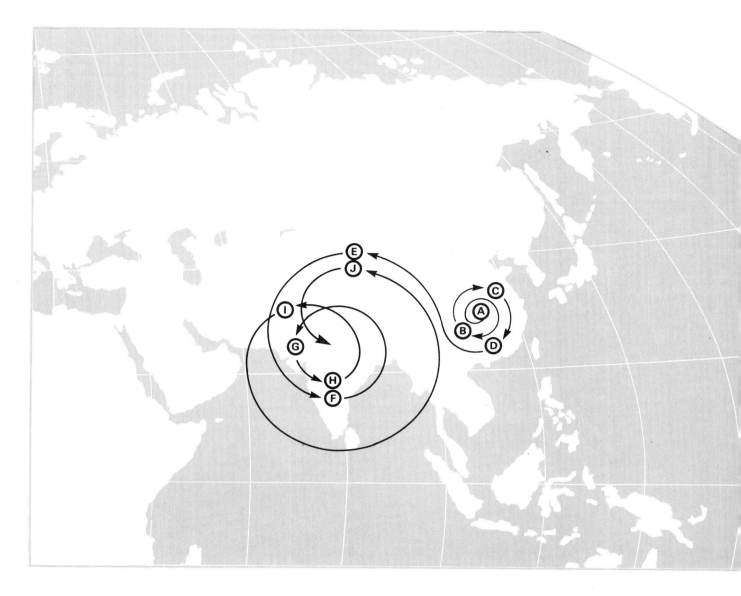

Figure 23   The course of the mental scanning line in time and space in
            M. Nordberg: The History of Asia, pages 15–48 (the period –
            100 A.D.). The letters refer to major historical phases.

A) The Shang (or Yin) civilization (1450–1050 B.C.) (pp 15–17)
B) China under the Chou Dynasty (1050–256 B.C.) (pp 18–24)
C) The Chin Dynasty (256–206 B.C.) (pp 24–27)
D) The Han Dynasty: China as world power (206 B.C.–220 A.D.)
     (pp 27–34)
E) The greatest territorial expanses of the Hun Empire (pp 29–30)
F) South India after 10000 B.C. (pp 35–37)
G) The Harappa civilization (3000–1500 B.C.) (p 38)
H) India of the Veda civilization (1500–500 B.C.) (pp 39–44)
I) Alexander the Great (327 B.C.) (pp 45–47)
J) Unrest of the Steppes (100 B.C.–300 A.D.) (p 48)

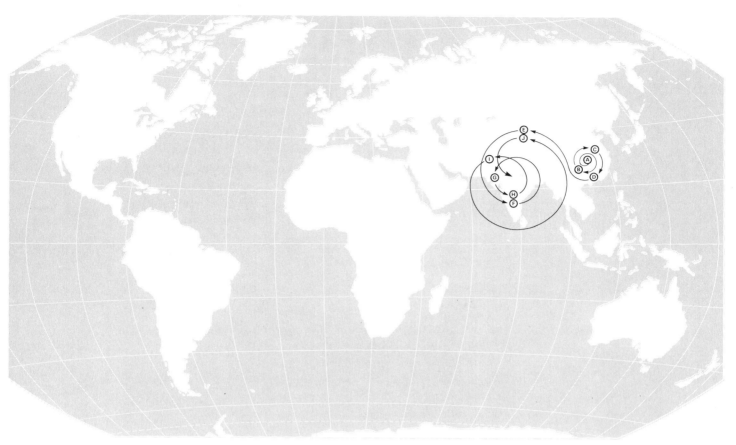

Figure 24   Figure 23 presented in the same map scale as figure 25.

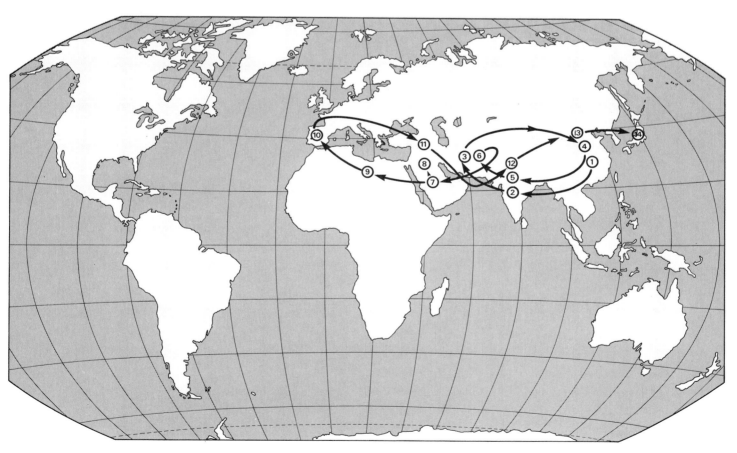

Figure 25   The main course of the mental scanning line in
M. Nordberg: The History of Asia, pages 15–149 (up to
the 13th century). Note the simplification in relation to
figures 23–24. (A–D in figure 23 = 1 here; F, G, H = 2
etc.)

The presentation is based on life paths of the various "sub-racial groups" which are mainly identified by their linguistic affiliation.

Flows through time-space; the text describes the flows; the maps show cross-sections

Once again we can view these ethnic groups as streams which flow upwards in time-space, streams which divide and flow along more-or-less discernible channels. We see ethnic groups which evolve with identities of their own, and whose actions we can follow during certain periods, but who disappear during others, displace one another and often intermingle. This process is often hard to interpret and vague, either intrinsically or due to lack of access to source material. McEvedy presents a textual account — with strong reservations for simplifications in the presentation — of the main features of this sequence of events, draws attention to some major characters and their actions in time and space — some dominant streams in time-space — and describes what he sees as the main features in the events of a specific period. It is in the text that we find the basic pattern of conditions and events during a specific period. At - fairly — regular intervals, he employs maps to make a horizontal section through a "flow diagram" of life paths, and draws the geographical boundaries of the flow channels — the spread of different ethnic groups.

Concentric waves of innovations

The expansion of material civilization lives its own life within this already complex picture. Nearly-concentric waves of innovation spread straight through the different ethnic groups (the art of producing bronze or iron, for example), and the maps also show how far these waves had reached at the time depicted by the map in question.

The intervals between the individual maps depicting the prehistoric period are at first extremely long — the earliest can be measured in thousands of years — but between 3000 and 1000 B.C. this is reduced to one or a few hundred years, and between 1000 B.C. and 360 A.D. to about 50-70 years. In the next volume (Medieval History), the average time space between two successive maps is only around 40 years.

The main body of the atlases consists of double-page spreads with maps on the right and on the left, the text which relates the events leading up to this moment in time and which comments on the geographical pattern illustrated there (see figures 16 and 17 in the colour supplement).

After every fifth or sixth such double-page spread the presentation is supplemented by two extra sections. One of them has an economic bias and gives an account of trading routes, areas of origin and markets for different commodities and towns which arise along the trading routes — (colour supplement figures 18 and 19).

The second section gives an account of cultural conditions, the spread of different writing systems and the routes along which they spread. In the volume on Medieval Europe, the map of the writing systems is replaced by a map of religious conditions — showing the spread of different religions and churches in Europe during these periods.

We can visualize these atlases as a deep shaft in the bedrock of the crystallized streams of time which we captured in the circular model we first presented. We see where the state of the flows was collected image by image which were then deposited one above the other. We observe the model first and foremost from an angle, through a sector which could be called political — the one having to do with territorial sovereignty and control. The main theme of the atlas is just that: the expansion of different ethnic groups, and the forces which produce but also change this pattern. We view the contents of our "shaft" by slicing out thin layers of the contents and superimposing them upon one another (see for example figures 16 and 17 in the colour supplement). We then compare them with each other — often by adjacent pairs, but sometimes choosing two which are quite a distance apart. Since such comparisons are difficult, we are aided by a verbal description of the flows between pairs of images. After each fifth-sixth "political" cross-section in time, we change "observation sector" — we move along the circumference of the circular model in a horizontal direction, and observe the same region from the viewpoint of the economist or trade historian and later on of the humanist and the theologian. In this way we really obtain three map series based on the same shaft: one where the cross-sections are close together and two where they are more widely-spaced.

A "shaft" is lifted out of the model and scanned

The third volume of this atlas — The Penguin Atlas of Modern History — has an equally consistent but more complicated structure. "In the medieval period, the nations of Europe and the Near East formed a community, the members of which constantly reacted on each other but were almost completely cut off from the rest of the world by physical barriers" (McEvedy 1961, Introduction). The great geographical discoveries expanded the limits of the world (then known by Europeans). Consequently McEvedy employs a double perspective in this volume: on the one hand he shows the world in its entirety, and on the other (on other maps) he limits his — and the reader's — field of vision to the European scene.

A double perspective: Europe as the centre and as a small part of the world

The pulse of the atlas: thematic, chronological, setting-related shifts

The maps' contents also vary thematically: although political conditions remain the core of the presentation, the observation sector on the circular model is varied more often and within wider limits.

The volume begins with four sections on the world around 1500: one on population distribution, one on the pattern of civilization on the Earth, a third on major political systems and a fourth on voyages of discovery which took place at or around this juncture of time.

Corresponding maps of the whole world are then presented for the segment of time around 1600, after which the presentation returns to the period around 1500 with a series of maps covering Europe alone during the period 1500-1650.

For the year 1483, one section (a double-page spread with text and map) deals with the population of Europe, a second with its trade, economy and towns and a third with political conditions, all for the same period of time. They are followed by three chronologically closely-spaced cross-sections

113

once again viewed from the "political sector" to present Europe's population and economic conditions in 1600. A series of maps on the internal political situation in Europe takes us to 1650 when the whole world is once again portrayed from the viewpoint of population and politics. The author continues in a similar systematic manner alternating between geographic and thematic perspectives in order to portray a complex course of events with two distinguishable settings: the world as a whole and Europe as its — supposed — central element.

Despite the rather more complex structure of the third volume, McEvedy applies the same systematic approach in all three volumes regardless of the great differences in the conditions illustrated: one (finally becoming two) clearly-defined setting; three (four in the third volume) chosen observation sectors (political, cultural, economic, discovery-oriented); a consistently-applied communications strategy (a text which describes the course of events + co-ordinated maps which show cross-sections of time); uniform, two-colour cartography (with black point, line and raster symbols uppermost) and a systematically-applied technique for locating cross-sections in time. He sinks a shaft into the past.

The composition of the atlas

Channels in time-space

McEvedy and Jones: Atlas of World Population History

"The aim of this book is to provide figures for the population of each country in the world at regular intervals through historical time. By countries we mean the nations of present day, their areas defined by the frontiers of 1975."

The formal unifying element in the three atlases by McEvedy we presented earlier was the horizontal cross-section in time repeated at regular intervals for a geographical region. In this book, it is the diagram of population development in individual countries which constitutes the equivalent formal framework (see figure 26). The horizontal axis represents the period from 400 B.C. until 2000 A.D. The vertical axis shows population size. An inset map showing the surface area of the country for which the population is being presented is inserted into the diagram.

The key element: the population of a country

It is interesting to note the tripartite division of the time axis. For the period between 400 B.C. and 1000 A.D., one horizontal unit corresponds to 200 years. Between 1000 and 1500 A.D. the same unit represents 100 years while after 1500 it only represents 50 years. This progressive abbreviation of units reflects our outlook with regard to both time and space: what is close at hand is perceived as more extensive than the same unit, the same phenomenon, which is further away. To halve the time-scale unit for different periods is a practical and easily-understood application of an approach which was developed by Torsten Hägerstrand (1962), and which found expression in the logarithmic distance scale applied to the surrounding world with Asby as the midpoint (fig 40:1). The same concept is

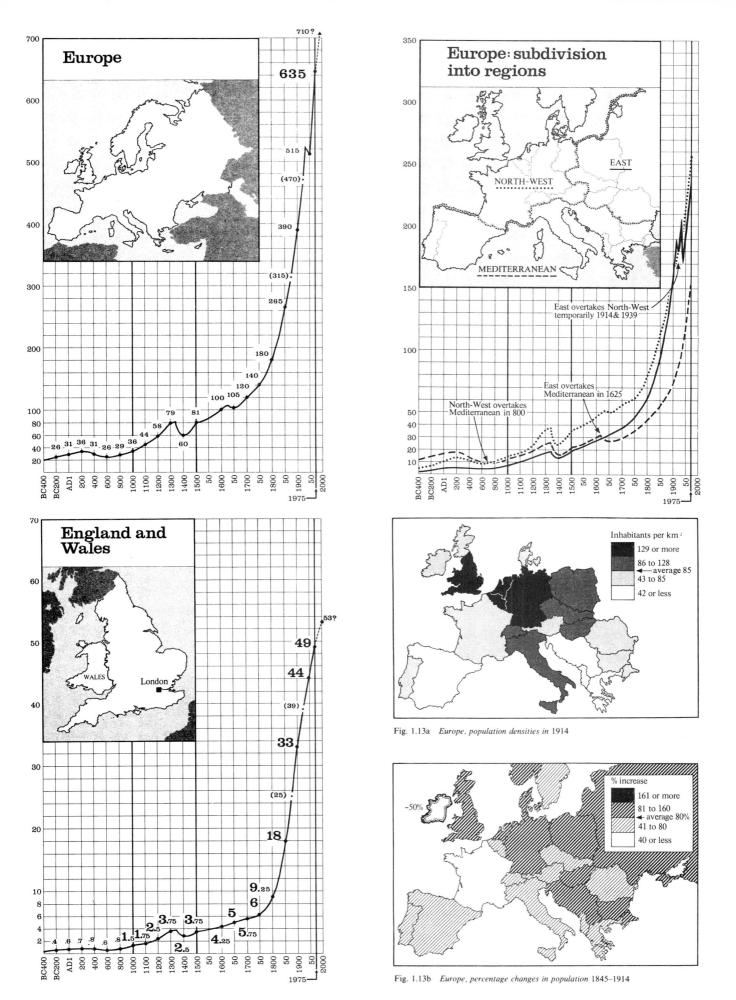

Figure 26   "Channels in time-space". Population development on a continent, in its different regions and in a single country according to C. McEvedy – R. Jones. Reproduced by permission of Penguin Books Ltd.

Fig. 1.13a   Europe, population densities in 1914

Fig. 1.13b   Europe, percentage changes in population 1845–1914

applied to time and space by the author when he attempts to formulate the way Man, especially the planner, views his surroundings. (Szegö 1974 and figure 41 in this book.)

Time-space
sliced into
vertical prisms

McEvedy and Jones employ the international boundaries of 1975 as a geographical reference system. Diagrams of population development within each such regional unit provide an easily-grasped picture of an area whose territorial expanse is probably familiar to the majority of the readers.

This technique gives a simple-to-understand picture of the development of a region, but it also breaks up a complex course of events into elements which are often artificial. Characteristic of the course of events from the viewpoint of time geography is that the clusters of life paths belonging to the actors — groups of people, ethnic groups or nations — occupy territories which expand or shrink and sometimes also move great distances. Age-old peoples and nations have also expanded their territories during certain periods and seen them reduced during others. When McEvedy and Jones apply the boundaries of 1975 to the nations of the earth, they split or divide up the time-geographical model into vertical prisms whose surface areas correspond with the land areas of 1975. These prisms, the cross-sections of which are irregular though unchanged through time, slice straight through the territorial changes which every country, every ethnic group, has undergone during the course of history.

The overall
structure of the
prisms

The fact that the shortcoming mentioned above does not cause the book to disintegrate into disparate units is partly due to the book's organization which is based on physical geography's own, less-changeable hierarchy. Population development is first presented for entire continents, then for parts of continents, and only then is the population growth of individual countries presented. However, the basis for the clarity created by this organization is a conceptual model applied by the authors. This follows the major population flows through time and geographical space, and studies the interplay between the different flows.

On the European scene, they first give a rough outline of the rapid population increase in Greece (1000-300 B.C.), and then the shift of population growth first to Italy then to the Roman Empire and afterwards to north-western Europe and eventually sliding over towards Eastern Europe.

Description of a
complex process

The authors do not express themselves in the manner of time geography. However, the composition of the text makes it easy to visualize population development in the form of streams flowing up through time-space. During one period they may be swift in some areas of the geographical setting only to ebb out there, but then to reappear with increased force in other parts of the setting. The text is accompanied by simple sketches showing population size, density and growth rates in different parts of Europe. The maps are small, cartographically simple and unpretentious, and are repeated for several significant chronological cross-sections. Together with the weighty but still vivid text — with which they are well-co-ordinated — they re-create the complex process in a highly-tangible way. This is summarized

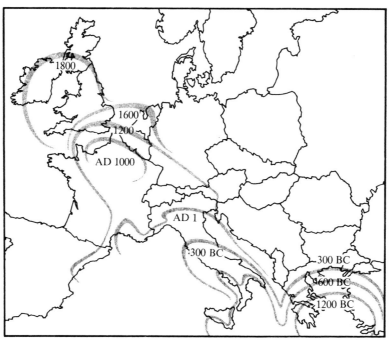

Fig. 1.12 *Europe, demographic development* 1200 BC–AD 1800. *The wave-fronts represent rapid multiplication to high levels of density – high for the date in question, that is. There is an obvious correlation between these demographic surges and social advance: the first four waves mark the development of the classical culture of Greece and its spread through Italy; the next two the establishment of the feudal order in Western Europe; the final pair the appearance of the early capitalist society of the Netherlands and the beginning of the industrial revolution in England*

Figure 27   The crest of the wave of population development passes through Europe. From C. McEvedy – R. Jones. Reproduced by permission of Penguin Books Ltd.

finally in a synthetic map, which illustrates where and when population development culminated in Europe in the form of an advancing wave. We can observe this wave from 1200 B.C. when it reached the Peloponnesian peninsula, follow its course to 300 B.C. towards the northern Balkans, continuing on to central Italy, see how it reaches northern Italy at the start of recorded time to arrive in France around 1000 A.D., Holland — southern England around 1600 A.D. and Ireland — northern England about 1800 A.D. The latter map is an interesting example of the potential of the synthetic map to summarize a complex process in nominal terms. The maximum growth rate of the population, which the wave represents, is not shown in connection with the map. Its nominal character does not prevent it from summarizing the essence of a complex process more distinctly than could have been achieved by much longer numerical presentations.

This outline presentation of developments in Europe is followed by a more detailed account of developments in the different parts of the continent. An outline of the main features of the development of a particular portion of the continent is followed by a detailed account of population developments within the individual countries there, or else the same material is presented in reversed order.

Historical data are also presented in order to provide perspective and enable comparisons to be made. For example, to supplement the presentation of population development in the area occupied by Austria in 1975, variations in population are shown throughout the entire Hapsburg monarchy 1525-1918. Population developments in today's France, Germany etc. are supplemented by corresponding population graphs for the kingdoms which existed within their borders during the course of history.

The book shows us that even longitudinal studies which are virtually chronological in nature can be incorporated into a time-geographical approach with the help of mental scanning lines which consistently follow the major lines of development through time and space.

Wanderings in time and space
The work of Martin Gilbert

The atlases presented in the previous sections were delimited in time and space in a formalized manner: their settings were defined once and for all, and even the intervals of time at which events were presented were largely predetermined.

The subject of the atlases: the life paths of nations and regions

Martin Gilbert displays a different approach in his many atlases. This is most apparent in the three atlases dealing with the life paths of three nations: the British, the American and the Russian (succeeded by the Soviet which was not available when this analysis was made). All three atlases provide a general picture of the development of these nations from prehistoric times up to the time the author completed his work on the atlas concerned.

How is the setting of a nation's existence demarcated?

We would expect that the history of an island people especially would be portrayed using the island's coastline to define the setting, and with correspondingly distinct demarcations in the chronological disposition of its history. But does this prove to be the case?

In order to answer this question — and to be able to apply the analysis not only to historical atlases but to other cartographic material as well — the following method has been developed.

A method for analysing the contents of an atlas

We imagine a map of the world in some suitable projection. Above this map are deposited new layers. Each such layer covers that part of the earth's surface which corresponds to one individual map sheet in the atlas being analysed. The thickness of each layer is given the value of 1 (at least in this first, simplified application of the method). We then superimpose layer number two corresponding to map number two on top of this first layer, and so on. We presuppose that these layers are fully elastic. What we thus obtain is a series of layers where the individual layers are equally thick, but where the thickness of the model varies because of the different

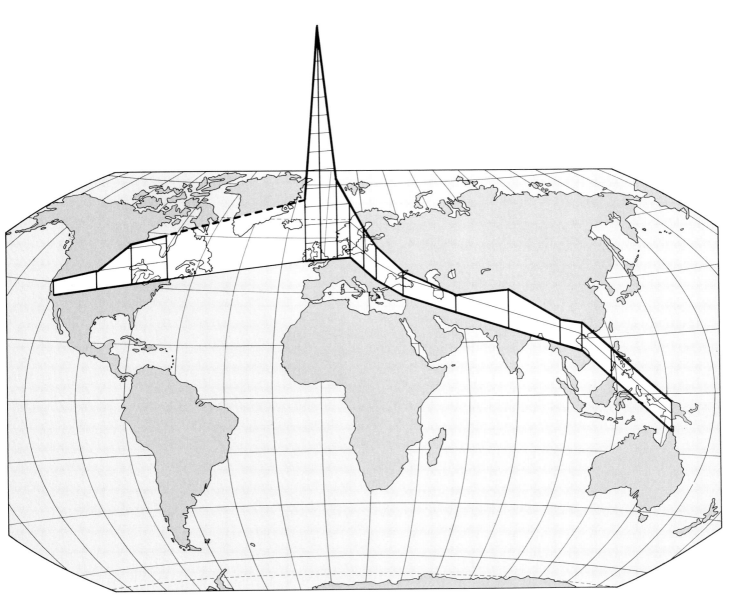

Figure 28   An "information geography" cross-section showing the
            informational content of Martin Gilbert: British History
            Atlas. Illustration in false perspective. For explanations
            see the text.

numbers of layers. The transition between different parts of the model with
varying thicknesses occurs along straight or curved lines. Every straight
line of this type corresponds to the edge of a map sheet.

The implica-
tions of the
method: maps
represent
information. A
model of the
distribution of
information

The idea behind this model is the following. Every individual map sheet
contains a certain amount of information. We assume that every map sheet
— regardless of scale and general appearance — contains the same amount
of information on all parts of its surface. In that case "layer" number one
which we superimposed on a map of the world represents the informational
content in map number one; layer number two the informational content
of map number two and so on. If we continue depositing layer upon layer

in this way until all the individual maps in an atlas are represented by a layer, we will finally obtain a three-dimensional model whose construction reflects the cartographic information contained in the atlas. The height of the model is greatest above that part of the Earth's surface for which the atlas provides the most information, and the volume of information supplied by the atlas decreases with reduced model height. If the thickness of a map layer is given the value of 1, the height of the model will then relate quite simply how many map sheets in the atlas under analysis cover different parts of the Earth's surface. In more sophisticated applications of the model, its contents and implications can be expressed in more complex, but also more precise terms.

This model can be illustrated in several ways. It can be treated as a digital terrain model whose height indicates informational density, and which can be represented by means of height contours. It can also be portrayed by means of a cross-section taken through the model. The attached analyses of Martin Gilbert's atlases of the history of the three nations mentioned above and of his first work "Recent History Atlas" were carried out in this latter manner.

In systematic applications of these analyses, a dense grid or other latticework, a triangular network for example (see Nordbeck and Rystedt 1972 page 37), is superimposed on the mapped surface, and the number of overlaps occurring at each point is calculated. Based on this information, height contours are then interpolated or a cross-section is constructed through the model.

A simplified application: cross-sections based on test areas

The cross-sections shown here were done in a somewhat more simplified manner. First, a general inventory was made of the contents of the atlas — a systematic examination of the area covered by the individual maps. Then a number of test spaces were selected covering areas which appeared to be significant after the preliminary analysis. These spaces were also chosen with regard to their proximity to a line on the Earth's surface. It was then noted which maps covered the area represented by each test space. The total number of maps on the test space was then presented in the form of cross-sections. Here it was assumed that the number of maps covering the surface of the Earth varied linearly between pairs of proximate test spaces. Figures 28 and 29 show two such cross-sections in axonometric perspective. The vertical lines indicate the approximate position of the test spaces. Each test space is named after the country where it is located or after a well-known place if the name of the country does not provide sufficient locational information. In order to improve the diagram's readability, levels equivalent to five map sheets have been marked as horizontal layers. The use of test spaces has been inspired by the methods applied within dialectic geography, e.g. Besch, Knoop et.al. 1982 and Hansson 1986.

The choice of test spaces necessitated a certain degree of subjectivity. However, this was accepted as a reasonable price to pay for being able to conduct this preliminary study with the resources available as a first stage in the development of new methods.

120

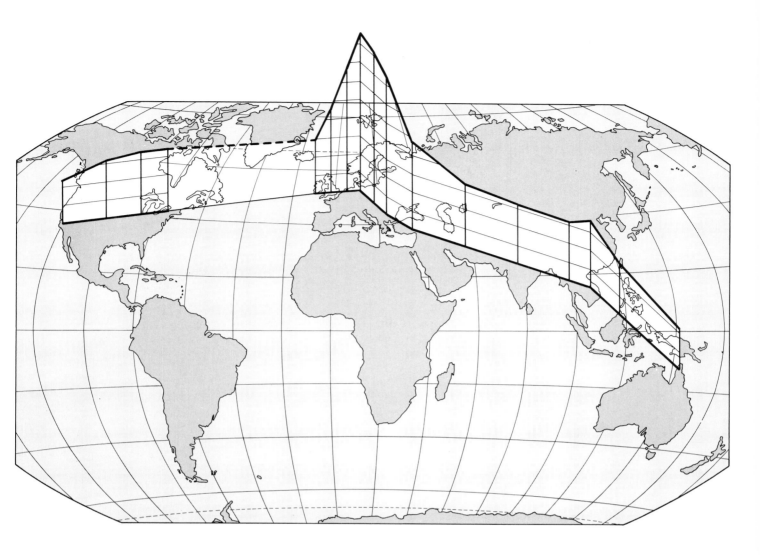

Figure 29   An "information geography" cross-section showing the
informational content of M. Gilbert: Recent History Atlas.
Illustration in false perspective.

"The British
History Atlas"
— the distribu-
tion of informa-
tion

The cross-section shows quite clearly how Martin Gilbert focussed his
attention mainly on England when designing his atlas. However, this focus
differs distinctly from the one employed by McEvedy in his survey of the
European setting. Even though a large part of the information relates to
England, considerable amounts of information about the rest of Europe
are provided as well, particularly with regard to its most westerly and
central parts. Informational density then diminishes towards Iran, rising
to a secondary peak in India from which it diminishes towards Malaya —
Borneo and Australia. A rather high density of information can be noted
for the east coast region of the United States, which then decreases towards
the western regions. It is interesting to note the similarity of the cross-section to a graph which plots the frictional effect of distance.

The height of the model and accordingly of the diagram can be said to
depict how many times, how frequently, the author's "field of vision", his
train of thought, has swept across the different parts of the geographical

space while preparing the atlas under consideration. The precise number of "mental scanning movements" can of course not be presented — a rather absurd idea. However, the scanning pattern, how the author divided his attention between different areas, is probably reflected quite well by the cross-sections or by a map drawn up according to the same principle.

We thus obtain a cartographic projection, a cartographic impression of the author's thought paths in the latter word's literal sense.

The internal structure of the model: information from different periods

In figure 30 we can study the composition of this cross-section more thoroughly. The periods to which the information relates are shown here in addition to the density of information. We see here — albeit with some difficulty due to the tightly-compressed sequence of layers in this particular section — how the maps for the period before 1000 are limited to Europe, how maps relating to the period 1000 and 1800 are mostly concerned with England while maps presenting the history of the period 1800-1900 give prominence to India and areas beyond.

The "sequence of layers", the thickness of different layers in the cross-section, is primarily an expression of the composition of the atlas as regards content, i.e. the way the author organizes his material. This is to some extent an obvious consequence of the historical course of events being portrayed, but it also has to do with the atlas author's approach to the material.

"The American History Atlas" — composition and organization

A corresponding cross-section of the informational content in Gilbert's "American History Atlas" is shown in figure 31. The density of information in the atlas is, of course, highest over North America, with a distinct peak above the east coast. Informational density is fairly high over the whole of Europe and on into Asia Minor, and it peaks again — not above India, as in the case of Great Britain — but in the Far East, in Vietnam. Once again a clear reflection of the historical events depicted in the atlas.

The same causal relationship can be discerned with regard to the sequences of layers in the model. A large portion of the maps relating to the American east coast originate from the period after 1500 A.D.; the history of the west coast in presented in maps which mainly depict the post-1800 period. The atlas' maps of Europe and Asia mainly concern the 20th century — an expression of the fact that interaction among the continents intensified during the 20th century.

"Imperial Russian History Atlas"

The cross-section of Tsarist Russia, figure 32, slices through Moscow in a largely east-west direction. Informational density is greatest over Moscow, diminishes slowly towards Poland, and then sinks to considerably lower levels towards Germany and France. The density of information decreases considerably faster towards Siberia where it reaches substantially-lower levels than towards the west. Once again: an expression of the contents of the atlas, depending partly on historical background, but also on the author's outlook. The same combination of circumstances can be traced in the composition of cross-sections of different historical strata (note the rather even stratification from the start of recorded time until after 1900).

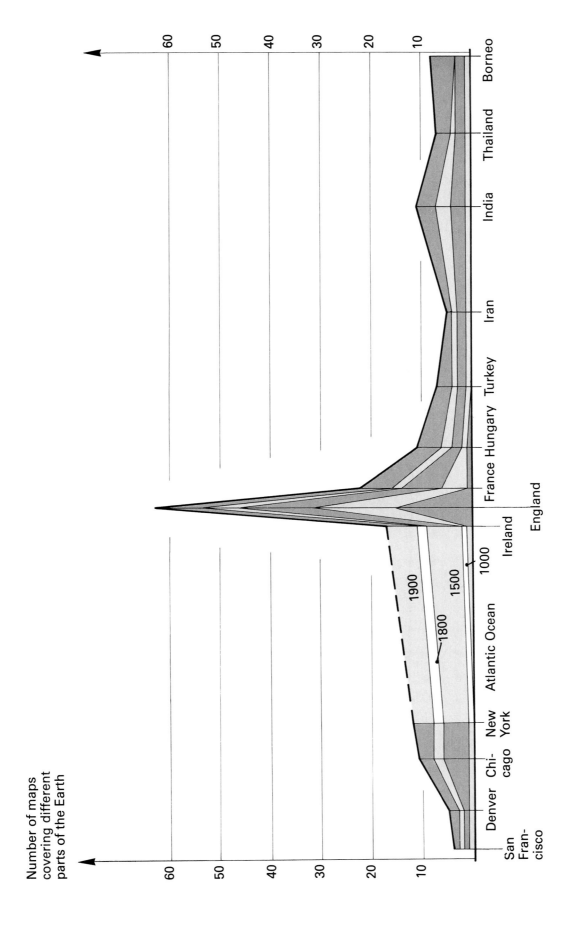

Number of maps
covering different
parts of the Earth

Figure 30　An "information geology" cross-section of the contents
of M. Gilbert: British History Atlas.

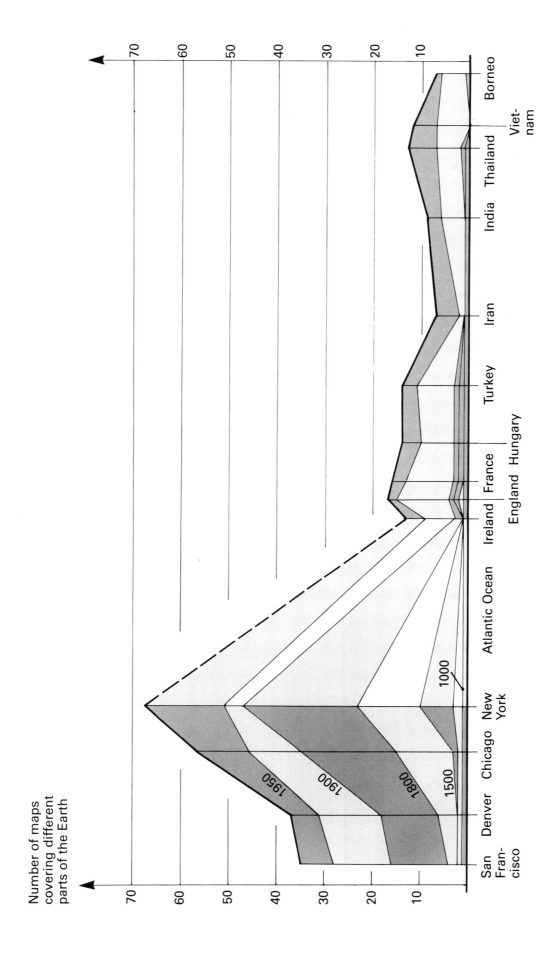

Number of maps
covering different
parts of the Earth

Figure 31   An "information geology" cross-section of the contents
of M. Gilbert: American History Atlas.

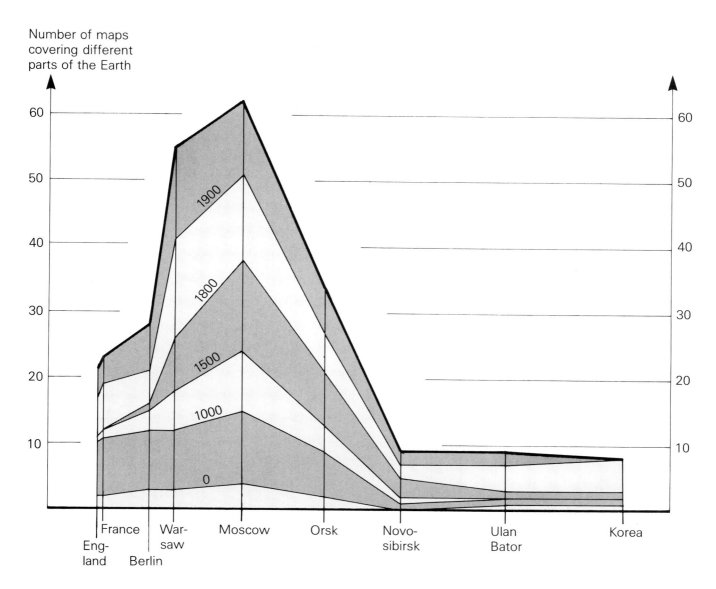

Number of maps covering different parts of the Earth

England / France / Berlin / Warsaw / Moscow / Orsk / Novosibirsk / Ulan Bator / Korea

Figure 32   An "information geology" cross-section of the contents of M. Gilbert: Imperial Russian History Atlas.

The frictional effect of distance on events — the frictional effect of distance on human thought

A basic concept of human geography is that geographical distance creates resistance to human actions. During certain periods in the history of mankind this resistance is very pronounced, and during such a period and in the regions where this resistance is manifest, human society disintegrates into small local communities. During other periods this resistance becomes less prominent, and then the human population becomes organized in increasingly larger, cohesive geographical units (see for example Spencer and Thomas 1969). However the distance factor never ceases to operate entirely, and it is therefore natural that the activities of individuals as well as of nations have distinct centres where activity is most intensive and from whence the level of activity diminishes with increased geographical distance. It is this relationship that is expressed by the graph of the friction of distance. It is also natural then that the contents of a historian's atlas of the activities of a nation should reflect this basic relationship.

125

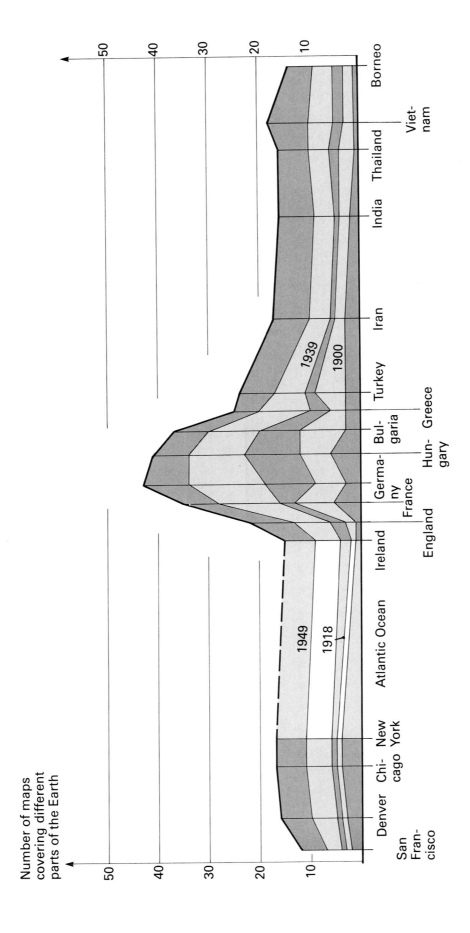

Figure 33   An "information geology" cross-section of the contents
of M. Gilbert: Recent History Atlas.

Martin Gilbert is the author of many more atlases than the three mentioned above. The cross-section of the contents of his first work — Recent History Atlas, 1966 — was designed according to the same principles as presented earlier in figures 29 and 31. It is interesting to note firstly that the friction of distance does not appear to be as pronounced as in the above-mentioned examples (the author's field of interest is much broader and less concentrated than in the two previous cases), and secondly that his field of vision is focussed on Germany. A secondary centre along this cross-section appears over Vietnam — a not-unexpected feature in a contemporary global history atlas. The construction of the cross-section can also be described somewhat differently, namely that it reflects the author's view that the setting disintegrates into a setting-centre and a less intensively-observed secondary zone which surrounds it. The focus on the European setting is not surprising with regard to a period when two world wars started and had their primary centres there. However, the shape of the curve would appear to reflect a European historian's view of world events.

The latter circumstance is expressed not least in the organization of the cross-section into different chronological strata. The inter-war years and the period during and after the Second World War in Europe obviously comprise the most central parts of the atlas.

Martin Gilbert has written several atlases which do not deal with individual nations or events during certain periods. Instead they follow different "projects" in the history of mankind, i.e. several major complexes of events in which human actions converge. Atlases of the First World War, the Arab-Israeli conflict, "The Atlas of Holocaust" are works which are constructed around rather clearly-demarcated events, the often terrible "projects" of history.

An enriched cartographic language
dtv-Atlas zur Weltgeschichte

The spring of 1964 saw the publication of the first volume of a historical atlas which even now, over twenty years later, stands out as an important leap forward in the development of the cartographic language: dtv-Atlas zur Weltgeschichte, later published in English under the title "The Penguin Atlas of World History" (see colour supplement figures 1 to 13). The pioneering nature of the book and maps become particularly evident when compared with another, almost classic atlas from the same country: Germany, namely Westerman Atlas zur Weltgeschichte (Swedish edition: Atlas till världshistorien, 1958, Stockholm-Braunschweig).

Westerman's atlas is a high-quality cartographic product, printed in a format close to A4. The atlas consists solely of maps with up to six maps on the same page. The design of the maps is characterized by high density of information and meticulous cartographic detail which make possible the presentation of large volumes of information on the often small maps. The entire atlas is printed in colour with many different hues, and reflects the printing methods in use prior to the introduction of four-colour technology. The colours cover the entire maps. The terrain on maps describing the setting is often illustrated by shading. This makes it easy to locate other map elements, and also makes the maps appear more animated. The maps also display meridians and parallels — one of the few historical atlases to do so. Representation of waterways, coastlines and place names is characterized by a wealth of detail and accuracy.

The impression this atlas makes is based to a great extent on its use of colour. The hues are often vivid, and many different nuances usually appear on a map. The colouring sometimes causes the observer to recall the maps printed during the inter-war years. Other maps appear to stem from a considerably later period to judge from their colour patterns and general design. To sum up: a standard work unsurpassed as to wealth of information, but somewhat overloaded and a trifle old-fashioned.

An enriched cartographic language

dtv-Atlas zur Weltgeschichte is a fundamentally different book. It was initially designed as a pocket edition (size 11 x 18 cm). Half of the contents consist of text: opposite every map page is a page of text with chronological information about the events depicted on the map. The size of the individual maps varies: one, two, three, and in some cases six maps find room within the comparatively small format. However, the maps are designed accordingly. Their contents are limited and unequivocal. The symbols and the text are small but distinct. They are placed on the map in such a way that each one stands out clearly, but they still combine to form a cohesive whole. The colouration makes a substantial contribution to the general impression of the maps. The colour scale is often limited, forms harmonious combinations and usually follows the logical pattern of the map. This is especially perceptible when it comes to the three aspects mentioned earlier: the depiction of points, lines and areas with progressively-fading zones of influence, the interaction among several such elements, and the representation of dynamic processes. The use of an air brush for applying progressively-fading colour tones and for designing the point, line and area symbols makes it possible to depict the interplay among actors in historic events with a subtlety and aesthetic quality which still today, over 20 years after the publication of the book, stand out as virtually unparalleled.

A new synthesis
The Times Atlas of World History

In autumn 1978 a new historical atlas was published with a comprehensiveness of information and a quality of design which are expected to set standards for the immediate future: the Times Atlas of World History.

With its large format (26×36 cm), nearly 300 pages of text and maps and an additional 60-page register, the book is also quantitatively impressive. The work covers the history of mankind from the earliest traces left by

Man on the surface of the Earth up to the year 1975. (The 1979 edition. Later editions have moved the closing date progressively forward).

Intention: an atlas of the history of the *whole* world

The book clearly endeavours to be an atlas of *world history.* "Most historical atlases of an earlier generation were marked by their Eurocentricity, ... Our aim has been to present a view of history, which is world-wide in conception and presentation and which does justice, without prejudice or favour, to the achievements of all peoples in all ages and in all quarters of the globe ..."

"... When we say that this is an atlas of world history, we mean that it is not simply a series of national histories loosely strung together. In other words, it is concerned less with particular events in the history of particular countries than with broad movements — for example, the spread of the great world religions — spanning whole continents."

"History is dynamic, not static; it is a process of change and movement in time; we have tried to avoid a series of static pictures of particular situations at particular moments in the past. In The Times Atlas a special effort has been made to emphasise change, expansion and contraction by the use of appropriate visual devices." (Introduction, page 13.)

An examination of the composition of the atlas shows that the intentions outlined in the introduction have been followed to a considerable extent.

The atlas covers the entire surface of the Earth

The atlas scans the world's surface in wide sweeps. First the Earth is observed in its entirety, then it sweeps over the Eurasian landmass together with Africa, continuing over to the American continents. This examination of the Earth's surface is completed in this first section with 20 pages on Australia and Oceania. (The world of early Man).

...through the entire history of the world

The atlas' "scanning line" retains its wide sweeps in the next section ("The first civilisations") where the great centres of civilization of the ancient world with their mutual relationships are presented jointly after which each is dealt with individually. A major section is also devoted to the Indo-European migrations which attack these great civilizations.

The process of scanning the Earth's surface is then continued along these lines throughout world history. (The classical civilisations of Eurasia; The world of divided regions; The world of the emerging West; The age of European dominance; The age of global civilisation.)

Laying out the mental scanning line: (=scanning strategy)

It is easy to follow the book's mental scanning line since it is used continuously and rather consistently: broad surveys of entire continents or organically-related zones which stretch across several continents; concentration on selected areas within one such survey and successive scanning of these areas one by one. This mental movement then continues up in time to the next epoch where it is repeated: broad general views where centres of civilization are presented in their respective contexts are followed by a focussed treatment of each one of them in turn. These mental scanning lines display a combination of patterns observed earlier: M. Nordberg's

129

scanning lines with their movements between centres of civilization and the summarizing, introductory sweeps across large regions employed by McEvedy and Jones.

The disposition of a theme

The atlas is designed around separate double-page spreads, each of which focusses on a theme. As a rule, each theme has a main map — usually accompanied by several smaller maps providing supplementary aspects — and text which form the backbone of the presentation. Figure 25 in the colour supplement (The colonisation of Europe) is an example of such a main map in the section entitled "Early Europe. The colonisation of a continent 6000 to 1500 B.C.".

The disposition of a map

The main map presents the setting and emphasizes its composition from the geographical viewpoint of the *subject* being illustrated. The spread of agriculture in Europe is thus depicted as seen from the centre of dissemination — Asia Minor. The map is oriented so that the compass point northwest, the major direction of the spread of agriculture, coincides with the key direction of the map — upwards. A suitable map projection was chosen for this purpose which even makes it possible to discern the curvature of the Earth. Superimposition of the graticule helps to further accentuate this curvature. The topography is presented by terrain shading; landforms can be perceived directly without any kind of intellectual interpretation. The transparent layers of colour indicating the progressive spread of the agricultural civilizations are then superimposed over the grey image of the terrain. Inset arrows help strengthen the impression of the spread of civilization.

The placement of the names of the different civilizations which arose in connection with the spread of agriculture make an important contribution to the comprehensive geographical picture. They do not merely identify each civilization and present its territorial expanse, but also suggest the fact that the limits of this expansion are only partially known. Two smaller, simpler, supplementary maps show the diffusion of metal production and the emergence of different centres of metal production in Europe during various periods as well as the rise of distribution centres and the spread of megalithic monuments.

Text and map; advantages, limitations, complementarity

The backbone of the double-page spread, however, is the text: the description of the dissemination process and the complexities of historical development is a further demonstration of the capacity of the written word to describe complex processes in time and space. This is accomplished with a flexibility, tangibility and concentration quite different from the maps in terms of orientation and contents, but in many respects not inferior to them. This verbal information with its factual descriptions of living conditions and how they changed thousands of years ago succeeds in evoking glimpses of human life, but also images of the changing scenery of a world of long ago. When we then combine this information with the maps, we are made aware of the great effectiveness of textual presentations co-ordinated with sophisticated cartography. The map — even at its best, and despite its concrete nature — provides a somewhat abstract presentation of the setting. Then too, excellent as it is, the cartographic description of the process of dissemination appears somewhat lifeless when compared with the images conjured up by the text. Together, however, the maps and text provide tangibility and wealth of information and make the presentation come alive so that a complex process can unfold with great clarity before the observer.

At the same time, the reader becomes aware that even high-quality accounts composed of text and maps are limited in some respects: they place very exacting demands on the reader's concentration and on his ability to combine two different kinds of information — text and visual images — which are organized in different ways. The text alternates between highly-concrete descriptive elements and very generalized ones. Highly-concrete elements suggest, allow the reader to visualize, individual people or perhaps small groups of people in concrete situations. Generalized elements use few words to place these individuals and groups in an extensive geographical context, in an expansive setting painted with a very broad brush.

The text and the map have different levels of abstraction

The map, on the other hand, falls somewhere between these two extremes: a comprehensive map of a continent presents the setting in a highly-concrete manner which is rich in detail within certain limits, but which is still generalized. The illustrated process is also depicted in a simplified manner even if its key pattern — the spread of agricultural civilization in different periods — is portrayed in an evocative way. It may be difficult for the reader to combine these two levels — the text and map levels with their different measures of generalization — into a whole.

This disposition — main map with accompanying text and outline maps for a theme on each double-page spread — is applied throughout the atlas. The focus of attention shifts constantly, and the scope of the setting varies from the multi-continental to the more limited local area, and together they form a mental scanning line which successively traces the history of the world.

A varied cartographic language is employed in the atlas. What is most apparent is the richness of the settings and the way they can be perceived directly. In figure 26 in the colour supplement (Germanic and Slavonic invasion of Europe) it achieves almost artistic heights. The descriptions of the actors and the play are usually distinct in the real meaning of the word: points, lines — sometimes arrows — and areas are most often presented with their areal coverage sharply defined. Together with the settings they often create a high-quality whole which effectively suggests dynamic courses of events. The possibility of portraying the dynamic character of events, the diffuse distribution of the actors and the progressively-fading effects of their actions, which was taken advantage of in the dtv-Penguin Atlas, is employed here only to a limited extent. Despite this, due to the ambitious disposition, the well-co-ordinated maps and text, the wealth of information which is still kept within reasonable limits and, finally, the high-quality of the cartography, this book stands out as a landmark which will be difficult to surpass.

131

A new synthesis
Some precursors

The Times Atlas of World History brings a new element into the world of atlases, but it did not lack precursors. The book which appears to be most closely related with regard to outlook and approach to the subject was published as early as 1967: *A World History* by William H. McNeill. This was intended as an experimental text book for general courses in world history where the main features in the course of history would be highlighted at the expense of individual events. The main theme of the presentation was the development of civilizations.

An experimental textbook about the history of civilization

"Human societies, distinguished from one another by differing styles of life, are very numerous .... Civilisations are unusually massive societies, weaving the lives of millions of persons into a loose yet coherent life style across hundreds or even thousands of miles and for periods of time that are very long when measured by the span of an individual human life. Being both massive and long-lived, civilisations must perforce also be few .... These facts allow an overview of the history of mankind as a whole.

A few high-level civilizations ...

The organizing idea is simple: in any given age the world balance among cultures was liable to disturbance emanating from one or more centres, where men succeeded in creating an unusually attractive or powerful civilisation.

...interacting with one another

In successive ages the major loci of such disturbance to the world altered. It therefore becomes possible to survey the epochs of world history by studying first the center or centres of primary disturbance and then considering how the other peoples of the earth reacted to or against what they knew or experienced of the innovations that had occurred in the prime centres of cultural activity.

In such a perspective, geographical settings and lines of communications between different civilisations became centrally important" (W. H. McNeill: A World History, 1967, Preface).

The introduction reflects a pronounced geographical approach to historical events, and strong echoes from innovation theory can be discerned.

The writing of history with pronounced geographical aspects

The book's method of approach can also be expressed in another way. It draws attention to the actors — not just entire civilizations, but also ethnic groups or individual people within a cultural trait cluster — and places them within the geographical setting. The author then monitors the play taking place there during periods when their actions form homogeneous patterns. He reproduces two types of patterns: static or balanced patterns and what could be called transitional patterns. Static patterns emerge when a civilization is in balance and often displays a repetitive pattern of activity. The transitional pattern arises when new forces — new actors under different conditions — upset this balance. As examples of a balanced pattern, McNeill paints pictures of the emerging, maturing, increasingly-

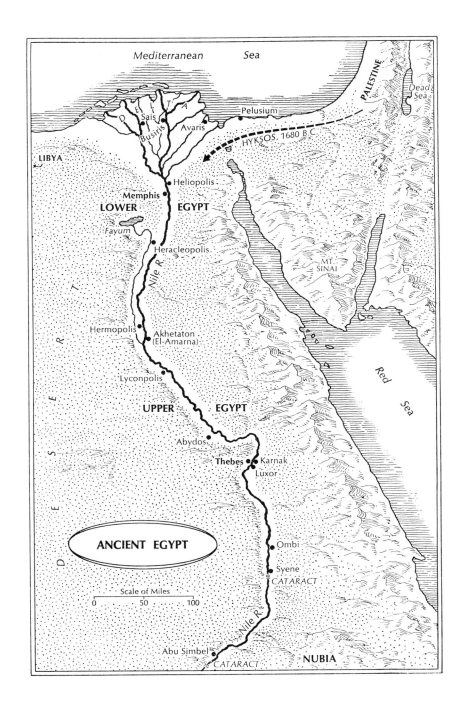

Figure 34   A "setting map" of Ancient Egypt from A World History by William H. McNeill, published by Oxford University Press 1967.

flourishing centres of civilization in Mesopotamia, Egypt and the valley of the Indus up to 1700 B.C. He illustrates a transitional phase in the chapter describing the attacks of the charioteers, iron-age barbarians and mounted bowmen on these advanced civilizations (1700-500 B.C.).

McNeill makes frequent use of maps to illustrate his textual presentation, and ends his book with a small atlas section. The text is the dominant element of his presentation though, and it scans the life paths of civiliza-

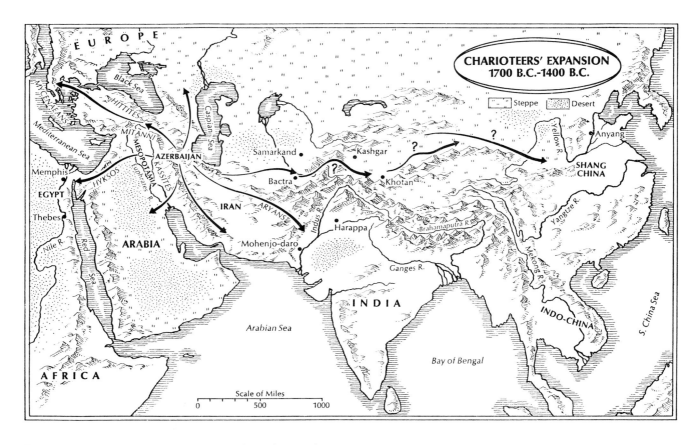

Figure 35   The play superimposed on the setting.

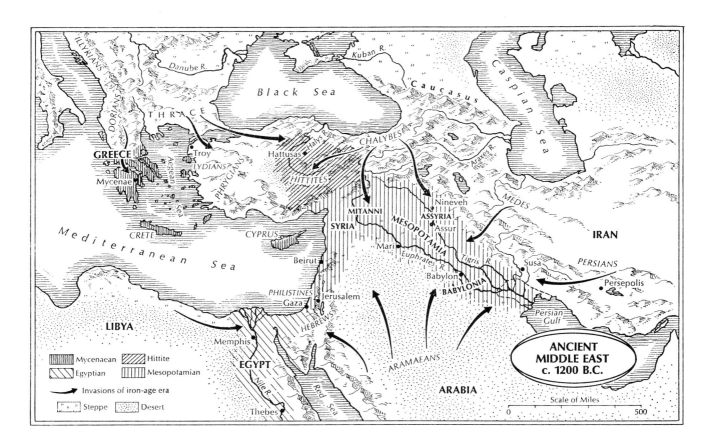

Figure 36   The setting, the actors and the play. From A World
History Atlas by William H. McNeill, published by Oxford
University Press 1967.

tions in different corners of the globe using broad sweeps in a manner very closely related to the disposition of the Times Atlas.

The maps themselves (37, usually full-page, text maps and a miniature atlas at the end of the book) deserve separate comment.

The design of the maps: unobtrusive articulation

Although these actual terms are never used explicitly, the elements setting-actor-play stand out very distinctly in the text. The text maps are not articulated in as accentuated a manner. They are line drawings with thin, inked lines of even thickness. Coastlines, lakes, mountain ranges and rivers are presented in a very unobtrusive manner with finely-drawn inked-in symbols. Despite the restrained character of the presentation, they give the settings an almost three-dimensional appearance. The majority of the maps (see figures 34 — 36) contain actors' elements as well, usually in the form of shading and raster, just as unobtrusively presented as the setting. The designations of the actors are barely visible on the setting. Thanks to the fine sense of balance of the anonymous cartographer-artist, the maps remain legible and distinct. Only the play — often in the form of clusters of arrows — is lifted appreciably above the visual level of the setting and the actors.

Map and text in organic inter-action

The intimate interaction between text and maps is striking. The maps contain no elements or details to which the text refers or is otherwise linked. But they still manage to follow, illustrate and make tangible the central concepts in the text in a way which appears obvious to the reader.

The presentation puts across its message not only through the unobtrusive but competent design of the maps, but also by means of the sharply-chiseled depictions of events in the text, and the organic way the maps are in agreement with the main patterns of the events described.

The third element — the illustration as complement

Van der Heyden and Scullard: Atlas of the Classical World

Maps evoke visual images

The atlases presented up to now have either consisted solely of maps or of a combination of maps and text, as a rule in the proportion of 1:1. The aim in the latter case is for the maps and text jointly to create a visual representation of events which took place in geographic space during a certain period of time. This presentation employs different levels of scale. At one extreme are illustrations which depict an entire continent and a time span of several hundred years. The illustrations are, however, often much closer to actual experience. They may refer to places, localities, sites of finds which are spatially limited, but which still serve as points of departure for the large overviews. They may also depict scenes where important events have taken place, and where the setting itself has played a crucial role. Or it may be a question of a combination of the two: maps depicting extensive

135

scenes are often provided with visual elements which are (probably) meant to make the maps more vital and tangible, and to adapt them to the frame of reference of the inexperienced map reader. Maps for children, for example, are often provided with drawings which are totally foreign to the abstract style of the map. Visual elements are, however, often inserted surreptitiously into the map where they soon become accepted features. The terrain, especially mountainous terrain, is often portrayed in a three-dimensional way which is more closely related to landscape drawing than to abstract, geometrically-grounded cartography (see for example figure 26 in the colour supplement). This is geometrically quite incorrect, but it helps give the reader the right associations.

Maps contain
hidden images

In addition to these visual elements which are "smuggled" into the maps, atlases are increasingly being supplemented by photographs or drawings. These illustrations often help make abstract maps more tangible by focussing on important details which are presented in a way which is closer to direct, personal experience.

The illustrations
provide supple-
mental informa-
tion

Although increasingly-elaborate illustrations can be found in atlases and related volumes, some of the best examples of effective use of illustrations are still to be found among earlier works. Van der Heyden and Scullard: Atlas of the Classical World (1959) is one such volume.

Atlas of the
Classical World

The book combines maps, text and illustrations. The maps have a wealth of detail which is largely denotative. They present a large amount of solid information about settlements and cult sites, communications networks, economy, trade routes, military and organizational conditions. In reproducing certain events — the Roman war with Carthage, Caesar and the civil war — the cartographic presentations become more dynamic in character.

By current standards, the maps are unsophisticated in design, but with their wealth of information and diversified perspectives, they are lively presentations which soon make the reader forget their simple graphic form.

Landscape
"paintings"
from the air

Still, it can be argued that the illustrations make the strongest impression. A considerable number of works of art are reproduced, but it is the landscapes which predominate — landscape photographs taken from the air and from ground level. These black-and-white photographs are often arranged in sequences which display landscapes from different perspectives and different distances so that their topographic features stand out much more tangibly than if the same thing were described only by maps. The aerial photographs of the Greek coastal and mountain regions make the conditions of Greek history come alive in a way which unites the tremendous density of information of the photographic image with the ability of the aerial photograph to capture broad swaths of the landscape on a single frame and the landscape painting's ability to convey the atmosphere of a setting. The aerial photograph of Delphi at the foot of Parnassus does not only show the geographic and topographic location of the temple. Because the photograph (an oblique view as are most of the others) is able to reproduce the scale of the landscape — the height of Parnassus, the steep

A visit to the
ancient world

cliffs of Phaedriadis above the temple and other relationships in the landscape in a way which even a reader unfamiliar with aerial photographs can understand — the picture is able to suggest the atmosphere still felt by the present-day visitor, and of course even more strongly by the ancient visitor, when approaching the temple. Supplemental information is provided by the photographs of the temple ruins taken from ground level and displayed side by side with reconstructions of the temple drawn from the viewing point from which the photographs were taken.

Picture sequences give a "zoom effect"

The fortification at Mycenea is, in the same way, illustrated both from ground level — viewed from a distant point on the plain and clearly marked on the photograph by a circle between two mountain peaks — as well as from a low-flying plane which proceeds to "zoom in" on Mycenea's walls, showing its construction from different angles. The experience is heightened still more by a reconstruction of the stronghold of Mycenea superimposed on a photograph taken from ground level, creating the illusion that the viewer is standing a few hundred metres outside the walls and looking up at them.

The illustration is an increasingly prominent component of the atlas

The visual image, visual presentations, play an increasingly powerful role in Western civilization, and illustrators have ever-greater resources at their disposal. Books published under the designation "atlas" often prove rather to be geographically-oriented picture books supplemented by a short text and a number of maps which comprise a relatively minor portion of the book. In some cases volumes of this sort succeed in balancing the text, maps and illustrations, and in co-ordinating the spatial and chronological aspects of the presentation on a very high level. Sven Lidman's book (50 sekler: Världshistoria i ord och bild) is a work which has successfully integrated the different components. Unfortunately these works often employ an imagery and style of illustration that appeals expressly to children. Adult readers are probably not encouraged to become more closely acquainted with the works even though the informational content is often of high quality.

Reconstruction drawings

Popularized scientific works and even other popular presentations sometimes contain illustrations, reconstructions of historic sites — ancient structures and entire towns, prehistoric cult sites etc. — which have a scope, a wealth of detail and a quality of reproduction far beyond the dreams of previous generations of scholars.

"...to whom honour is due"

In spite of this, Heyden's and Scullard's work, and especially their way of using aerial photography, is still qualitatively in a class by itself.

The map in its context: a comparative summary

The fifteen-odd atlases and other books analysed in the preceding sections constitute a relatively small portion of the total number of atlases and quasi-atlases published during the 1960's and 1970's. It appears that atlases with a historical orientation have been published at a steadily-accelerating rate during this period. A systematic compilation proved, however, that the rate of increase remained relatively constant (see figure 37). When the rate of publication diminished during a certain period, production during subsequent years appeared to level out the depression (for example the period 1974 to 1977). The diagram illustrates the development of the number of atlases available in Sweden. Due to Sweden's pronounced bias towards the Anglo-Saxon culture, the diagram primarily contains English-language atlases, and to a considerably lesser degree German-language works. The diagram cannot profess to completeness even with regard to the Anglo-Saxon world.

The examination of an atlas should answer four questions

1) How are its contents delimited in time and space and with regard to subject?
2) What are the proportions of historic and geographic aspects (perspectives) respectively?
3) What "scanning strategies" are used?
4) What are its "presentation strategies"?

The answers provided here refer primarily to the atlases analysed in the preceding sections with some glances at other works which have not been treated as thoroughly, but which are included in the diagram.

The multilinear system: perpendicular and oblique streams

The fifteen-odd atlases presented here exemplify different types of illustrations of multilinear systems. The system contains the two previously-mentioned main types of element: vertically-rising, interwoven streams of individual life paths and oblique waves which reproduce themselves through the vertical streams like pressure waves through a liquid. The oblique waves represent the diffusion of different types of knowledge, technical advances, religious beliefs but also things. These waves may also coincide with and be carried by the movements of ethnic groups such as in the case of migrations.

The balance between static and dynamic components of atlases

Atlases which present the history of mankind always balance between these two components. Some of them stress the static, the stationary elements: the vertically-rising streams. They often focus on the expansion of the different ethnic groups, the structure of settlements and the conquering of different territories. Other atlases stress the dynamic aspects instead: the changes, the movements which bring about increased diffusion of certain types of technical know-how or religious beliefs. The first group focuses on the political aspects; the second on the economic, cultural,

138

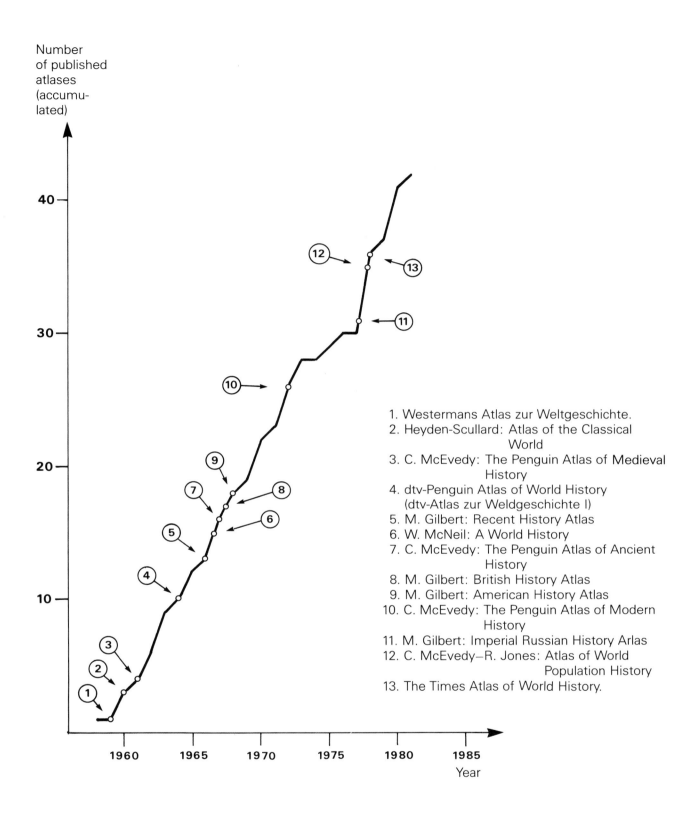

Number of published atlases (accumulated)

40

30

20

10

1960   1965   1970   1975   1980   1985

Year

1. Westermans Atlas zur Weltgeschichte.
2. Heyden-Scullard: Atlas of the Classical
        World
3. C. McEvedy: The Penguin Atlas of Medieval
        History
4. dtv-Penguin Atlas of World History
        (dtv-Atlas zur Weldgeschichte I)
5. M. Gilbert: Recent History Atlas
6. W. McNeil: A World History
7. C. McEvedy: The Penguin Atlas of Ancient
        History
8. M. Gilbert: British History Atlas
9. M. Gilbert: American History Atlas
10. C. McEvedy: The Penguin Atlas of Modern
        History
11. M. Gilbert: Imperial Russian History Arlas
12. C. McEvedy–R. Jones: Atlas of World
                        Population History
13. The Times Atlas of World History.

Figure 37   Increase in the number of atlases of historical events
                available in Sweden between 1960 and 1980.

religious components of history. All atlases contain both major components but in varying proportions.

Uninuclear and multinuclear presentations

The spatial demarcation of atlases also varies between two extremes: the uninuclear and the multinuclear presentation. Both types deal with perpendicular streams as major elements. The uninuclear presentation focuses its account on the main channel of one single stream - often the history of a nation. All events and situations which are described are linked to this main channel. The greater part of the presentation deals with conditions and events which take place in the region under consideration — often a country, sometimes an entire continent (see McEvedy's work). Since the inner workings of a region are always influenced by its environment, these atlases often include surveys and supplements which show the interaction between the core area and its environment (see figures 28-33; diagram of the distribution of information in M. Gilbert's atlas).

Demarcations of the setting

Behind the demarcation of a region — the choice of setting for an atlas — is often an express or unspoken belief that the chosen setting forms an organic whole which makes it distinguishable from the rest of the world. This belief is articulated especially distinctly by McEvedy in the introductory chapters of his atlas.

The multinuclear presentation points out several major streams on the Earth's surface — for example the great, contemporary civilizations — and the presentation swings back and forth between them. The mental scanning line often traces the major connecting movements between these centres — migrations, flows of commodities, the expansion of an empire, a religious or economic system. The multinuclear atlas often deals with the entire surface of the Earth as a single unit.

Time-related aspects

The majority of atlases describe their subjects from the first trace left by Man in the region under consideration to the author's own period, sometimes — as in the case of McEvedy and Jones — to a not-too-distant future. In other cases the authors of the atlas let the time periods coincide with the major, generally-accepted historical epochs, largely in the perspective of European history (ancient history, the middle ages, the modern age, the contemporary period). However, even the definition of historical epochs shows a displacement towards a global perspective: the structure of more recent atlases (such as the Times Atlas) follows different epochs of interaction between the great civilizations of the Earth.

Scanning strategies

Not surprisingly, scanning strategies appear to follow the demarcation techniques of time geography, or more correctly, they are based on the same perspective which guided the geographical demarcation of the main setting and main section of the atlas.

Perpendicular channels	The purest longitudinal scanning technique is displayed by McEvedy and Jones who follow vertical channels in time-space — the national land areas of 1975 traced back through world history. The presentation of each sequence of channels is introduced, however, by a spiral-shaped scanning of the time-space above an entire continent presenting the region's major time-geographical features, and holding together the longitudinal analyses.
A shaft in time-space	McEvedy's other atlases are also quite pure in approach: he lifts out a shaft from time-space, a shaft which follows the "fault lines" of the European setting — zones through which hardly any communication occurs. He makes horizontal cross-sections through the volume of the shaft at regular intervals, and links these sections by mapping the movements — events — among them.
Spiral-shaped scanning lines	Uninuclear atlases with less-sharply demarcated boundaries are, as a rule, scanned by spiral-shaped movements through time-space. The scanning is often done in the vicinity of the core area, but time and again, the scanning lines make wider swings out towards the surroundings. The spiral movement starts with sparse lines, but becomes denser, its slope less steep the closer we come to the present.
The core areas are demarcated and displayed	The multinuclear model defines the core areas — the great civilizations — and demarcates them into epochs with the aid of horizontal cross-sections. By being scanned one at a time, the multinuclear, synchronous, complex stream of events (a number of events which take place simultaneously) is transformed into a simpler, mainly linear presentation. This approach can be studied in its purest form in Nordberg's work — because of his almost exclusive use of textual presentation — but the same model can also be found in almost as pure a form in McNeill and in the Times Atlas.
Shifts in thematic approach	Scanning strategies also imply shifting approaches — in the thematic sense of the word. A strategy which is completely straight-forward and free of shifts in approach can be found in McEvedy and Jones who focus their investigations on population growth. McEvedy's other atlases treat, in addition to the expansion of ethnic groups, the economic links between different regions and the spread of certain cultural and religious beliefs. Gilbert's main interest is the political setting while dtv-Atlas and the Times Atlas exhibit continual shifting of perspective, though with a certain dominance for political-territorial aspects.
The scope of the atlases: from the history of the world to the atlas of events	The works analysed up to now have, as a rule, dealt with the whole of world history or the history of certain regions from prehistoric times until the present. Corresponding atlases have sometimes been produced dealing with more limited historic periods. M. Gilbert's atlases of the history of the First World War and of the Arab-Israeli conflict and Oppen: The Riel Rebellions: A Cartographic History (1978) are some examples of atlases dealing with events which are much more narrowly delimited in time and space.

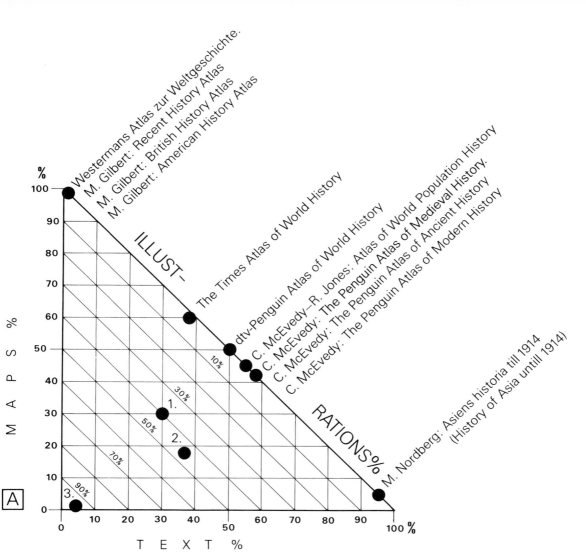

1) S. Lidman et.al.: 50 sekler (50 centuries)
2) Heyden-Scullard: Atlas of the Classical World
3) Ph. Clucas: Britain. The Landscape Below

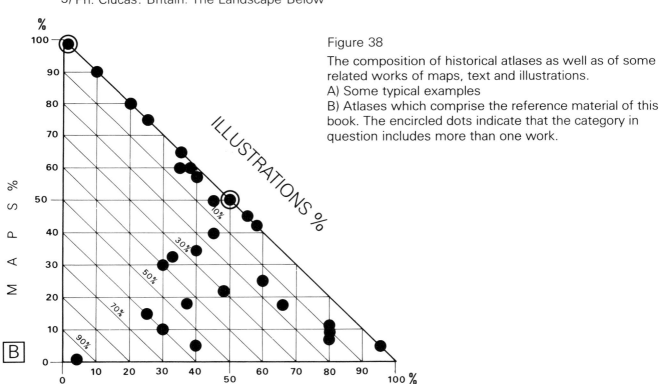

Figure 38

The composition of historical atlases as well as of some related works of maps, text and illustrations.
A) Some typical examples
B) Atlases which comprise the reference material of this book. The encircled dots indicate that the category in question includes more than one work.

Presentation strategy

The works which have been analysed employ text, maps and — in some cases — illustrations to reproduce the scanned contents of the model. These instruments can be used individually or in combinations (see the triangle diagram, figure 38).

Pure presentations: map, text or illustration

No atlas is completely devoid of text — a title-page, a table of contents, etc. are self-evident features in all such publications. In many works of this type, however, the body of the atlas consists entirely of maps (see the top part of diagram 38 A). Processes in time geography — which are here assumed even to include historical processes in a geographical perspective — can, on the other hand, be reproduced almost exclusively through the printed word. Michael Nordberg's book has been chosen to represent this type of work.

In recent years, geographically-oriented picture books have also been published. They often consist entirely of photographs taken at oblique angles from aeroplanes — a kind of aerial landscape photo — with insignificant amounts of text (picture captions) or a few outline maps with some commentary. P. Clucas: Britain — The Landscape Below exemplifies this type of work (see the triangle diagram, figure 38 A).

Combinations

Many of the atlases use two, and sometimes all three of these elements. A large percentage of the analysed works use maps and text in the proportion of 1:1 (for example McEvedy's atlases and dtv-Penguin Atlas) or with a slight preponderance of maps (the Times Atlas). Van der Heyden's and Scullard's Atlas of the Classical World represents a mixture of all three elements with a preponderance — based on number of pages — of illustrations, and — again based on number of pages, but hardly on wealth of information — with maps as the smallest component.

The presentation strategy is a mirror image of the scanning strategy and — in the cases investigated — it follows one of three main strategies.

Three main strategies

A. A chronological account of courses of events in geographically-demarcated areas (McEvedy and Jones, but also several chronological tabular works, such as J. Hawkes: The Atlas of Early Man). The text and outline maps unify the presentation making it complete from the point of view of time geography.
B. Horizontal cross-sections through the time-geographical world model or selected parts of it presented in the form of maps. Processes taking place between two cross-sections are described in the text. (McEvedy's atlases are of this type.)
C. Dynamic processes are illustrated, i.e. many, closely-spaced, horizontal cross-sections as in B. are combined into one single map. Simple chronological cross-sections from other fields help illuminate, along with the text, the process being described and its implications. The Times Atlas is an example of this type of atlas.

143

Most atlases contain a combination primarily of B. and C. Type B. dominates among the older atlases. The dynamic processes (C) play an increasingly-prominent role in the more recent publications.

One or more
mental scanning
lines

When either text or maps (or illustrations) are used alone as means of communication, their sequential placement represents the mental scanning line of the work/the author. When combinations of maps and text or map/text/illustration are employed to present the results of the scanning process, the situation may be different. Often the text will comprise the mental scanning line around which the maps are positioned. Or the maps, along with supplementary commentary, may represent the mental scanning line of the presentation. The text and the maps may also appear side by side as two independent mental scanning lines which are linked at certain points, but living their own lives (dtv-Penguin Atlas). The mental scanning line may be formed by the interaction between the text and maps (McEvedy's atlases) or between text, maps and illustrations (for example Lidman 1981).

Successful
co-ordination?

These strategies of co-ordination can be implemented more or less successfully. A chosen strategy can be carried out so well that the author's conception is transferred to the mind of the reader. Sometimes, this is not the case, however. The text may for example run along paths which hardly coincide at all with the contents of the maps. Correspondence between text and map can be lost due to incorrect reference methods or different approaches to text and maps. Painstaking co-ordination of text, illustrations and maps may prove meaningless in practice if the body of the text is so voluminous that it is not often read. A well thought-out presentation strategy is probably the best guarantee for avoiding mistakes of the kind mentioned above. It should also help make the meeting between atlas and reader such that the reader is enabled to reconstruct the author's train of thought.

A very important element in a presentation strategy is the choice of the contents and design of the maps and their co-ordination with text and illustrations in the layout.

Nordberg chose the least pretentious solution: a few outline maps in the form of line drawings. The free-hand style of the sketches is emphasized, and they provide only the most essential references about the different parts of the Asiatic continent and about the expanse of certain territories.

Line drawings

McEvedy and Jones are nearly as unassuming with regard to means of communication: simple diagrams with outline-map insets portraying the areas of individual countries against the background of the outlines of continents or against other major geographical features in the environment. Simple but often ingenious outline maps contribute to the geographical clarity.

From the viewpoint of reproduction, McNeill's textual maps are equally unpretentious: in the first double-page spread of the book, his anonymous cartographer employs only black print. Skillful use of the artist's pen still makes it possible to shape the setting, actors and play which are confidently articulated with unobtrusive means. Gilbert's cartographer, Arthur Banks, also uses black print exclusively in his maps. His cartography is rich in contrasts, strictly structured and distinct with the setting suggested schematically and emphasis placed on the thematic content, i.e. the actors and the play. In some of the maps, this gives excellent, distinct solutions (see for example figure 2 in the Imperial Russian History Atlas which portrays migrations) while certain others maps threaten to disintegrate due to the sharp contrast between their various elements. A frequent problem in these maps is that the ocean, an important element of the setting, often ends up on the same visual level as the thematic elements which are illustrated by shading. These maps are often difficult to grasp. A special feature of Gilberg's and Bank's maps are the insets with commentary. They are often very informative, but in some cases they impair the map's visual effectiveness.

Two-colour and four-colour solutions

McEvedy uses a two-colour presentation technique in his atlas: ocean and lake surfaces as well as waterways are coloured blue while the thematic elements are done in black, often in the form of shadings. The topographic structure of the setting map — and major elements in the deployment of the actors — are presented separately on two special introductory maps. These provide the terrain information (setting description) which cannot be supplied by the main maps with their various screen patterns for different ethnic groups.

The most advanced techniques have been employed by dtv-Penguin Atlas and the Times Atlas. Both have four-colour print and utilize the presentation capabilities of the air brush. In the Times Atlas the terrain is usually moulded in three dimensions while the theme is most often depicted by distinct lines and surfaces. dtv-Penguin Atlas sometimes uses the capabilities of the air brush to reproduce the terrain in three dimensions, but most often to suggest the dynamics of historic development and the progressively-fading character of point, line and area symbols.

The text and maps are presented together on double-page spreads in most atlases. The profound co-ordination of all graphic elements which Lidman has achieved in his book *50 sekler* (50 Centuries) and in his reference works (such as Combi-visual) are still rather unusual among atlases.

In summary:

Atlas cartography in a historical context means that the author distinguishes and demarcates organically-related segments of the time-geographical world model. Thereafter, a linear scanning sequence is determined within and between the segments thus defined. The scanning process is rendered into a combination of text, maps and illustrations and these are grouped so as to form a linear pattern.

Part II: From today's map to tomorrow's

Human cartography in practical applications

Census cartography for urban and regional planning

Introduction

On the border between the past and the future

We live on the upper surface of the time-geographical model. For each unit of time which passes, a new layer is deposited there extending the life path of every living individual, every object or other element which comprises an image point in the model. We attempt to see into the future to a time-space as yet unformed, to predict events and situations there, and to guide the development of the existing world in directions we consider desirable. We are conscious of the great power exerted by the past on the future, and we glance backwards to see in which direction developments are headed, and to search for points of departure from which we can attempt to form the future the way we think best. We look upon the present, that which exists at this very moment, as the last element of the past, and, consequently, as a base for the future. We attempt to capture it in various ways: through verbal descriptions, in pictures, in figures and also in maps. The manner of description varies along with the intentions of the author. If the author is an urban or regional planner, his activities all aim at co-ordinating as many individual desires for the future as possible. His plans may concern future physical structures — buildings — or some of their specific functions such as social planning, school planning, health-care planning. No matter what the orientation of his activities, as a rule he will strive to construct a comprehensive picture of the present — comprehensive in the context of his specific vantage point. The statistician who

A task for census cartography

compiles data about the present aims to provide *primary data* for constructing a very large number of conceivable comprehensive pictures. Among the mass of figures collected for this purpose are concealed an infinitely large number of *latent* pictures. To transform these latent pictures into actual ones, to present them in such a way that they even suggest the basic structure of the other images still concealed among the mass of figures — this is one of the most important tasks of the field called census cartography.

In the following sections, a major field of application for census cartography is studied first, namely that of urban and regional planning. Good cartography requires that the results be adapted to the application, to the conceptual world of the environment and its demands concerning the tools of the trade. Thereafter three projects are described in which these demands have been observed: the design of a planning atlas for a town, a map series for regional planning illustrating the census of population and housing, and prepared with the aid of computer cartography and finally, the production of a census atlas on the national level — all three in Sweden. Taking these projects as point of departure, and against the background of the theoretical analyses carried out in the first part of the book, consideration also being given to the technological advances being made in computer graphics, a developmental programme is outlined for the field of census cartography.

Background: The field of activity of urban and regional planning

A model-town in time-space

Figure 39 shows an imaginary, circular town at three different times, cut from the cylinder-shaped time-geographical model. The horizontal plane "t" represents the point in time "now", and the area of the circle shows the extent of the town at this point in time. The outlines of the town thus lie within the uppermost surface of the cylindrical model which represents the past. "t-1" is a point in time in the (recent) past, "t+1" in the future. The planning now in progress in the town aims at preparing guidelines for the (possible) expansion of the town until t+1 (see the bulge on the circle) as well as plans for various activities which are necessary for the continued existence of the town.

Tasks in urban planning

The planning work deals with two major aspects: external and internal conditions. Dealing with external conditions means describing and analysing the town's relationship and interaction with its environment today (time t); in the past (t-1, possibly t-2 etc.) and the changes which have occurred in the intervals. In addition an evaluation is made — based on the previous analysis — of how these relationships are expected to develop until t+1, into the future. The same analysis should be implemented for the town's internal conditions. Since a town is not homogeneous, it must be studied section by section — it is these sections which are symbolized by the implied grid in figure 39. The development which has taken place and its expected continuation must be analysed (see the channel in time linking a district at three different points in time), and the results of this series of analyses must be summarized in a comprehensive description. In the next stage, goals for planning are formulated, measures for achieving these goals are proposed and the consequences of these measures are studied.

The work schedule above is grossly simplified. In the real world, this work process seldom takes place in this simplified form. The complex processes leading to the preparation of different types of plans do, however, include these elements though they may often not be apparent. In spite of its simplifications, and whether or not it is actually printed on paper, the model should still be suitable for portraying the role of the geographically-oriented description in the planning process. This applies whether or not the planning area comprises an urban district, an entire town, a municipality, a region or an entire country.

150

TIME

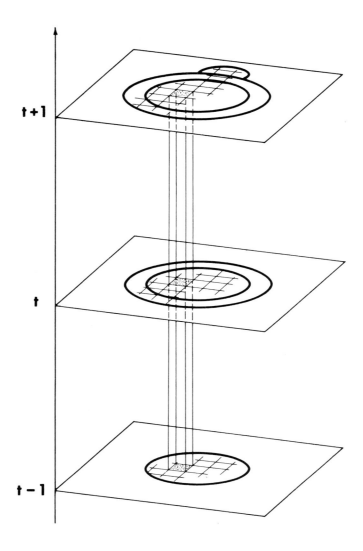

Figure 39   A city today, yesterday and tomorrow – an example of
the sphere of activity of urban and regional planners.

Statistical
information for
planning

Planning documents consist of qualitative as well as quantitative elements.
The quantitative elements play a central and often predominant role —
though qualitative elements appear to be gaining ground. To satisfy the
needs of urban and regional planning for quantitative information, population censuses and similar registrations of buildings, communications etc.
are carried out. The data so obtained are in the form of geographically-
oriented statistical information — i.e. statistical information compiled for
small areas which can be aggregated into larger areas more relevant for
planning. The field of activity of census cartography is then the formation
of statistical areas for data acquisition and the presentation of the compiled
data in ways which draw attention to their geographical significance.

151

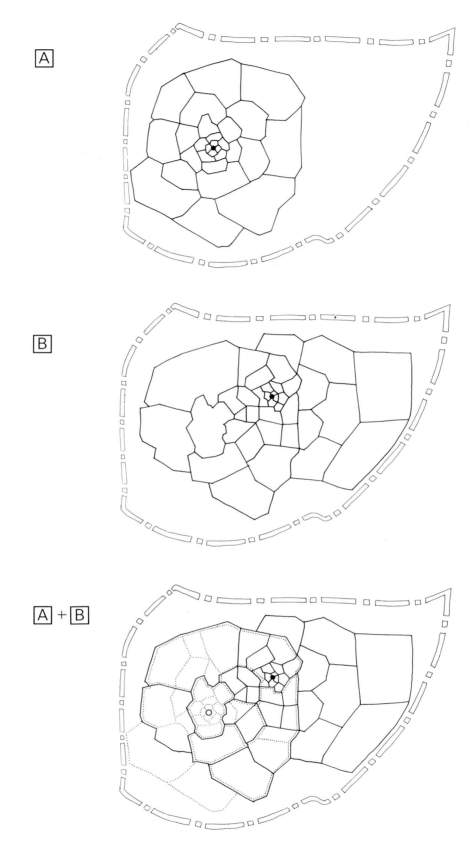

Figure 40   The field of vision of the urban and regional planner is
             centre-oriented — the highest resolution is required in the
             immediate vicinity of the current planning object. A fictive
             example with two planning objects.

Background: The planner's environmental image

One of the most vital requirements concerning planning data appears to be the demand for *flexibility*. The term refers to the spatial versatility of the statistical information as well as to its content. By spatial flexibility is meant here that the same data can be acquired (with limited effort) for very small, somewhat larger and large areas within a single planning region.

The demand for flexibility probably stems from an outlook which appears to be fundamental among planners but which is probably also applicable within a much larger context. This outlook can be likened to the centre-oriented or "central" perspective, i.e. the manner of registering visual information which can be observed in its purest form in the operation of the camera, but which also is fundamental for the workings of the human eye. An image reproduced according to the rules of the central perspective accentuates that which is found in the foreground closest to the observer or the camera, while phenomena further away diminish rapidly in size with increased distance. It is this perspective which is reflected in Hägerstrand's logarithmic distance scale (Hägerstrand 1962, see also figure 40:1).

The planner's view of the environment is centre-oriented

The planner sometimes focuses his image on small, individual objects, a building or an element in the traffic system for example. Its most immediate surroundings are illustrated with a great amount of spatial detail, but the further away we come, the briefer the presentation (see figure 40). The population in the vicinity of an intersection slated for reconstruction, for example, is presented property by property. A little further away the presentation is limited to blocks. At a greater distance, population distribution is analysed only on a district basis. If one wishes to take into account traffic flows originating outside the area, this is done on the basis of entire towns or other urbanized areas. The geographical resolution thus diminishes very rapidly with increased distance from the planning object.

If the planning object is an entire town, its internal population distribution must be presented in a detailed fashion block by block; its immediate surroundings are shown with slightly less detail, while its more distant environs are perhaps studied on a municipal-wide basis and the rest of the country is analysed county by county.

Up to now this type of planning analysis was implemented manually — and this still applies to many of the analyses currently being carried out. This is possible to accomplish within a reasonable amount of time if the primary data are available on different regional levels. For the centre of the planning area, the data must be available for very small reference areas; for its other sections, data are usually required for increasingly-large areas the further we come from the centre of focus (figure 40). If data organized in this way are available, i.e. for large as well as small reference areas, an aggregate picture corresponding to the centre-oriented perspective can then be constructed manually with a relatively limited number of operations.

153

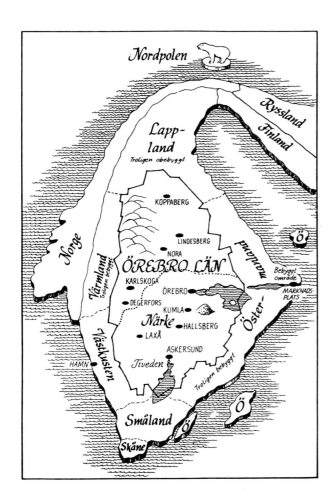

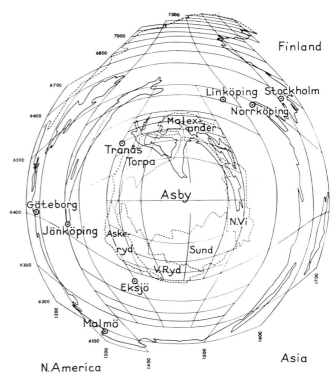

Fig. 38. Location of more important places in the migration field of Asby.

Figure 40:1

Three examples of man's centre-oriented ("egocentric") view of his environment. Torsten Häggerstrand's logarithmic maps and two maps which joke about the local chauvinist's view of the relative importance of his own territory.

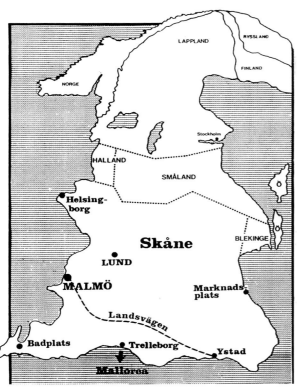

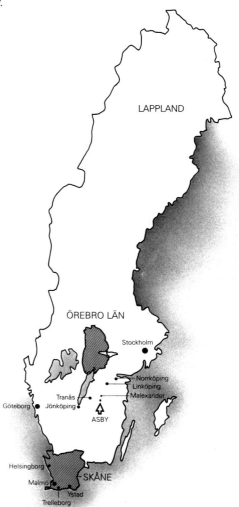

In dealing with a multitude of different objects of varying size, the planner shifts the midpoint of his centre-oriented perspective around to different locations within his field of activity. Consequently, the *entire* field must be presented with different levels of detail. This is probably the main reason why the hierarchic subdivision has been so well-accepted within (Swedish) urban and regional planning.

The centre-oriented perspective also applies to the dimension of time

The centre-oriented perspective — focussing on the immediate vicinity and devoting rapidly-diminishing interest to more distant phenomena — appears to apply to the planner's sense of time as well. Developments taking place within the planning area in the recent past are often studied exhaustively while the somewhat-more-distant past is dealt with more cursorily. The same can be said about the future: the immediate future is often treated as relatively tangible while a more distant future is outlined in an extremely schematic manner.

Double-logarithmic time-space

It was on the basis of observations such as these that the double-logarithmic time-space was formulated as a co-ordinate system for describing the urban and regional planner's approach to reality or his view of the environment (see figure 41 from Szegö 1974). The main point is that tha planner's demands regarding spatial detail in the primary data diminish with the logarithm of the distance from the planning object calculated in time as well as in space.

This hypothesis, an extension of Hägerstrand's logarithmic map, is not based on a systematic analysis of planning documents or similar material, but is rather an intuitive summary of conversations between planners recorded during a period of many years, in which the author took part either as active participant or as interviewer.

The centre-oriented perspective with regard to thematic concerns

The centre-oriented perspective also applies to the data content of urban and regional planning. The requirements concerning the amount of detail in the data are very high in the vicinity of the planning area's focal point, but sink rapidly with increasing thematic distance. When planning for child care, one wants detailed information for each separate age group (one-year groups). Parent and sibling relationships and household-formation around children served by child-care facilities are studied almost as exhaustively, while the rest of the population, the broader context of child-care planning, is treated more cursorily.

In consequence the data are structured hierarchically even with regard to thematic content, with increasingly-smaller classes of objects and with increasingly-numerous categories in the vicinity of the planning object.

Figure 41

System of co-ordinates for man's, and especially the urban and regional planner's, mental map of time and space.

The vertical axis represents time; the horizontal plane space. "The present" arises as a space between the recent past and the proximate future (see the two horizontal planes).

The main point made by the figure is that man's view of his environment is dominated by the recent past and the proximate future as well as by geographic proximity.

Objects and events which appear to be twice as distant in spatial terms as nearby objects (see the distance circles with radii = 2) are actually 10 times further away from the observer. Objects and events which appear to be three times more distant are actually 100 times further away etc.

The same phenomenon applies to time. Events which appear to be twice as remote in time as the most recent events are actually ten times more remote; those which appear to be three times as remote are actually 100 times more remote. The same "perspective abbreviation" also applies to our view of the future.

The perceived distance in space as well as time is thus a common logarithm of the objective distance. Man's subjective perception can thus be described as the double-logarithmic time space: logarithmic in regards to the distance from "here" and "now" in time as well as space.

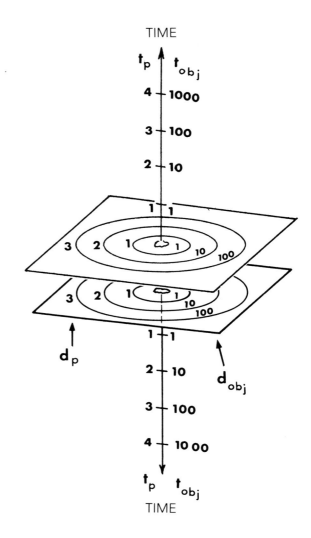

d_{obj} = objective distance
d_p = percieved distance
t_{obj} = objective time
t_p = percieved time

Background: The demans of urban and regional planning concerning planning data: Flexibility versus ease of use

Demands for flexibility create large amounts of data

It is the demand for flexibility which — together with other demands — has lead to widespread use of subdivisions which are geographically as well as thematically hierarchic. A hierarchic structure necessitates the acquisition of great amounts of data, however, which can either be compiled in the form of printed tables or stored in data bases from which tabular presentations are created on a computer screen as needed.

Within this large mass of data, the planner can find all the individual information needed to create the centre-oriented analyses which are required in conjunction with concrete, individual planning projects.

The planner can also use the data in another way, however. He must be able to carry out broad-stroked, comprehensive analyses of the planning area and monitor the geographical developmental trends there. The planner is, of course, not completely dependent on statistical data for forming an impression of what is going on in the planning area, but the statistical data can display trends which are not discernible through direct observation or personal contact with the inhabitants. Statistical data can also supplement the latter methods.

A comprehensive view is necessary — not only flexibility

If the planner is seeking new approaches to the planning area, or seeking new clues for solving concrete planning problems, he needs an overview. One of the routes goes via statistical information. He must then have a clear overview of the entire material and of the geographical and other problems which are concealed within the mass of statistical data.

A comprehensive view — why?

Anyone who has come to grips with these matters has in all probability experienced how difficult it can be to discover geographical patterns of even the simplest and most basic kind in statistical tables without first rendering the tables into maps. These patterns are, moreover, essential, not only when seeking new approaches to problems, but also for testing concrete planning proposals which are often based on statistical arguments. It is often necessary to pose questions of the type "Is this argument correct?" "Is this pattern (of population distribution, age, employment etc.) which is implied in this proposal correctly interpreted?" "Is it not possible to interpret it differently?" etc. That the data are flexible is not a sufficient prerequisite for posing questions of this type or having similar exploratory discussions — it must also be easy to handle. It must be easy to reshape the material, to reorganize it, to see whether it then reveals new patterns.

Flexibility versus ease of handling

Flexibility is achieved when the smallest subdivision of the material is very fine. Consequently, a large amount of labour is required for reorganizing the material. *Ease of handling* certainly presupposes that the material is flexible, but also that it still can be regrouped without major effort — which implies that it may not be too finely distributed. How can these

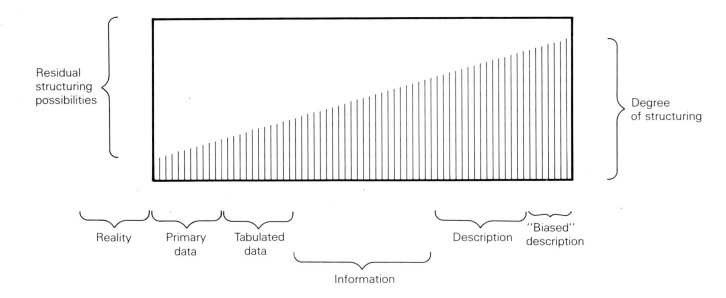

Figure 42   Different levels of informational organization.

conflicting demands be balanced against one another? In other words, how must statistical information be *organized* to satisfy the demands placed on it by urban and regional planning?

Background: Organizing information

Organization
versus residual
structur-ability

Reality is infinitely complex. It can be described in many different ways. A description implies among other things drawing attention to some of the many structural elements of reality. In our description we give reality a simplified, more articulated structure — we organize it. Before beginning our descriptive efforts, we have the entire range of descriptive possibilities — 100% — at our disposal. At this stage the level of structuring is 0% — we have not yet begun to organize the material — while the *residual* structurability is 100%. In the instant we decide which attributes to use to describe reality, we have begun organizing the material. For example, a population is defined and certain of its characteristics are deemed important for describing it while other attributes of the chosen population and of other populations are considered irrelevant in the present context.

Reality has been organized but its residual structurability is still great: if we collect data based on these definitions of the population and its characteristics, there are a number of different ways in which we can present the *primary material* which we have acquired (see "primary data" in figure 42). If we transform the primary material into work tables, for example, we increase the level of structuring: the design of tables for presenting the primary material draws attention to certain aspects of the compiled data while imparting to others a less prominent role. The degree of organization of the material has been raised still more. We have created *data*. An analysis

158

of this material can, however, be carried out from several different points of departure and give different types of results. Thus the residual structurability of the material is still great.

If we/the researcher/the investigator/the planner do an analysis of this type and it results in a *description* of the chosen population, as a rule, this will mean that we have selected a portion of the registered data, and also that we have chosen an approach which tinges the description. Certain attributes and certain aspects are then considered to be fundamental and essential, others are looked upon as less important. A description based on analysis therefore means that the material becomes highly organized and tinged by the analyst's outlook and his method of approach to the original material. A good description supplies so much factual material, however, that a constructively-critical reviewer of the description can apply alternative approaches to the subject under consideration. Thus the material still has a substantial amount of residual structurability, but its presentation is characterized by a high degree of organization.

A description can be positioned along lines of thought which its author considers to be the only conceivable interpretation of the facts he presents. His factual presentation is such that it is very difficult to make alternative interpretations. The material is highly-organized, its residual structurability is low. We are dealing with a one-sided *biased description*.

A presentation of a proposal for solving a planning problem can be said to fall within the category of "description". As a rule, such a proposal presents the circumstances which make it necessary to prepare a proposal, after which the proposal itself is presented. finally, an impact analysis is usually made, i.e. a description of an expected future situation which realization of the proposal would bring about compared with the original situation.

Statistical data are compiled in part to make possible descriptions of situations, conditions which make certain planning measures necessary. In some instances, the planner's education and experience provide guidelines for constructing a description of reality and for selecting facts to be presented there. He finds the statistical data for the presentation in statistical tables or in statistical data bases.

In other cases he must find his own points of departure for specifying existing problems and for continuing on to the preparation of the planning proposal. In these cases statistical tables with finely-distributed data presentations and the flexibility which this implies are not enough. What he needs is a broad idea of the outlines of the structures concealed within the large mass of data. He must have access to *comprehensive information* about the basic structure of the data mass. Those who examine plans and their prerequisites have the same need. Mistakes in details are seldom found in concrete planning proposals. However, it is often valuable to question the views on which the on which the proposal is based. The person set to examine a planning proposal thus needs comprehensive information in order to question the planner's approach.

What is needed are comprehensive data presentations with good balance between the level of organization in the material and its residual structurability. The requirement can quite simply be expressed as *information* presented in a flexible and easily-grasped way (figure 42). In the following three sections are presented three different projects which use census cartography to create information of the type outlined above.

Census cartography of today:
Three levels — three implemented projects

The acquisition of statistical data for urban and regional planning has developed and become standardized in Sweden during the latest three decades approximately. The work is increasingly systematic, and is carried out by the producer of statistics (Statistics Sweden) in co-operation with the users — statisticians and planners employed by local and central government and private firms. The process of standardization taking place in the field appears to have developed organically on the basis of a dialogue between producers and users. Excerpts from these discussions can be found in some reports, but only a tiny portion has been compiled. Virtually no theoretical codification has been undertaken of the underlying conceptual structure of the process.

While the manner of production of statistical data has been standardized and is generally accepted by Swedish planning bodies — primarily the municipalities who enjoy considerable independence with regard to choice of planning method — the mapping of statistical data in a planning context (census cartography) still finds itself at an early stage of development, and the forms of presentation are not yet fully developed. In an attempt to systematize certain ideas as a basis for continued developmental work, three different projects are presented in the next section.

The first concerns the mapping of statistical data (census data) on the local level by which is meant mapping of conditions within a single town. This project was carried out entirely with manual methods of cartographic presentation.

In project number two a co-ordinate method was applied with the aid of computer cartography on a level which can be termed regional — municipalities and counties — with the aid of computer cartography.

In project number three a census atlas was produced on the national level (A Census Atlas of Sweden) employing manual as well as computer-based cartography.

The purpose of this presentation is three-fold. It aims firstly at placing experiences and methods (in several instances newly-developed ones) at the disposal of the practising planner. Secondly, by systemizing concepts, the study provides a basis for the author's continued work within the field. A number of attempts of this type are presented in this book. Thirdly, it is also meant to be a contribution to the discussions and developmental work now in progress in this field.

It must be stressed that the presentation of the three projects mentioned above cannot claim to be scientifically objective. Since the author of these lines is also the author of the above-mentioned local and national atlases as well as being responsible for the cartographic aspects of the third project, it is the author's own intentions and experiences which are being presented. It is hoped, however, that intimacy with these projects, first-hand familiarity with their backgrounds and implementation, will outweigh the lack of distance to the subject which accompanies personal attachment.

Case I: A local atlas based on a hierarchic subdivision and manual cartographic methods

The municipality of Lund, located on the densely-populated Lund plain in southernmost Sweden, was in the early 1960's composed solely of the town

A town ...

of Lund itself. With 50,000 inhabitants, it ranked 15th in size among Swedish towns (urbanized areas according to current terminology). With the largest university in the Nordic countries, a large and advanced industrial sector and an otherwise extremely varied business sector, the town already occupied a much more important position nationally than was suggested by the size of its population.

... and its previous planning

This was also reflected in the planning of the town. As early as the 1930's, systematic analyses of the town's population and trade and industry were carried out as a base for comprehensive planning. In preparation for the rapid urban expansion which was expected in the early 1960's, the town's planning organization was modernized and expanded.

Preparing for data acquisition ...

Within this newly-organized administration, the systematic analysis of urban expansion was developed further. Lund was one of the first municipalities outside a metropolitan area to introduce a hierarchic subdivision of its territory. All acquisition of statistical data was based on and adapted to the new statistical areas as were other planning activities.

... and implementing it

The new subdivision was put to the test for the first time in connection with the census of population and housing in 1965. The results appeared in the form of a pile of raw tables — a few thousand pages describing the population, employment and the housing stock on different geographical levels. The tabular material occupied 1.5 metres of shelf space. By current standards it was a moderate amount of data; however, at that time it raised

161

the still-valid question of how the informational content in such a huge
mass of computer-produced data could be put to use.

Two roads were open:

1) to establish a "statistical source" to which one could turn for
specific statistical information for clearly-defined geographical
areas
2) to create some type of index of the data mass which not only
summarizes major features of the statistical material, but which
also could be of assistance in the use of the above-mentioned —
and in all cases necessary — statistical source.

After a groping start, the work stabilized around alternative 2. The general
outlines of the work crystallized step by step. If the goals which emerged
during the course of the work had been clear at the start, they might have
been formulated in the following way:

Goal:

Statistics are compiled for making quantitative descriptions of the geographical composition and functioning of the town (Lund). This numerical

material is essential for different categories of professional planners —
some of whom lack training in the use of statistical and/or geographical
planning methods — as well as for political decision-makers who must be
able to examine, test and even question the prerequisites of proposed
technical solutions. Create, therefore, a statistical-geographical description
of the town (Lund) which not only illustrates the main structure of the
town as it appears in the compiled statistics, but also introduces the statistical terminology which is employed in the acquisition and presentation of
the statistical material. This latter element should enable the presentation
to serve as a guide for approaching and penetrating the entire statistical
material.

Means:

The basic element of this type of work should be maps. They should show
the division of the town into statistical areas, and indicate different features
in each area with the help of symbols. The maps serve as an index and
provide an overview. They should be supplemented by figures — tables —
which present the exact significance of the symbols of the statistical maps.
Text should be provided to facilitate the study of the maps and tables, and
to guide those who are unfamiliar with statistical maps. In addition the
text should provide information about the limitations of the maps and the
risk for mistaken interpretations, define professional terms employed and
give references regarding supplemental information.

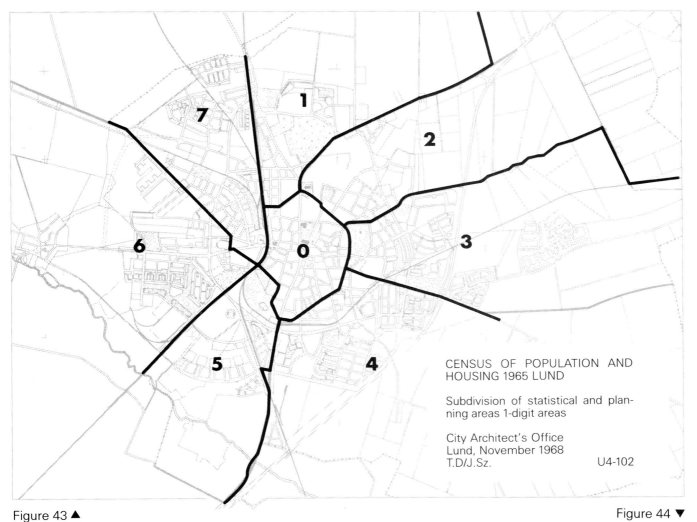

7 **1** **2** **6** **0** **3** **5** **4**

CENSUS OF POPULATION AND
HOUSING 1965 LUND

Subdivision of statistical and planning areas 1-digit areas

City Architect's Office
Lund, November 1968
T.D/J.Sz.   U4-102

Figure 43 ▲   Figure 44 ▼

7 **1** **2** **6** **3** **5** **4**

76 70 75 74 12 10 20
73 72 11 21 22 30
60 64 09 31 32
65 71 03 04 05 33
61 08 02 01
63 51 07 06 41
62 52 42 43
53 44
50 45
54 40

CENSUS OF POPULATION AND
HOUSING 1965 LUND

Subdivision of statistical and planning areas 1 and 2-digit areas

City Architect's Office
Lund, November 1968
T.D/J.Sz.   U4-103

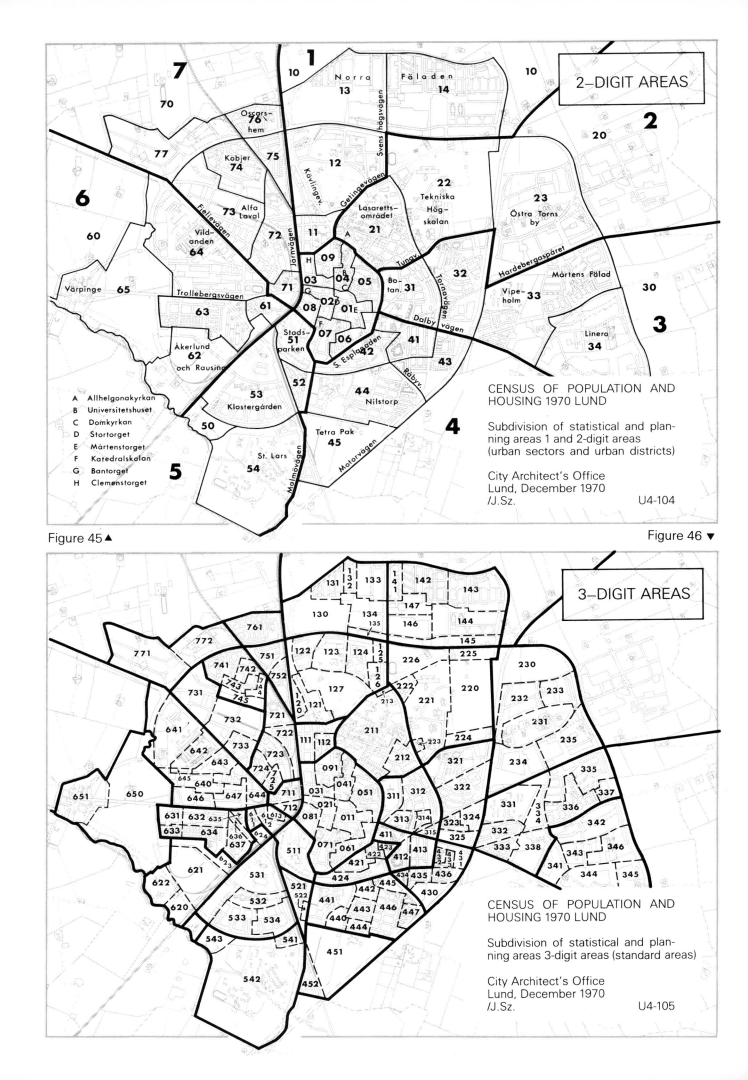

Figure 45 ▲

7
10
1
70
Norra 13
Fäladen 14
10
Oscars-hem 76
2
20
77
Kobjer 74
75
12
Svens högsvägen
6
Fjelievägen
73 Alfa Laval
72
Getingevägen
Lasaretts-området 21
22
Tekniska Hög-skolan
23
Östra Torns by
60
Vild-anden 64
11
A
09
H
Tunav
Hardebergaspäret
Mårtens Fålad
Värpinge 65
Trollebergsvägen
71
03 G
04 B C
05
Bo-tan. 31
32
Vipe-holm 33
30
61
08 02 D 01 E
Tornavägen
3
63
Stads-parken
F 07
51
06
Dalby vägen
41
Linero 34
Åkerlund och Rausing 62
S. Esplanaden
42
Råbyv.
43
52
53 Klostergården
44 Nilstorp

A Allhelgonakyrkan
B Universitetshuset
C Domkyrkan
D Stortorget
E Mårtenstorget
F Katedralskolan
G Bantorget
H Clemenstorget

50
St. Lars
5
Tetra Pak 45
Malmövägen
54
Motorvägen
4

CENSUS OF POPULATION AND
HOUSING 1970 LUND

Subdivision of statistical and planning areas 1 and 2-digit areas
(urban sectors and urban districts)

City Architect's Office
Lund, December 1970
/J.Sz.   U4-104

Figure 46 ▼

131 132 133
141 142
143
130
134 135
147
146
144
145
761
772
751
122 123 124
125
126
226
225
230
771
741 742
752
127
213
222
220
232 233
731
743 745
744
120 121
211
221
224
231
235
641
732
721
722
212
223
642
733
723
111 112
091
321
322
234
335
643
724 725
041
051
311 312
331
337
651
650
640 645
646 647 644
711
712
031
021
011
313 314
315
323
325
324
332
336
342
631 632 635
613 612
624
081
071
061
411
423
412 413
431 432
333 338
343 346
633 634
636 637
623
511
421 422
424
434 435 436
341
344 345
621
531
441 442 445 446 447
430
622
620
532
521 522
440 443 444
451
533 534
541
542
452

CENSUS OF POPULATION AND
HOUSING 1970 LUND

Subdivision of statistical and planning areas 3-digit areas (standard areas)

City Architect's Office
Lund, December 1970
/J.Sz.   U4-105

The maps, the tables and the text should be organized so as to facilitate the search for information, and so that it is easy to relate the contents of maps, tables and text to one another.

The solution:

The work resulted in a systematically-organized local atlas. Its disposition was as follows

1) The subdivision which forms a link between the setting — the physical structure of the town — and the actors and their play which are reproduced in the census. (See figures 43-46).
2) The night-time population — actors in their housing environment described by sex, civil status, age, employment etc. (See examples in figures 47-49).
3) The gainfully-employed daytime population according to the location of their employment and their journeys between dwelling and place of employment (actor and play description, see examples in figures 51-53).
4) The housing stock according to size, composition, standard, etc. (specific setting and actor description).

The basic component of the atlas is a double-page spread developed around a theme such as the age-structure of the night-time population. To the right is the map showing the town, its subdivision and the population in each area symbolized by the size of a circle (pie chart) which is divided into sectors to show the percentage share of each age group (see figure 48). To the left is a table showing the designation (number) of each area, the number of people in the three age groups described and their total (total population). The link between the table (*with* area numbers) and the map (with symbols, *without* area numbers) is an orientation map at the back of the atlas which can be folded out and viewed side by side with the map and the tables. The text is found behind the tables and must be leafed through. (When the table is folded over, the comments can then be read.)

The principles which crystallized during the course of the work, and which were given concrete form in the planning atlas *Population and Housing in Lund*, can be summarized in the following way:

1) Describe the setting well. (In the case of Lund it was assumed that the reader was well-acquainted with the geography of the town. The plate of the town's tourist map which shows the boundaries of the blocks and consequently also the street network was employed as setting map. It was assumed that the reader either could orient himself with the aid of this limited information or that he could supplement it with the tourist map itself.)

2) Construct a subdivisional network *step by step*. This network is then the link between the setting on the one hand and the actors/the play, i.e. the theme, on the other. Show how the hierarchy is built up level by level, and emphasize this hierarchy in the subsequent thematic maps as well (see maps 47 and 48).

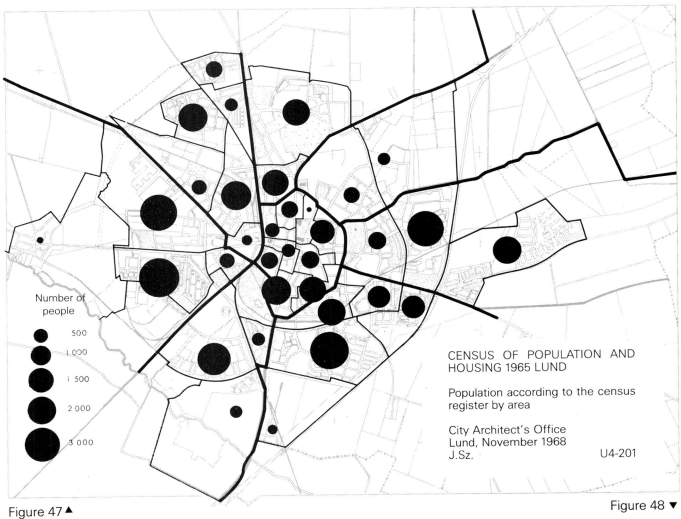

Figure 47 ▲

Number of
people

● 500
● 1 000
● 1 500
● 2 000
● 3 000

CENSUS OF POPULATION AND
HOUSING 1965 LUND

Population according to the census
register by area

City Architect's Office
Lund, November 1968
J.Sz.   U4-201

Figure 48 ▼

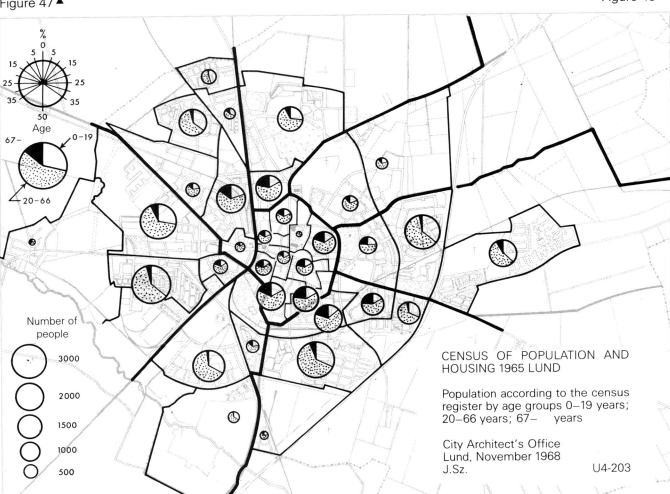

%
0
5   5
15   15
25   25
35   35
50
Age
67 —   0–19
—20–66

Number of
people

○ 3000
○ 2000
○ 1500
○ 1000
○ 500

CENSUS OF POPULATION AND
HOUSING 1965 LUND

Population according to the census
register by age groups 0–19 years;
20–66 years; 67–   years

City Architect's Office
Lund, November 1968
J.Sz.   U4-203

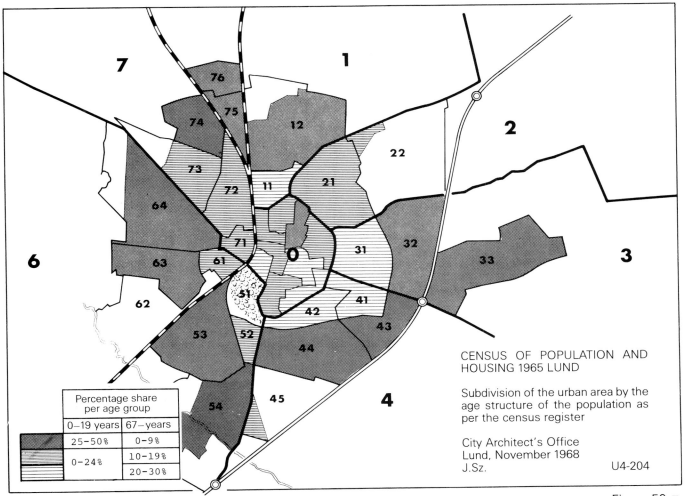

CENSUS OF POPULATION AND HOUSING 1965 LUND

Subdivision of the urban area by the age structure of the population as per the census register

City Architect's Office
Lund, November 1968
J.Sz.   U4-204

Figure 49 ▲   Figure 50 ▼

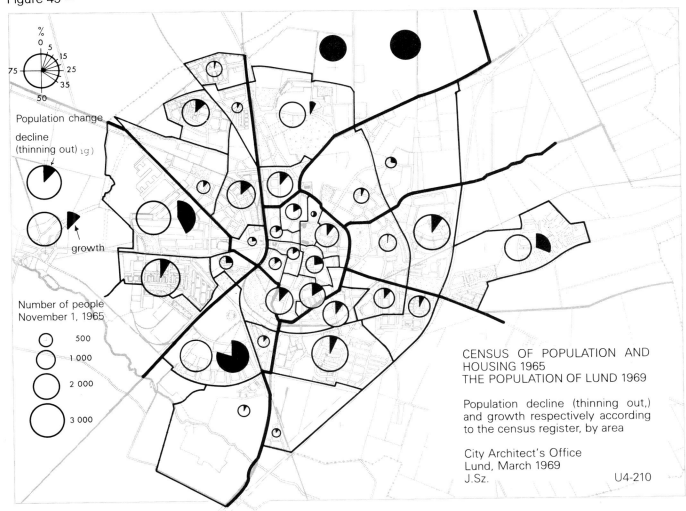

%
0
5
15
25
35
50
75

Population change

decline
(thinning out) 1g)

growth

Number of people
November 1, 1965

500
1 000
2 000
3 000

CENSUS OF POPULATION AND HOUSING 1965
THE POPULATION OF LUND 1969

Population decline (thinning out,) and growth respectively according to the census register, by area

City Architect's Office
Lund, March 1969
J.Sz.   U4-210

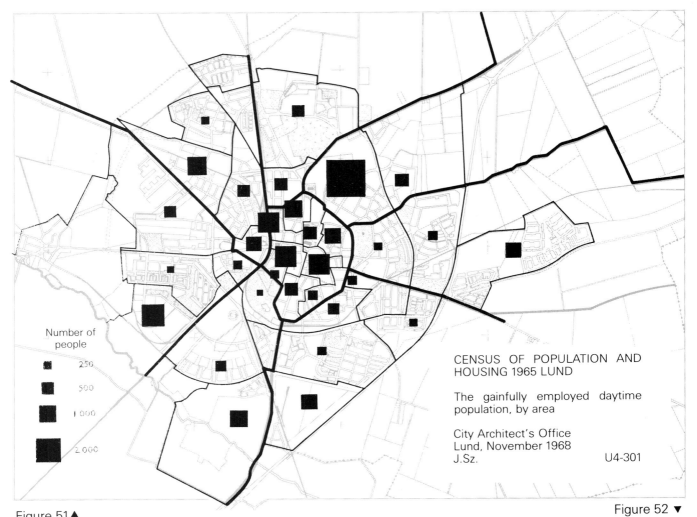

Number of people

- 250
- 500
- 1 000
- 2 000

CENSUS OF POPULATION AND
HOUSING 1965 LUND

The gainfully employed daytime
population, by area

City Architect's Office
Lund, November 1968
J.Sz.   U4-301

Figure 51 ▲

Figure 52 ▼

Manufacturing
Retail sales
Other, services

Number of
people

- 100
- 500
- 1 000
- 2 000
- 3 000

CENSUS OF POPULATION AND
HOUSING 1965

The number of people employed in
manufacturing, retail sales and
other services

City Architect's Office
Lund, November 1968
J.Sz.   U4-303

3) Anchor the subdivisional hierarchy — i.e. the boundaries of the statistical areas — in the reader's mental map. In the atlas entitled *Students in Lund 1970* this was done in a systematic way employing Kevin Lynch's urban elements (Lynch 1960). Area boundaries which followed distinct and well-known "edges" or "paths" were provided with names. The names of a selection of well-known "areas" were also printed on the map along with the locations of characteristic "landmarks". This link with the inhabitants' mental maps was expected to make it easier for the readers to comprehend the practical significance of the subdivision (see figure 45).

4) When designing the thematic maps, retain the link (the subdivision) at full strength, tone down the setting description and draw attention to the theme. Use multi-colour printing if necessary (the original was grey + black) as well as other contrasting elements so that the setting on the one hand and the subdivision (= link) + the theme on the other appear on two distinctly-different visual levels.

5) Limit the informational content of the maps — do not overload them. Use the subdivisional hierarchy for this purpose. Simple symbols — for example point symbols — can be employed in great numbers on a low hierarchic level (here the block level). More complex symbols — for example pie charts — must be limited in number, and can only be employed for a small number of areas — on a higher hierarchic level (see for instance figures 51-52). Very complex symbols should be used solely for the town as a whole (without any geographical background).

6) Use only a few levels so that the different maps can easily be compared with one another.

7) Maps with complex contents can be presented in stages. Show for instance population first with the aid of graduated circles which are then divided into sectors corresponding to main age groups etc. This helps accentuate the logical composition of the components and their interrelationships (see figures 47-48).

8) Articulate, organize the maps carefully. The significance of the symbols should be obvious, their various components should be immediately perceptible. This significance should be emphasized by the disposition of the legend as well. Provide the necessary aids there (see the percentage distribution adjacent to the pie charts in figures 48 and 50). Separating the setting and the theme on different visual levels is an important element.

9) Articulate the text well. Use a logical-consistent disposition. For instance start by stating what the map proposes to illustrate, describe the composition of the map and explain the terms employed there. Risks for misunderstandings should be pointed out. Then the contents of the map should be described verbally, and finally references should be given to other sections containing supplemental information.

10) Use typographical means for accentuating the composition of the text. Organize the body of the text so that each major section appears as an independent unit.

169

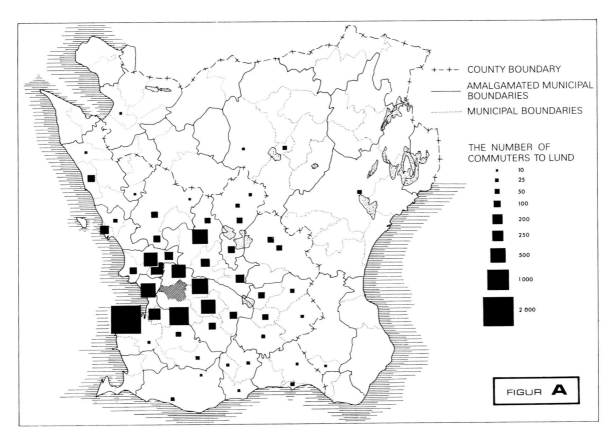

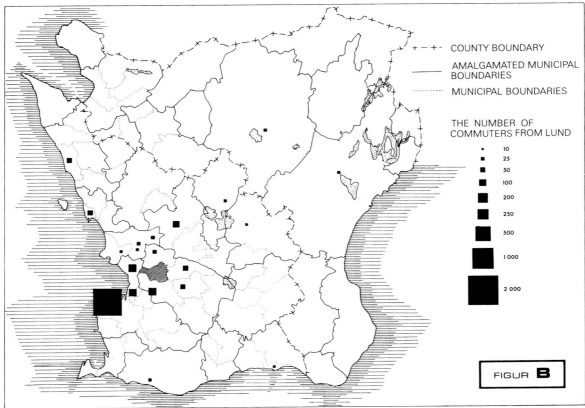

CENSUS OF POPULATION AND HOUSING 1965

The number of commuters to Lund by place of residence (fig. A). The number of
commuters from Lund by place of employment (fig. B) and the relationship
between the two groups, by municipality (fig. C).

Figure 53

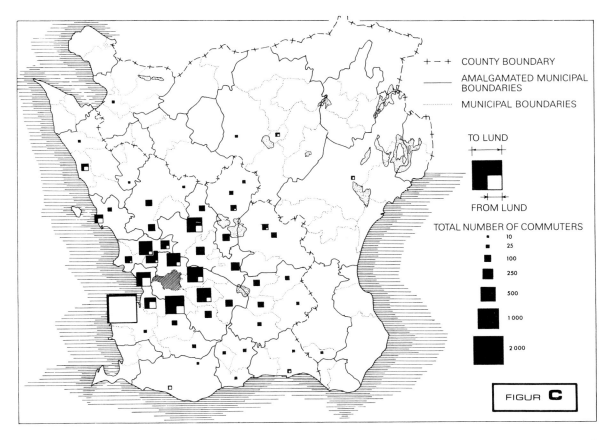

COUNTY BOUNDARY
AMALGAMATED MUNICIPAL BOUNDARIES
MUNICIPAL BOUNDARIES

TO LUND

FROM LUND

TOTAL NUMBER OF COMMUTERS

10
25
100
250
500
1 000
2 000

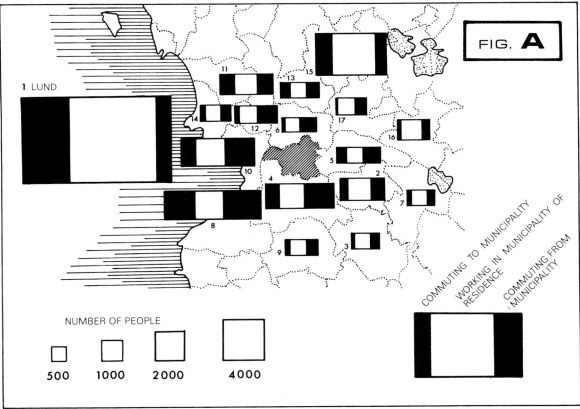

FIG. A

1 LUND

11
13
15
14
12
6
17
10
16
5
4
2
8
7
9
3

COMMUTING TO MUNICIPALITY OF
WORKING IN MUNICIPALITY OF RESIDENCE
COMMUTING FROM MUNICIPALITY

NUMBER OF PEOPLE

500   1000   2000   4000

CENSUS OF POPULATION AND HOUSING 1965

Commuting in the area surrounding Lund

Fig. A. The number of people commuting to and from each municipality
as well as working in municipality of residence

171

11) Use plain language. Technical terms — where unavoidable — should preferably be explained immediately. Avoid if possible references to lists of explanations of terms — even if one is provided.

12) Organize the different themes (double-page spreads) in order of logical succession which progressively illuminates the major theme.

Case II: Maps for regional planning based on the computer cartography of the 1970's

Implementation of the real-property data reform in Sweden began in 1971. In practical terms it meant that transferral of cadastral registers of the administrative and legal status of units of real property to data media was then begun. A government body, the Central Board for Real-Estate Data (CFD) was created solely for the purpose of transferring the manually-kept registers to an EDP system.

One of the first steps in the reform was to assign co-ordinates to the properties. The assignment of co-ordinates is based on survey data of the geographical position of a number of characteristic points within each property unit (the midpoint of the property's surface area, the midpoint of each building and the position of each ancient monument). Boundary lines which separate the property from neighbouring property units are *not* measured, however (see figure 54).

The geographical positions of the points mentioned above are determined within the framework of the national grid. This is a pair of perpendicular axes based on the Gauss Hannover Projection, i.e. a transversal cylindrical projection where the horizontal (Y) axis lies on the equator and the vertical (X) axis is located approx. 1,200 km. west of Sweden's west coast. The position of each point is recorded by a pair of co-ordinates, two 7-digit numbers which indicate to the nearest metre, the distance of a point from the respective axes.

The pairs of co-ordinates which record the different geographical positions of the characteristic points of a property unit are termed *property co-ordinates*.

One of the most important applications of property coordinates is in the production of *thematic maps*, for instance census maps. These maps are produced by integrating property co-ordinates with the contents of different administrative registers. This integration is made possible by the fact that the property unit is the basis of registration for virtually all Swedish registers containing spatial information.

As a rule, when thematic maps are being produced, a single point within the real-property unit is chosen to represent the entire property unit and its location (see figure 55A). If co-ordinates of a property unit are integrated with population data for this property for instance (figure 55B), we

The computerization of property registration in Sweden

The co-ordinates of properties are recorded

Thematic maps ...

... based on spatially-referenced data

172

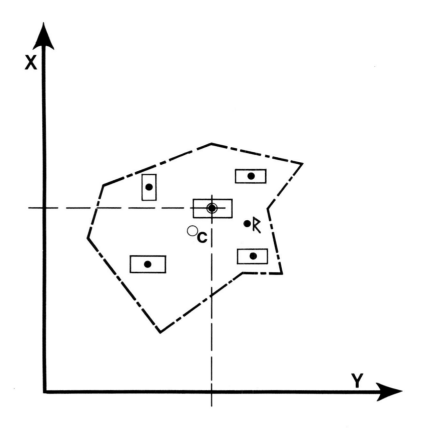

Figure 54   Determining co-ordinates of property in Sweden. The spatial midpoints of properties are determined as well as the location of buildings and ancient monuments.

obtain *spatially-referenced* population data for the property (figure 55E). We can then produce population maps based on these data (figure 55H). Similarly, we can produce spatially-referenced building data and from these, building maps (figures 55C, F, I), spatially-referenced agricultural data and from these, agricultural maps (figures 55D, G, J) etc.

Tools for urban and regional planning

When the real-property data system was set up, it was expected that physical planners would develop their own methods for using property co-ordinates in their work. There are signs that this is happening today. As a rule, however, this work is so demanding in terms of resources, that it became necessary to establish a special research and development unit at the Central Board for Real-Estate Data to develop these methods. In the mid-1970's certain types of maps and other geographical processing methods became predominant. Dot maps, grid maps and isarithmic maps (see figures 57 and 58) were the most important map types, and they could be used with great flexibility. These maps can be produced in different geometric scales and with different contents. They can describe the distribution of different categories of objects — population as well as ancient monuments, large farms as well as holiday homes etc.

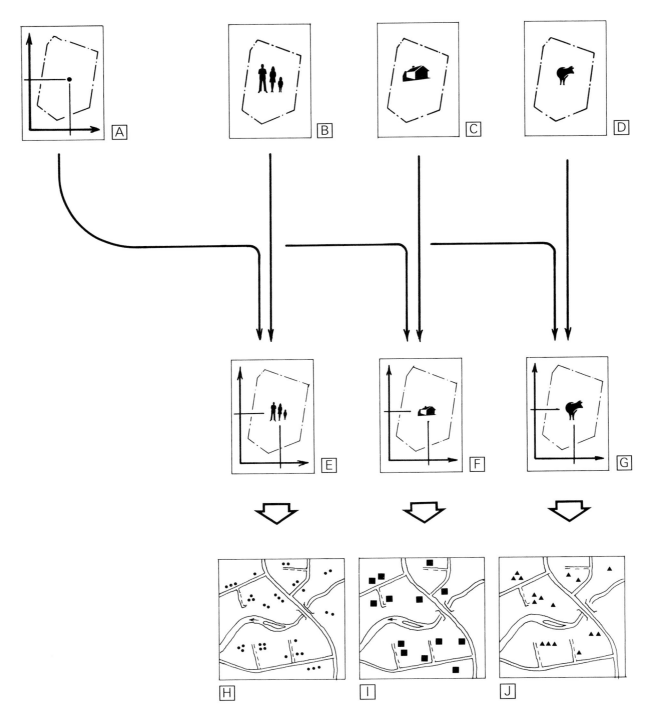

Figure 55   A representative point for each property unit (A) and
population data referenced per property unit (B) provide
spatially-referenced population data (E) and then also a
population map (H). In the same way maps can be
created from other property-related registers in Sweden.

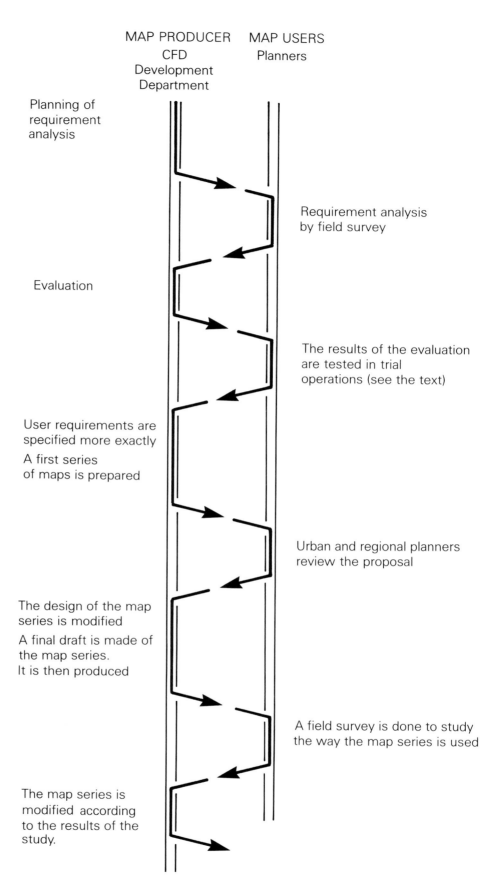

MAP PRODUCER   MAP USERS
      CFD   Planners
Development
Department

Planning of
requirement
analysis

Requirement analysis
by field survey

Evaluation

The results of the evaluation
are tested in trial
operations (see the text)

User requirements are
specified more exactly

A first series
of maps is prepared

Urban and regional planners
review the proposal

The design of the map
series is modified

A final draft is made of
the map series.
It is then produced

A field survey is done to study
the way the map series is used

The map series is
modified according
to the results of the
study.

Figure 56   Development of a map series in collaboration between
              map producers (CFD) and map users (planners).

175

In early 1977 a project was launched with the aim of effectively applying these methods in municipal planning. The key questions were: How can we apply these cartographic methods to obtain results useful for practical planning? Or to put it more concretely: Which cartographic products should be developed for practical use; how should production be started and developed? These questions led first to the Municipal Project (which began in 1977 at CFD) and later to the co-operative effort by CFD, Statistics Sweden (SCB) and the National Land Survey which resulted in a several-year-long project in census cartography which was in many ways quite unique. This project is described below.

Familiarity with these tools must be increased

Four main phases can be distinguished within the project

1) Requirement analysis
2) Trials
3) Full-scale production
4) Evaluation

These main phases constitute a process called (half tongue-in-cheek) the "interactive developmental process". Of course interactive usually refers to a continuous interaction between computer (system) and its (human) users. In this case, however, it refers to the interaction between on the one hand map users, in other words physical planners in municipalities and counties, and on the other map producers — employees of CFD, Statistics Sweden and the National Land Survey (see figure 56).

Requirement analysis

Requirement analysis was carried out in the form of an analysis of planning work. In Sweden, the preponderance of urban and regional planning is carried out within the municipalities. Therefore, a municipality was chosen for analysis, and within the municipality, a number of departments were selected where it could be assumed that the working procedures would involve geographical components. These were the departments in the municipality's comprehensive planning group. The municipality was the above-mentioned town of Lund — which by this time, the year 1977, had considerably enlarged its territory. In addition to the Lund urbanized area, it included seven smaller urbanized areas and 430 sq. km. of rural area. With its large, highly-developed planning organization and a rather small surface area and large population by Swedish standards, Lund was not a typical Swedish municipality. However, it provided examples of a large number of planning elements and planning problems which could not otherwise be found within a single municipality. Above all, Lund was selected because of the project leader's familiarity with local conditions and his personal relationships which were a prerequisite for penetrating the problems at hand.

A study of a municipality's departments

The requirement analysis was implemented in the form of interviews. Officials with planning tasks within the selected departments (the town

176

architect's office, the social welfare department, the department of education, the property management department, the town engineer's office and the bureau of statistics) were asked to describe their work and their methods for carrying it out. From these descriptions, basic tasks were sorted out containing geographical elements of the type that could conceivably be facilitated by cartographic aids and other planning aids based on property-co-ordinates.

In addition, the project leader participated as observer in actual work situations, and sometimes as co-worker. A corresponding but more limited study was carried out in another, smaller municipality.

The results of the study have been summarized in a report (Szegö 1978). The results were, in a nutshell:

The planners want

> easily-accessed
> easy-to-understand
> well-indexed
> easy-to-manipulate
> composite
> up-to-date
> but not necessarily exact

background information for planning work. What they do *not* want are *solutions* to planning problems based on this information.

The types of data called for most frequently concerned

> the population, its composition according to age, employment, its journeys to work

> the building stock, its composition, coverage and utilization for dwelling, work and service

> transportation matters, including the structure of the street network, car ownership, traffic flows

> the boundaries of administrative and planning areas, properties located there, land-use regulations in force etc.

They called for two different types of presentation

A)   General views, i.e. well-arranged, concise, not-too-detailed maps of the distribution and composition of the population, employment and buildings. These maps should preferably be in A4-format (210×297 mm) for use in overhead projectors or for printing.

B)   Work sheets in larger scale
(1:10,000 — 1:20,000 — 1:50,000) of the same conditions with a much higher level of detail. These maps should be suitable for placing on a drafting table for use as base maps for sketching or as sources from which data can be obtained.

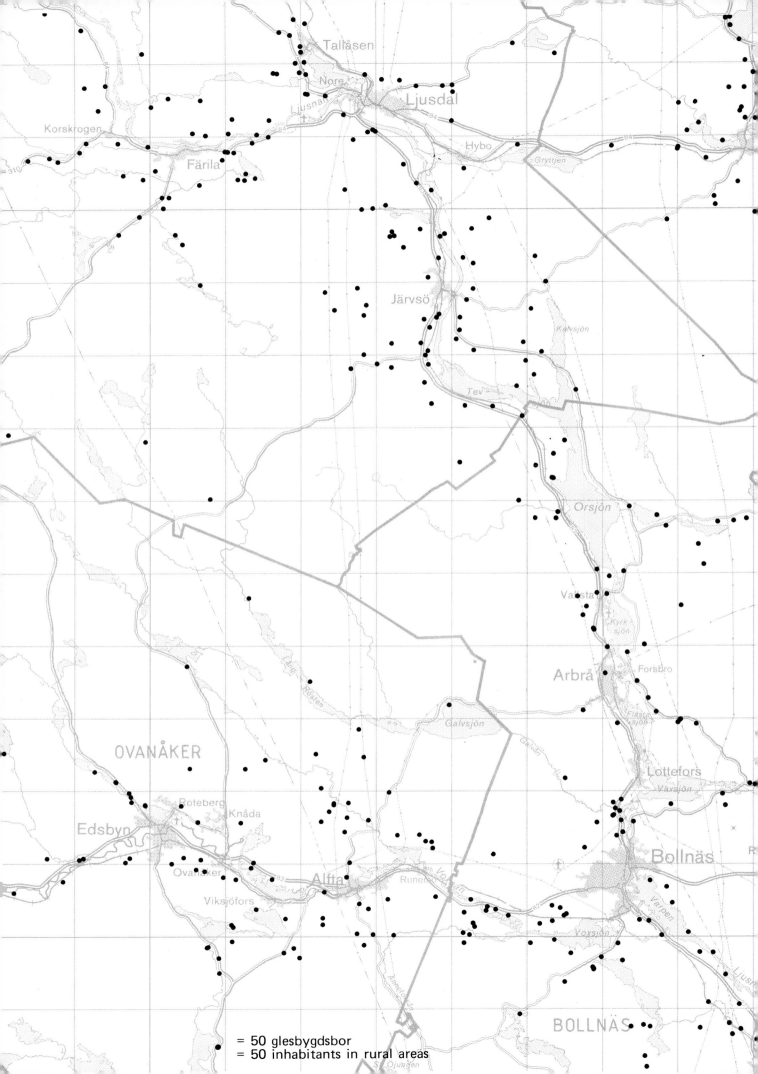

= 50 glesbygdsbor
= 50 inhabitants in rural areas

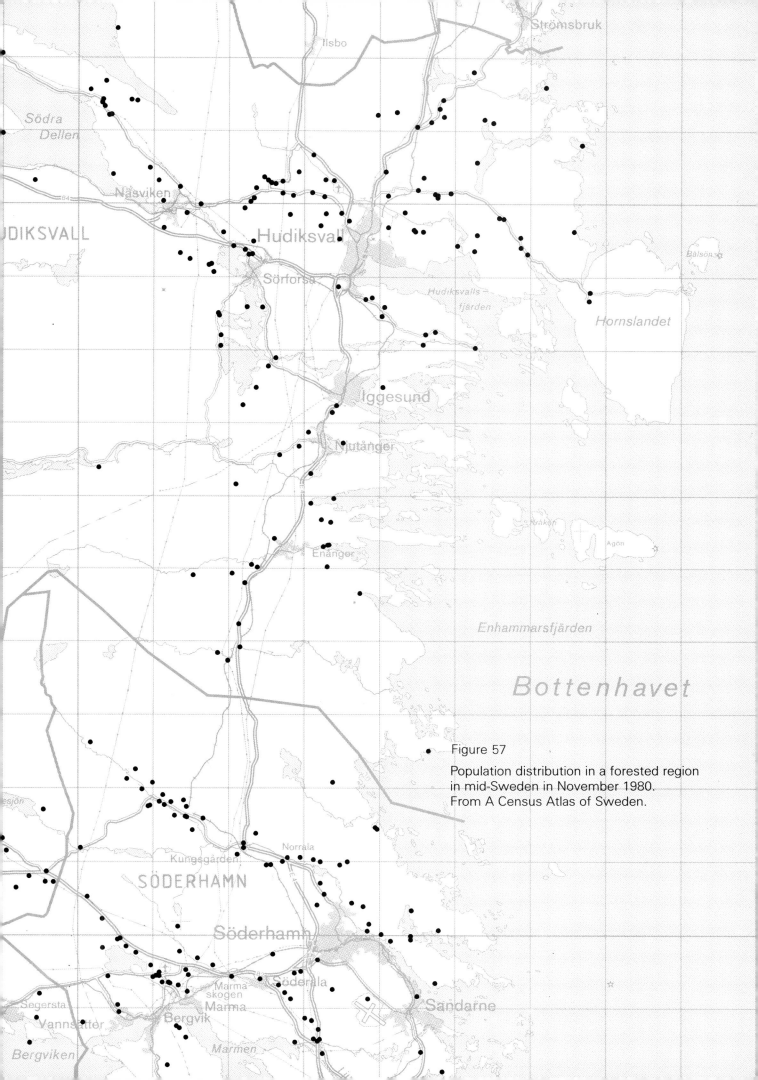

Figure 57

Population distribution in a forested region
in mid-Sweden in November 1980.
From A Census Atlas of Sweden.

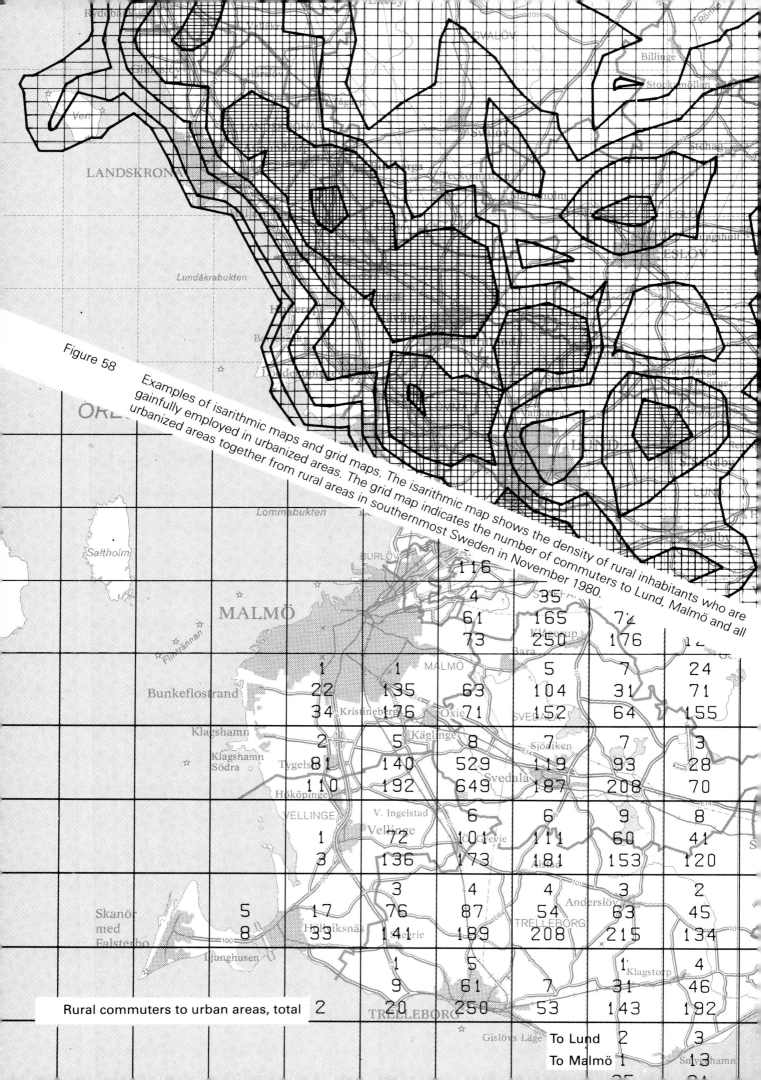

Figure 58

Examples of isarithmic maps and grid maps. The isarithmic map shows the density of rural inhabitants who are gainfully employed in urbanized areas. The grid map indicates the number of commuters to Lund, Malmö and all urbanized areas together from rural areas in southernmost Sweden in November 1980.

Rural commuters to urban areas, total

To Lund
To Malmö

Trials

During the requirement analysis it became evident that it was very difficult
even for experienced planners to state precisely what qualities they needed
in a new map. 50-odd maps were therefore produced by CFD on a trial
basis for a selected test municipality (Sandviken). These maps were designed to satisfy the demands which cropped up most frequently during
the requirement analysis, and which the majority of municipalities appeared to share, namely demands concerning population data.

Each map produced was accompanied by a "log", i.e. a questionnaire
glued to the map. Each time the map was used, the time and purpose of
use were to be recorded on the log. At the end of the test period of approx.
8 months, the logs were retrieved to CFD's developmental unit for analysis.
In addition, the planners who had access to the maps were interviewed
about their experiences and general impressions concerning the usefulness
of the different maps.

The next step involved trial production for an entire county (the county of
Malmöhus). A joint order of population maps for the entire county was
placed at a planning conference with representatives for urban and regional planners in the county and map producers: Statistics Sweden, CFD and
the National Land Survey. In connection with the production of the population maps which had been placed on order, a run-through was made of
the entire process. It ranged from the creation of spatially-referenced data
through the production of plastic sheets containing symbols representing
population (dot maps and grid maps) to the linking of the thematic map
elements with the setting elements, i.e. the maps of the physical landscape.

Approx. one-half year after the planners had received the maps, a field
survey was undertaken to assess the reactions of the users, and their favourable and unfavourable viewpoints were recorded (see the report of the
ASKA group).

Production

After user requirements had been analysed in this way and the whole
process of map production had been tested, the next step was to progress
to the systematic production of population maps. An offer was made of all
municipalities for which co-ordinates had been measured in the year 1978.
These municipalities were invited to purchase a map series consisting of 13
population maps. The maps presented the entire population distributed
within the territory of the municipality in question and also the distribution of certain age groups of special significance for planning (pre-school
children, children of school-age, etc.).

The orders received were considered to be expressions of the users' evaluations of the proposed maps. When the offer was renewed during succeeding

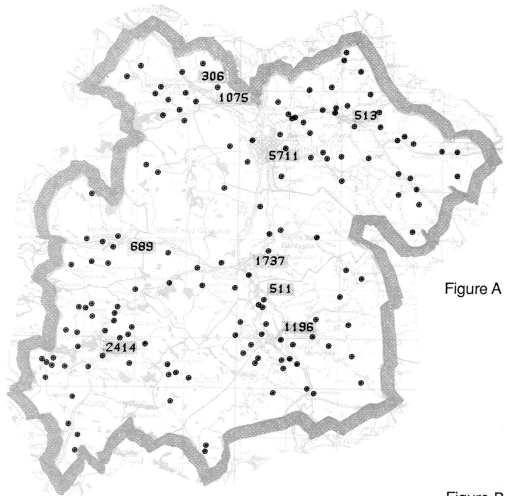

Figure A

Figure B

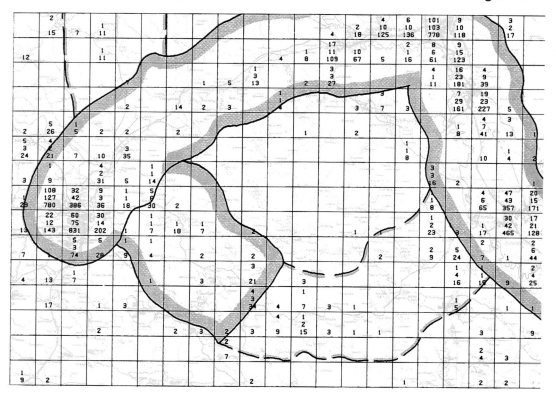

182

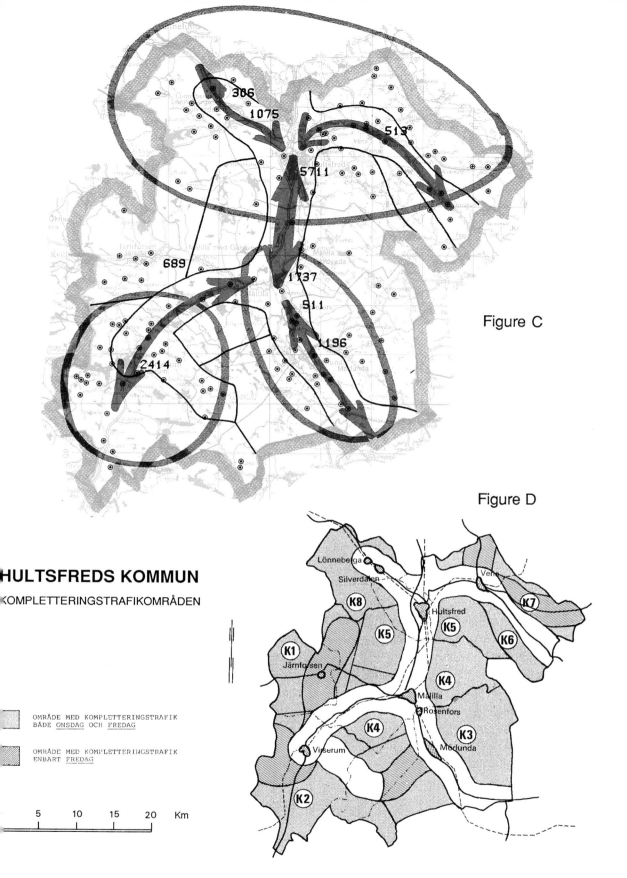

Figure C

Figure D

HULTSFREDS KOMMUN

KOMPLETTERINGSTRAFIKOMRÅDEN

OMRÅDE MED KOMPLETTERINGSTRAFIK
BÅDE ONSDAG OCH FREDAG

OMRÅDE MED KOMPLETTERINGSTRAFIK
ENBART FREDAG

5   10   15   20   Km

Figure 59–60 Example of the employment
of population maps in
regional planning.

The planners in Hultsfred in southern Sweden analyse
population distribution with the aid of a dot map (figure A.
The figures show the population in urbanized areas). The
main pattern of the traffic flows is studied (figure C) and
detailed calculations are done of travel demands (figure
B). The municipality's rural areas are divided into transportation districts for subsidized taxis. The map is sent
out to the households (figure D). A reconstruction of the
work process based on interviews (Szegö 1982).

years — an offer was sent to planners once each year — it was modified in accord with the results of the analyses.

Repeat orders from individual municipalities show that these municipalities are amassing cartographic information. The sequential data provides a basis for creating time series. The repeat orders also suggest that the maps being ordered are actually being used — which is not at all self-evident in the case of individual orders. These municipalities can be looked upon as centres of innovation in the use of this new information for planning decisions.

Maps for the Census of Population and Housing 1980

The requirement analysis showed that urban and regional planners called for *diversified* background data presented on maps. The best sources of such planning data are the censuses of population and housing. In connection with the 1980 census, studies were again undertaken concerning ways to organize such a voluminous material.

The following goals were set with regard to the presentation of maps illustrating the 1980 census.

Goal

The maximum amount of, and most essential, geographical information must be produced on the least number of maps. This must be accomplished without sacrificing good legibility on the part of the maps. Map production must be carried out in as short a time as possible so that the maps reach the planners while their contents are still up to date.

"Sketch pads" ...

The work was done with the aid of "sketch pads". Concepts were presented on the sketch pads and distributed to selected reference persons for comments. The term "sketch pad" was chosen to suggest the character of the presentation.

... for organizing problemsolving

Sketch pad no. 2 covered the problem formulation phase. The aim was to inventory and organize the prerequisites of map production. The questions dealt with at length in sketch pad no. 2 were

A) "What" questions — What variables from the 1980 census ought to be presented in map form?
B) "How" questions — How can we construct maps which would satisfy the planner's needs as well as the existing prerequisites of production?

"Icons" of different types of maps

In sketch pad no. 2 a broad frame of reference was outlined for map production. The factors pointed out in this outline were given concrete form in sketch pad no. 3. A table of contents of a map series meant to satisfy the needs of county and municipal planning was displayed here. In order to provide an overview of the whole map series, a series of symbols has been developed where each symbol represents one type of map, for example a * represents dot maps (see figure 61). This type of symbol is related to the

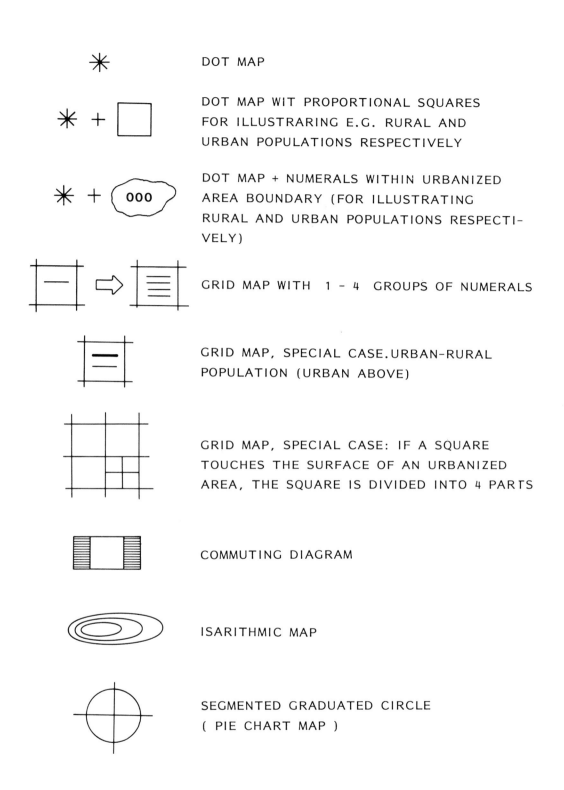

Figure 61   Shorthand notes for different types of maps

	COUNTY		MUNICIPALITY		URBANIZED AREA (= LOCALITY)	
GAINFULLY EMPLOYED DAYTIME AND NIGHTTIME POPULATION COMMUTING	MAP IN A3/A4 FORMAT	WORK SHEET 1: 250 000	MAP IN A3/A4 FORMAT (1:100 000 – 1:250 000)	WORK SHEET 1:50 000	MAP IN A3/A4 FORMAT (C:A 1: 30 000)	WORK SHEET 1:10 000 1: 5 000
GAINFULLY EMPLOYED DAYTIME POPULATION	**1**	**3** 000	**4** 20–34 / 20– hours per week	**5** 1 km	**6** 20– hpw	**7** 20–34 hpw; **8** 20– hpw; **9** 20–34; **10** 20– hpw (hours per week)
	2					
GAINFULLY EMPLOYED DAYTIME POPULATION IN URBANIZED AREAS AFTER DISTANCE TO DWELLING (0–4; 5–9; 10–19; 20– KM)		**11** 5 km		**12** 1 km REPLACED BY A DIAGRAM FOR EACH URBANIZED AREA		
COMMUTERS TO SELECTED URBAN AREAS (DOT MAP WITH PROPORTIONAL SQUARES)				**13**		
GAINFULLY EMPLOYED NIGHT-TIME POPULATION IN RURAL AREAS AFTER DISTANCE TO PLACE OF WORK (0–9; 10–19; 20–49; 50– KM)		**14** 5 km		**15** 1 km		

Figure 62   A "table" for planning a map series for the 1980 Census of Population and Housing. The table is based on the use of "icons" (symbols) of different types of maps.

so-called "icons" used in certain computer systems. Both are based on the concept that the visual symbol supplies diversified information — here: the description of the character of the map, in the case of the computer, an operation — more effectively than a written message.

"Map" of maps for ...

The symbols are then inserted in a table. Each page of tables represents a major section of the 1980 census such as population, households or the like. Each row in the table represents a more narrowly-defined part of a major section such as the gainfully-employed daytime population (see figure 62).

The table is divided into three main columns. The first of them contains maps covering an entire county, the second entire municipalities, the third individual urbanized areas. All three main columns are divided into two additional columns. The first of these shows A4 maps which are specially designed as illustration maps for reports, plans or the like to be printed in this format (210×297 mm) or shown as overhead projections. In the second are work sheets which are more detailed and larger in format and scale. These are meant to be used as reference material from which data could be collected during the preparation of concrete plans, the planning of various measures, etc. When the symbols mentioned above are added to this table, we obtain a relatively well-arranged reference document. When the symbols, moreover, are supplemented by certain numerical information, the reader is provided with a rather complete conception of the contents and design of the planned map. For instance, 2.5 km. indicates the size of the grid on a map or 20-34 hpw (hours per week) states that the population presented on the map is equivalent with the number of the inhabitants who worked between 20 and 34 hours during the week surveyed by the census.

A series of tables of this type is actually a "map of maps". A map presents large amounts of information which are often impossible to organize conceptually in other ways. A map *series* therefore contains vast amounts of information. In order to make it possible to comprehend the magnitude of the information categories contained in a proposed map series and what information is *not* included, a kind of "second level map" is needed — a map of maps. These tables are an attempt at constructing such a map. The tables show not only *what* is presented in map form, but also the design of the different maps. The employment of "icons" makes the information more accessible as does the use of maps compared with a tabular presentation.

... planning map series

This method ought to be of broader interest since systematized work methods for the design of map series of this type have, as far as is known, not been presented previously. The use of this method should facilitate the construction of similar map series in other contexts.

The sketch pads were used as a basis for discussions in the working party which made preparations for production of the census maps and also in similar preparatory discussions with urban and regional planners.

187

The work resulted in two series of maps. The first which consisted of 27 maps was aimed at municipal planners. 12 of these maps dealt with the population and with age groups of special relevance for planning; 9 maps treated the gainfully-employed population and their journeys to and from work; 6 covered the dwelling stock and the households inhabiting the dwellings. The maps included small A4 maps as well as large-scale work sheets, grid maps, dot maps and isarithmic maps and special commuting maps.

The second map series dealt with entire counties and presented their populations and employment in the form of grid maps.

Both map series were offered to all the municipalities and counties which had property co-ordinates at the time of the 1980 census.

The result: an offer

Case III: A census atlas on the national level

based on co-ordinate data and areal data on all regional levels, presented with the aid of computers — and manual cartography

Nils Holgersson over Sweden

" 'What on earth is that enormous patchwork quilt I am looking down upon?' Nils Holgersson, the main character in Selma Lagerlöf's fairy story *Nils Holgersson's Wonderful Journey through Sweden* obtains his first, literally, bird's-eye view of the world. 'Arable and pasture land, arable and pasture land' answered the wild geese led by Akka from Kebnekajse. And before the bemused eyes of both the bewitched dwarf boy from Skåne and the reader, pass first Skåne and in due course the whole of Sweden, county by county."

Goal: a dynamic, lively overview

The above quotation with its allusion to Selma Lagerlöf's book: *Nils Holgersson's Wonderful Journey Through Sweden* comprises the introductory passage to the *Census Atlas of Sweden* and its presentation of the 1980 Census of Population and Housing for the whole of Sweden. The introduction alludes to the impression one gets of a country viewed from a great altitude while in motion. It also refers to a landscape — not a map or satellite image. These introductory lines reveal some of the most important intentions behind the atlas: to try to create a dynamic, living, tangible picture of Sweden with the help of census data.

The tool employed is the map, primarily the statistical map and related presentations (diagrams). However, the atlas is intended to appeal to a wide range of readers from the individual citizen, unversed in statistical matters, to the highly-trained specialist — who may, however, not be familiar with the language of statistical cartography. The maps are therefore supplemented by analytical text.

Dynamics from static maps — how?

The individual statistical map is static in character. By showing the country from various observation altitudes, drawing attention to limited portions of it and shifting among thematic approaches, the author attemp-

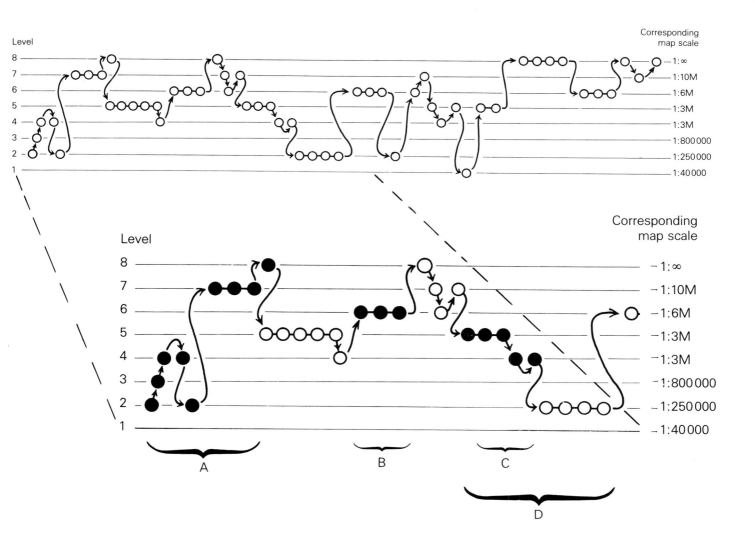

Corresponding
map scale

8 ——————————————————————————— 1:∞
7 ——————————————————————————— 1:10M
6 ——————————————————————————— 1:6M
5 ——————————————————————————— 1:3M
4 ——————————————————————————— 1:3M
3 ——————————————————————————— 1:800 000
2 ——————————————————————————— 1:250 000
1 ——————————————————————————— 1:40 000

Level

Corresponding
map scale

8 ——————————————————————————— 1:∞
7 ——————————————————————————— 1:10M
6 ——————————————————————————— 1:6M
5 ——————————————————————————— 1:3M
4 ——————————————————————————— 1:3M
3 ——————————————————————————— 1:800 000
2 ——————————————————————————— 1:250 000
1 ——————————————————————————— 1:40 000

A   B   C

D

Figure 63   "Itinerary" of A Census Atlas of Sweden. Each circle
represents a theme. The different levels indicate the
observation altitude (see map scales on the right).

ted to make his presentation more dynamic. With the help of these variations, but also by means of variations in cartographic language (symbols,
colour scale, etc.), the aim was to give the book a rhythm which would
make it attractive to read and make its contents come alive to the reader.

The atlas opens with a description of "A piece of Sweden", a section of
south-west Skåne in southernmost Sweden observed from — what can be
Shifts in   looked upon as — "a low flying altitude". This map reproduces the land-
perspective   scape with a relatively high degree of detail (1:250,000, level 2 in figure 63)
where the distribution of the rural population is illustrated with a corresponding degree of detail (1 dot = 100 people). Already by the next section
("A broadening view") Skåne appears before the observer in its entirety on
a map sheet (1:800,000, level 3 in figure 63 and figure 15) with individual
urbanized areas easily discernible in the landscape. In the third section the
reader is enabled to observe "The full scenery: the landscape of towns" in

the form of a map of southern Sweden in a scale of 1:3 million — with an equivalent map subsequently provided for the northern part of the country where all 1,820 urbanized areas are presented according to population size. After a plunge to the initial level (1:250,000) covering southern Norrland in order to study how the pattern of population distribution differs there (see figure 57), the reader ascends to even greater altitudes in order to observe the country in the form of three three-dimensional models in a map scale of approx. 1:10 million. Here the county is the smallest discernible unit. By way of compensation for the low level of geographical resolution, the reader is afforded a well-arranged summary of the major features of patterns of population distribution in Sweden (see figure 16) where column heights indicate population density, and where the distribution of the volume of the model is proportional to population distribution in Sweden. Following the presentation of two additional cartographic diagrams of similar type, the flying altitude is again increased, the country shrinks to a speck and is replaced by a diagram which lacks a base map. In the next section the observer "plunges down" to a level corresponding to a map scale of 1:3 million, but here it is a municipality, not an urbanized area, which is the smallest discernible unit. The municipalities are coloured in accordance with their percentage share of rural inhabitants (or, in subsequent maps: the percentage of children, of pensioners, of foreign citizens etc.). Figure 63 where each circle represents a theme in the book, shows how the reader is transported between different "flying altitudes" (including level 1 where he can even make out parts of an urbanized area, corresponding to a map scale of approx. 1:40,000, see figure 71:1).

Thematic construction

The construc-
tion of a theme

The atlas is constructed around 52 themes. "The landscape of towns" (Sweden's urbanized areas ranked according to population), "Work — with what?" (the gainfully-employed population distributed according to occupation,) "Commuting to and from urbanized areas", "How large are the households we live in?" are some examples of themes in the atlas. Most themes occupy two double-page spreads. The first one deals with southern Sweden, the second with the northern part of the country. Each left-hand page presents a map or diagram; each right-hand page has text in Swedish and English, and gives the title of the map. Regional-study inserts cover a whole double-page spread on which the text is reduced to a narrow column on the right. In figure 64 each black dot represents such a theme. One-third of the themes in the atlas deal with the country's population; around one-fourth with household formation and housing. The rest of the atlas is devoted to commuting.

Themes are
linked together

Each theme is independent and can be read separately. However, in the greater part of the book, these themes are linked together to form short chains. These interconnected themes benefit from being read together, and provide additional illumination for one another. It is these sections which are joined together by broken lines in figure 64.

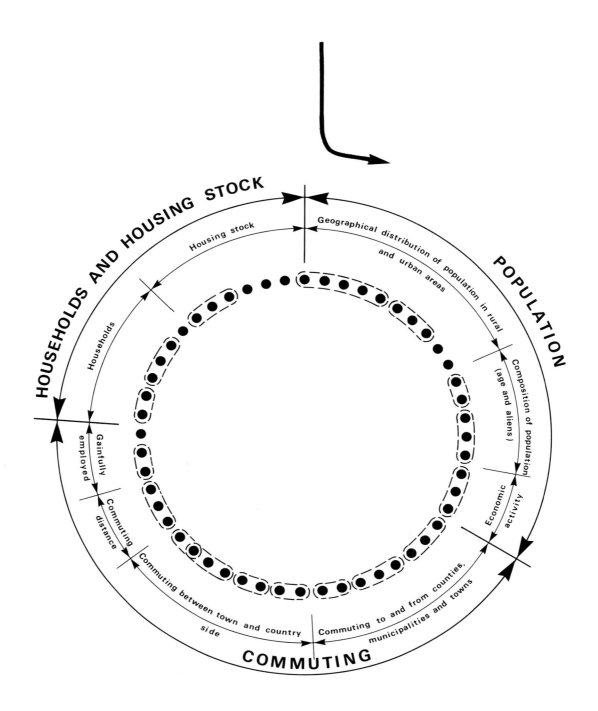

Figure 64   The development of A Census Atlas of Sweden from
various themes. Each black dot represents a theme.
Series of themes are closely related (se the broken lines).
Together they consitute sections and parts.

The role of the text

The text describes the construction of the relevant map or diagram, and comments on how it should or should *not* be interpreted. The text also summarizes the map's contents, and refers to other sections for supplementary information.

191

Although the book can be used as a reference work, it can also be read as a "text book". If it is skimmed section by section — and not studied in detail — it should, within the space of about one hour — provide a general picture of Sweden and the major features in the geographical structure of its population. The reader can then delve more deeply into the sections which are of particular interest to him.

Organizing information

The design of this atlas is governed by two principles

1) The primary goal of the design of the maps is maximum clarity and expressiveness on the part of the individual map.
2) The individual maps should as far as possible form dynamic sequences. The dynamics may result from

Creating
dynamics —
four routes

A) hifts in "observation altitude" ("flying altitude"), i.e. changes in the geographical scale and the geographical level of detail connected therewith,
B) shifts in the geographical level of detail without any alteration of the map scale, "the flying altitude",
C) shifts in thematic content,
D) combinations of A), B) and C).

Shifts in
observation
altitude

The first seven themes in the atlas which were discussed above are examples of A). (A section of south-west Skåne expands to the whole of Skåne in the next section, to the whole of Sweden in a scale of 1:3 million with discernible urbanized areas in the following one, and then shrinks into a three-dimensional model with a geographical scale of approx. 1:10 million with the county as the least discernible unit to finally appear as a pure diagram without a base map. See "A" in figure 63.)

Shifts in the
amount of detail
with unaltered
scale

Sections 2.4-2.8 are examples of the shift mentioned in B). Sections 2.4-2.6 show municipal commuting — each municipality's area is coloured according to the percentage of incoming and outgoing commuters and commuting balance in the municipality concerned. In figures 2.7 and 2.8 incoming and outgoing commuters are presented per urbanized area. The geographical resolution — i.e. the smallest geographical unit shown shifts from municipality to individual urbanized area without the map's scale being altered (see "B" in figures 63).

Shifts in
"thematic
resolution"

Certain sequences in the section on population are examples of C), for example sections 1.14-1.16 (see figures 31-33 in the colour supplement). First the population is divided hierarchically into the categories employed — unemployed (figure 31). The employed (with a working week of over 20 hours) constitute the entire mapped population of the next theme (figure 32), and are divided among those employed in industry and two other categories, while the industrial employees alone constitute the mapped population in the next map (figure 33). Note the use of colour: in figure 31 the orange-yellow hue designates both two categories of employed people (those with 20-34 working hours per week *and* those with over 35 hours) of

192

which the mapped population in figure 32 is composed. In figure 32 the blue colour designates workers in mechanical industry as well as other branches of industry. These groups make up the entire mapped population of figure 33.

A combination of all three

A combination of all three elements — shifts in observation altitude or in geographical or thematic resolution — is employed in sections 2.1 — 2.12 (see "D" in figures 63). Commuting is here presented for the country as a whole followed by long-distance commuting, commuting over county boundaries, municipal commuting and finally commuting in urbanized areas — in other words, studies of commuter movements of progressively-diminishing length and increasing complexity. This sequence is completed with the highly-detailed presentation of the commuting pattern in a small portion of a rural area in south-west Skåne (see figures 27 — 29 in the colour supplement.) Note how difficult it is to make a visual comparison of the two arrow clusters which designate commuting to the two urbanized areas; note also how easy it is to analyse the same patterns when they are combined to form a whole as in figure 29.

In summary:

A "zoom technique" has been employed in the design of this atlas in order to give the presentation a dynamic, pulsating character. The zoom method consists in part of the fact that the surface of the Earth is observed from different altitudes (shifts in map scale and/or geographical level of detail) and in part of variations in the thematic resolution of the maps.

The latter means that the maps and diagrams follow a terminological hierarchy with ever-increasing thematic detail. Shifts in geographical and thematic perspective (level of detail) are usually simultaneous. The images thus alternate between two extremes. At one extreme the country is observed from a great altitude where many of the geographical details disappear. On the other hand, the level of thematic detail can be high. Figures 31-33 in the colour supplement present examples. Even more pronounced examples of such presentations can be found in the atlas. At the other extreme we find examples of images with a high level of geographical detail ("low flying altitude"), but where the thematic detail is very limited (see figure 57 for example).

References and presentation method

Point co-ordinates as well as areal references (presentations of data on an area-basis) were used in the production of the maps.

The point co-ordinates used were

    A) Property co-ordinates
    B) Parish co-ordinates
    C) Urbanized-area co-ordinates
    D) Municipality co-ordinates
    E) County co-ordinates

The reference areas employed were

A) "Key-code areas" (enumeration districts)
B) Municipalities
C) Counties
D) The entire country

Co-ordinates

The urbanized-area co-ordinates were used as *object co-ordinates*. Values applying to an urbanized area (population size, number of employed, number of incoming commuters, etc.) were linked to the co-ordinate of the urbanized area. During the mapping process, these values were represented by symbols which were placed directly above the urbanized-area co-ordinate — above the actual object. Point symbols as well as other composite symbols were employed (see figures 15 and 17).

The property and parish co-ordinates were used as data carriers from which the positions of the point symbols were *interpolated*. The property co-ordinates were thus the basis of the production of dot maps, arrow maps, and the circle diagrams placed in a grid (see figures 27-29 in the colour supplement and the black-and-white figures 18 and 57).

Municipal and county co-ordinates were used as representative points for the population or housing of an entire municipality or county. The symbols were positioned as closely as possible to the centre of gravity of these populations.

The most important *reference areas* are the territories of municipalities and counties. These areas were either coloured in accordance with the values of the variables or were made the bases of three-dimensional presentations (see figure 30 in the colour supplement and black-and-white figure 16).

Methods

Both manual and computer-aided cartography were used to produce the plates; photographic as well as electronic technology for colouration and colour separation. Maps with a large number of symbols have been created with the help of computer-guided drafting machines. Dot maps, arrow maps, and diagrammatic maps have been constructed using CFD's pen plotter and drafting system (figures 27-29 in colour and 18 and 20 in black-and-white). Maps in which the territories of municipalities are printed in colour were produced with an ink-jet plotter at the University of Lund, and the software was produced at Statistics Sweden (see colour figure 30). Presentations for which no programmes were available such as the three-dimensional diagrams were drawn by hand (see figure 16).

Colouration and colour separation were in part done electronically using the Scitex system and partly through the conventional peel-coat method.

The atlas emerges

The complex structure outlined above was not planned in detail from the beginning. It was allowed to evolve in an organic manner during the course of the analytical work. Its basic structure, an elusive yet still concrete conception of the dynamics of the book, began to emerge during the work described in cases 1 and 2. Important "cornerstones" — key sections — of the atlas were produced during the course of the analytical work, several of them during the initial stages of the work. The elements which became the links between these cornerstones revealed themselves during the continued analytical work and sketching. The volumes of information which had to be dealt with in this design process were vast and the choices innumerable. If they had been treated in a strictly logical fashion, so many different alternatives would have been revealed that we would have been forced to retreat to an entirely conventional solution. To create a systematic yet lively presentation, it was necessary to combine strict analytical work with an intuitive search for solutions in the way alluded to above.

Towards the human cartography/census cartography of the future

Development routes and development potential

Technical prerequisites — a brief outline

The three projects described in the previous section reflect some important characteristics in the development of thematic cartography during the past decades.

At the end of the 1960's manual methods were still predominant. During the 1970's and the early 1980's some computer-aided cartographic methods became available. However, the methods for both vector and raster graphics were largely developed before 1975 (see the Fris project, Nordbeck and Rystedt 1972, Bergström and Nilsson 1977).

Another important characteristic is the limited availability of these methods. The technology — hardware, software and the requisite expertise for their application — are concentrated to a few institutions and not available to the user without intermediaries.

An important limiting factor is that this technology can only be used where there is a homogeneous supply of data. This implies a requirement for uniformly high-quality geographical references (such as co-ordinates, area descriptions in the form of boundary polygons, etc.) and registers from which attribute data is obtained (e.g. different attributes of the population or of buildings).

The explosive development currently underway in computer technology appears to focus heavily on graphic data processing. These tendencies are reinforced by advances within other fields of electronic technology which affect the acquisition and processing of images.

There are several different circumstances contributing to the rapid development of computer-graphics technology and to its almost equally rapid dissemination.

1) New high-capacity memory circuits are being developed. They make it possible to store the large volumes of data which are needed for electronic image processing.
2) New processors, often special-purpose graphic processors with large capacity, are being developed which contribute to rapid and efficient image processing.

		Cartographic methods	
		Today's	Tomorrow's
Technological prerequisites	Today's	I	II
	Tomor-row's	III	IV

Figure 65   Four steps towards the future, based on the cartographic methods and technology of today and tomorrow.

3) Image-processing software is improving with regard to both quality and quantity.
4) User interface is improving, i.e. both software and hardware are becoming easier to handle.
5) The price of software, and to an even greater degree of hardware, is falling thus making the technology available to a growing number of users.

Scanning

Important in this connection are both input and output of information. Input census data are often in the form of digital data from registers. Scanning technology now makes it possible, however, to input data from maps, satellite images etc., and base maps (settings) for a theme can be created from census data.

"Hard copy" — a critical step

The development of the ink-jet colour plotter, the laser printer and the electrostatic printer was essential for making "hard copy" illustrations of the often highly-variegated images composed of many different hues which appear on the colour monitors of the computers, and which display the results of graphic information processing.

In contrast to the 1970's, it appears today that the results of technological development reach the users in a very short time. The prerequisite for this is the rapid spread of powerful personal computers.

What efforts are necessary in order to take advantage of the development potential created as a result of the technological advances outlined above?

197

The conceivable activities can be classified in four groups, namely,

I)   efforts which neither require development of the methods of thematic cartography nor the application of new technology for map production

II)   efforts which involve development of the *methods* of thematic cartography, but which are based on the map-production technology of today

III)   efforts which are based on today's cartographic methods but which apply the technology of tomorrow

IV)   new cartographic methods, based on new technology

The link between the technology and cartographic methods of today and tomorrow and the above four stages of development can be expressed as a matrix. This is shown in figure 65.

Four steps towards the future

Developmental efforts according to I. Cartographic development based on the cartographic methods and technology of today

Development can occur without any special developmental efforts through more effective use of available methods and existing technology.

This can take place on three different levels:

1) More effective information strategy.
2) More effective choice of map types, symbols, etc.
3) More effective organization of the individual map.

1) More effective information strategy

The examination of the selected historical atlases demonstrated clearly that some of the most effective, distinct presentations are based on very simple reproduction methods and — in certain cases — simple cartographic methods as well. The outline maps presented by McEvedy and Jones, for example, are often extremely simple, but they are organic parts of a well-organized conceptual whole. In concert with the text, they manage to visualize courses of events in ways that are easy to comprehend. McNeill's maps are also simple from the point of view of reproduction methods (although very well articulated). Above all, they serve as organically-related parts of a conceptual chain. They are effective not least for that reason.

Census cartography as ritual

The main practical application of census cartography is in the presentation of comprehensive plans. These planning documents often give the impression that the presentation of population, employment, housing stock, etc. is done in an obligatory, almost ritualistic way. The presentations are often schematic, as a rule static. The flows through time-space which are so representative of a population system even when observed for a short span of time, are usually not suggested in these presentations.

The population of an area — a town, a region, a country — forms a dynamic system which fluctuates rhythmically during the course of a day, from season to season, etc., and exhibits a slower dynamic development when observed in a broader chronological perspective. Very little of these dynamics can be discovered in the schematic, static depictions of population common to many planning documents. The reason for this is probably two-fold. In the first place, urban and regional planners do not often

The dynamics
of the popula-
tion not taken
into considera-
tion, not
depicted

employ the approaches and models which deal with the development and activities of the population in the context of a long span of time. Secondly — even when such an approach is employed — it is only the final results of the thought processes dealing with the dynamic elements which are presented, and these final results are, as a rule, static. The most common type of result is a discrete area with sharply-drawn, abstract boundaries within which regulations apply and possibly with an intended pattern of development (a detailed development plan, a regulatory area or the like). In most cases, the dynamics of the plans are the human activities on which the regulations are based. But although these activities are often the basic element in the construction of the plans, and although the activities often appear during the planning process in the form of sketches of patterns of movement or the like — they are virtually never presented in the final documents. Instead, the result is correct, often well thought-out, but in the eyes of the observer dead, lifeless presentations of plans. Specialists familiar with the planning methods employed, and equipped with intimate knowledge of local conditions are able to fill in the omitted thought processes. All others concerned are unable to fully fathom the plans.

The development of census cartography should be based first and foremost on the use of models of the dynamics of the observed or planned area on the long term as well as the short term. Look upon the population and its various activities as a part of a vertically-rising stream in time-space with oblique tributaries of movements in a short chronological perspective and a longer one (for example, daily journeys to work and migratory moves respectively). Utilize these dynamics as basic conceptual elements — in the analysis of the past as well as in the planning of the future. Document this approach with text, tables, diagrams and maps in a co-ordinated manner. Let all these elements create a linked chain around the basic concept. Do not sort out too much: present even the less-formalized thoughts, sketches, etc. if they help reproduce the dynamics.

2) More effective choice of symbols and map types

It is seductively easy to employ certain map types in a routine manner: dot maps for one type of information, pie charts for another, bar charts for a third, etc. Instead, take as point of departure the actual phenomenon which the map is supposed to reproduce. Look upon it as a portion of the time-geographical model. Try to visualize the population in a bird's-eye view, and seek cartographic means of expression which correspond to this image. Attempt to separate the setting, the actors and the play. Determine which of these elements are to be included in a single map — is there room for them there without sacrificing clarity, or do they need to be distributed among several maps? If a map of a certain type is still the point of departure, try to see the reality behind it, the actual landscape with activities in progress.

An example: when the commuting map for the 1980 census was to be constructed, practical considerations dictated a certain point of departure:

the dot map which would show the place of residence of people who commuted in to an urbanized area. Since the programme for a dot map was available, it was not necessary to construct a special programme, and time was thereby saved. But it was also obvious that the map would be lacking in dynamics. In an absent-minded fashion, the author sketched some small arrows next to the dots and graduated squares which represented the commuters (see figure 60, WORK SHEETS FOR MUNICIPALITIES, COMMUTERS TO SELECTED AREAS). These arrows proved to be very useful for helping to explain the significance of the map to others. Finally there was a moment in which the idea of people in motion from rural areas into a town coincided with the arrows sketched beside the dots. The result can be seen in figure 18 and figures 27 and 28 in the colour supplement.

When it comes to statistical maps, study the interrelationships of the component values in graphic terms. A study of the gainfully-employed daytime and night-time populations done in this way resulted in maps with commuting diagrams (see figures 20 and 53). Do a graphic analysis of whether the statistical component values in a conceptual chain can be reproduced with good legibility on a single map or whether they need to be distributed among several maps. Study how to create a visual relationship among them. Devote much attention to the mapping of dynamic processes. How should they be illustrated? Should several factors be mapped at certain intervals (i.e. several horizontal cross-sections through the time-geographical model)? Or should the process of transformation itself be reproduced on the map (i.e. oblique movements in the model such as migratory moves)? Or should net change be depicted?

We can now formulate the working hypothesis that the greater the discernible similarity between the situation found in reality (or the process in progress) and its cartographic depiction, the more effective map we obtain. If the similarity is sufficiently great we can *perceive* the contents of the map directly. In other cases we must interpret them with the help of the map — a slower and more time-consuming process.

A dynamic illustration of a process is usually superior to a series of static pictures or a picture of net change from which one must conceptualize the process of change.

3) More effective organization of the individual map

When designing a map: employ the concept of setting/actor/play. Determine which of the map's elements belong to the three levels, what their interrelationships are, which of them should dominate, which should be subordinated, which should be omitted. What are the means necessary to achieve a separation of levels? What types of contrast are available? black print; two, three, four colour print? Study the various alternatives, and make sketches. Maps are too complex for us to visualize them comprehensively without a supporting sketch.

201

In summary: Employ the geographical and cartographic models consistently. Consider the map to be part of a cohesive conceptual framework constructed around the time-geographical model. Organize the individual maps with the distinguishable elements setting/actor/play.

Carry out the educational programme which is a prerequisite for achieving this goal.

Developmental efforts according to II. New cartographic methods based on today's technology

Is cartographic development in the doldrums?

Some cartographers are of the opinion, perhaps without having analysed the matter, that the methodological development of thematic cartography is poised on a threshold. According to this notion, these methods have developed as far as existing technological prerequisites will allow, and continued advances can be resumed only following dramatic technological developments.

A few types of maps are predominant

The "old" cartographic methods can be refined

It is a fact that the map types in computer-aided cartography which are frequently used — especially in the field of statistical cartography — are few in number. Dot maps, grid maps, isarithmic maps drafted with pen plotters, isopleth maps produced with ink-jet colour plotters are some examples. The same applies to manual cartography — despite its greater flexibility — a small number of map types are predominant. The reason that new types of maps have not been developed to any great extent is, however, not that the cartographic technology of the 1970's has exhausted its possibilities. The reason would appear rather to be that the new technology segregates the steps of map production, assigning them to different people, and that a chain of individuals can only develop new types of maps under the most favourable of circumstances.

In this section two different ways of developing cartographic methods in the field of thematic cartography are presented with the aid of some examples. The two are

1) further development of individual map types
2) development of systems for cartographic analysis.
   Example 1: A system for analysing influences on a dynamic population.
   Example 2: A system for providing an overview of cartographic information.
   Example 3: Development of maps of change.

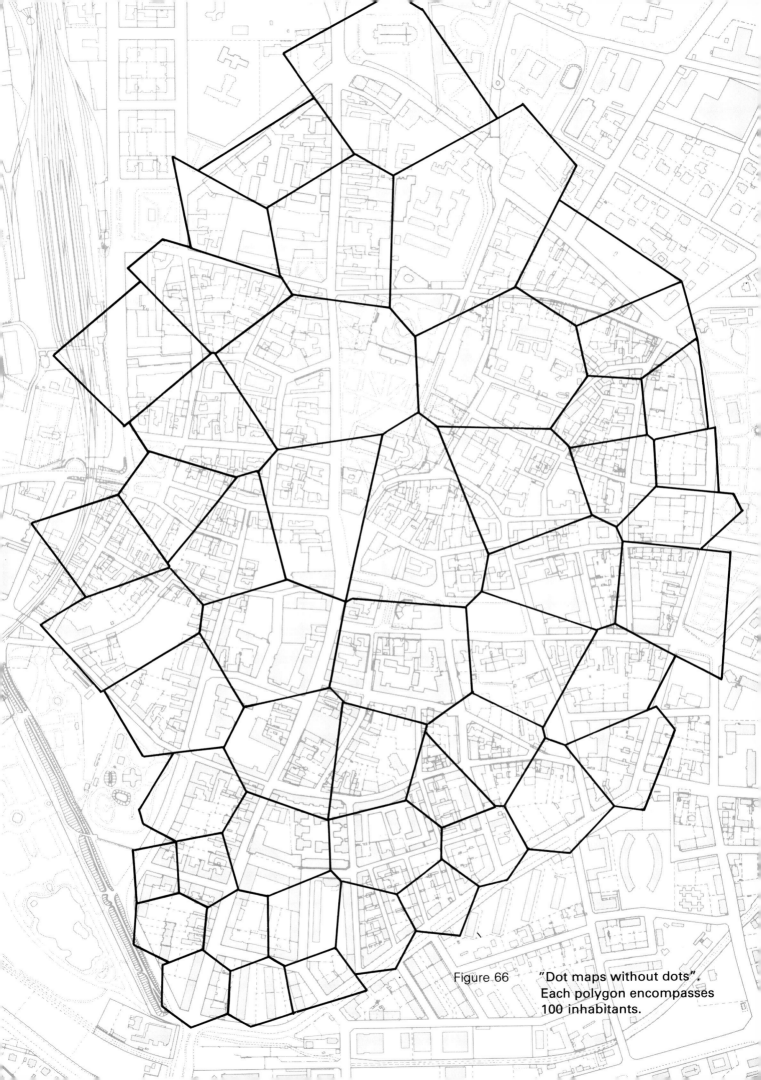

Figure 66   "Dot maps without dots".
Each polygon encompasses
100 inhabitants.

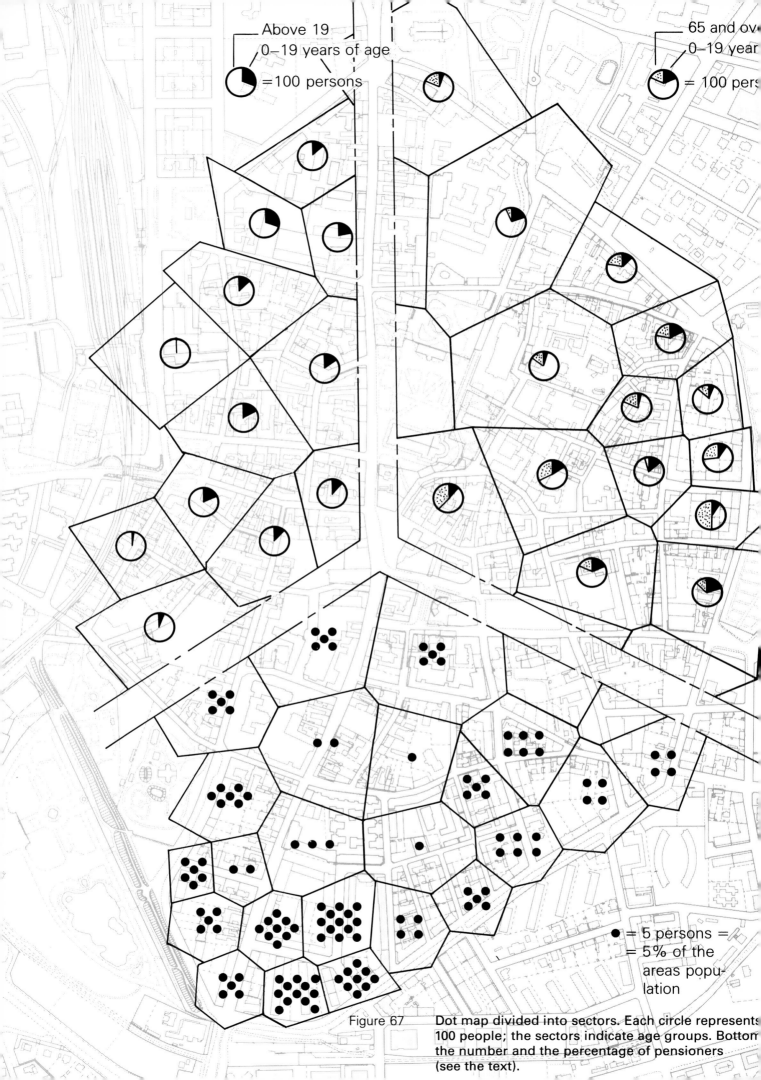

Above 19
0–19 years of age
=100 persons

65 and ov
0–19 year
= 100 pers

● = 5 persons =
= 5% of the
areas popu-
lation

Figure 67 Dot map divided into sectors. Each circle represents
100 people; the sectors indicate age groups. Bottom
the number and the percentage of pensioners
(see the text).

1) Further development of individual map types

Example A) *Development of dot maps*

The shape and implication of the dot symbol

The dot map is one of the most frequently-used types of map. It illustrates a population without presenting its internal structure and without determining the exact geographic position of the individual dots. The point symbol is — almost without exception — discrete, with a precisely-defined geometric shape. Geographically it may signify diminishing force or frequency — the point symbol may indicate the centre of gravity of a population with repetitive patterns of movement, the frequency of which diminishes with increasing distance from the position of the point (example: presentation of the population). The map may also show a population which lacks this fading quality, but whose precise territorial expanse is not presented (example: map with point symbols depicting the number of buildings.)

The dot map thus reproduces a homogeneous population in absolute terms. Dot maps are static in nature and reproduce movement only in exceptional cases. They present neither the internal structure of the mapped population nor its relationship with any larger population of which it may be a part. For example: when we map the total population in an area, we do not obtain its age structure. If a dot map depicts the distribution of school pupils in an area, we are not informed about how large a percentage of the entire population these children constitute.

Some examples of development potential:

a) *A dot map which is simultaneously an absolute and a relative map*

Figure 66 presents a map whose surface is divided into polygons. Each area enclosed by a polygon contains a certain, given number of units, here 100 people. This is, therefore, a special kind of map: "a dot map without dots". It supplies more information than can be provided by the traditional dot map: it not only shows the presence of population groups consisting of 100 people each, but also their (approximate) geographical distribution. In contrast to the conventional dot map where the dots tend to absorb the map reader's attention, the polygon lattice makes it easier for the reader to observe undisturbed the physical landscape, i.e. the setting where the actors are present, and to study the interaction between the setting and the actors. If we then introduce traditional dots above some component population in each area, we obtain a dot map which is simultaneously absolute and relative.

The point symbols on the next map (figure 67 below) are an example of this type of map. Each dot on this map represents 5 pensioners (65 years of age or more). Since each symbol constitutes an even multiple of a percentage (here: 5%) of the population within each polygon, the map presents

> firstly, the number of pensioners within each area enclosed by a polygon
> secondly, their percentage of the total population of each area.

205

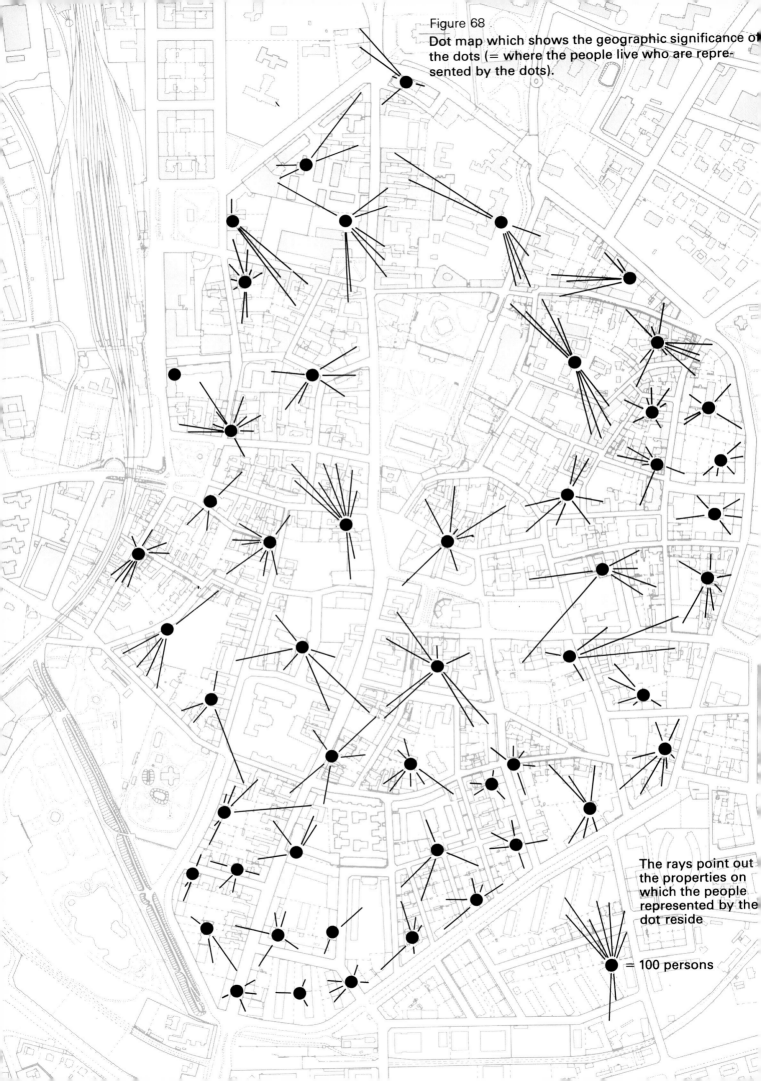

Figure 68.
Dot map which shows the geographic significance of the dots (= where the people live who are represented by the dots).

The rays point out the properties on which the people represented by the dot reside

= 100 persons

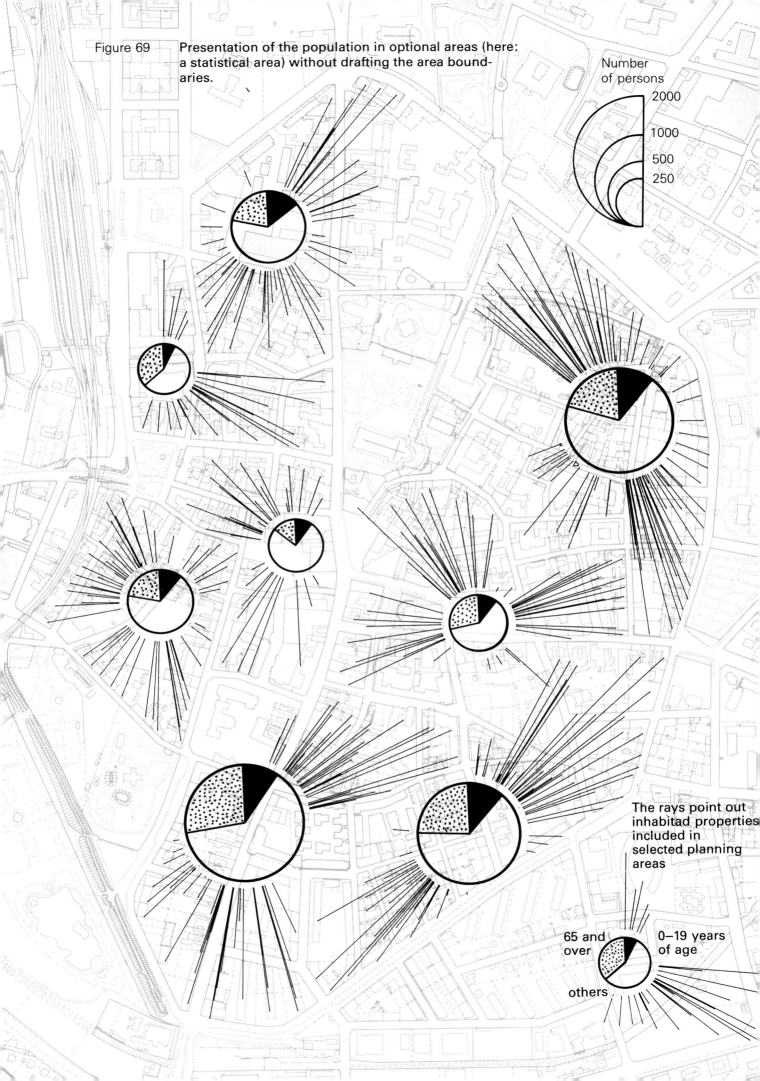

Figure 69   Presentation of the population in optional areas (here: a statistical area) without drafting the area boundaries.

Number of persons

2000

1000

500

250

The rays point out inhabitad properties included in selected planning areas

65 and over   0–19 years of age

others

The map thus presents the mapped population in itself and also as a part of a larger population. Similar maps can be produced for other units (such as dwellings, manufactured goods, etc.).

b) *A dot map which shows the internal structure of the population.*

The upper part of figure 67 shows the settlement patterns of inhabitants in the centre of the town of Lund. Each symbol represents 100 people. The sectorial division of the circles shows the age structure of each group (black sector: 0-19 years of age; dot screen: 65 years of age or older). The sectors' percentage values (which are easy to estimate) show the relative shares *and* the absolute numbers of people simultaneously since each percent equals 1 person. The geographical distribution pattern of the population does not appear as clearly as in a dot map. Since each symbol represents the same value, the map is still relatively easy to read. The circle sectors provide valuable supplemental information. The polygon subdivision indicates, moreover, the areas where these 100 people reside — an important piece of information.

Similar maps can for instance show the distribution of a population among different categories of employment occupation, etc.

c) *Dot maps which show the geographical implications of the point symbols.*

A number of lines radiate out from the point symbols in figure 68. Each line connects the point symbol with a property where there reside people who are represented by the symbol. Since the number of people re-presented by a symbol is predetermined to be 100, it is not possible to identify a property within which a particular individual resides. The personal integrity of the mapped population is thereby protected. The readers of the map still obtain a clear conception of the geographical distribution of the population represented by each point symbol.

d) *A dot map which reproduces movements.*

Arrow maps — i.e. dot maps whose point symbols are shaped like arrows — suggest movement by their graphic design. This feature can be rein-forced. An arrow map which reproduces movements between two points can be designed in the following way.

Each arrow represents a certain, predetermined number of persons which originate from the same area, move towards the same destination, and are assumed to travel as the crow flies and *simultaneously.* It is also assumed that the starting times and the speed of the movements are known. In this case we can reproduce graphically the path of movement traced by these per-sons per unit of time — for example each 5th minute. The image will be highly-simplified: the map will show the path of movement projected along a line representing the shortest distance between the origin and the destina-tion. Such a map can be constructed for predetermined points in time. The map will show the location of all persons in motion and how long they have been in motion as well as their points of origin. If journeys to work are

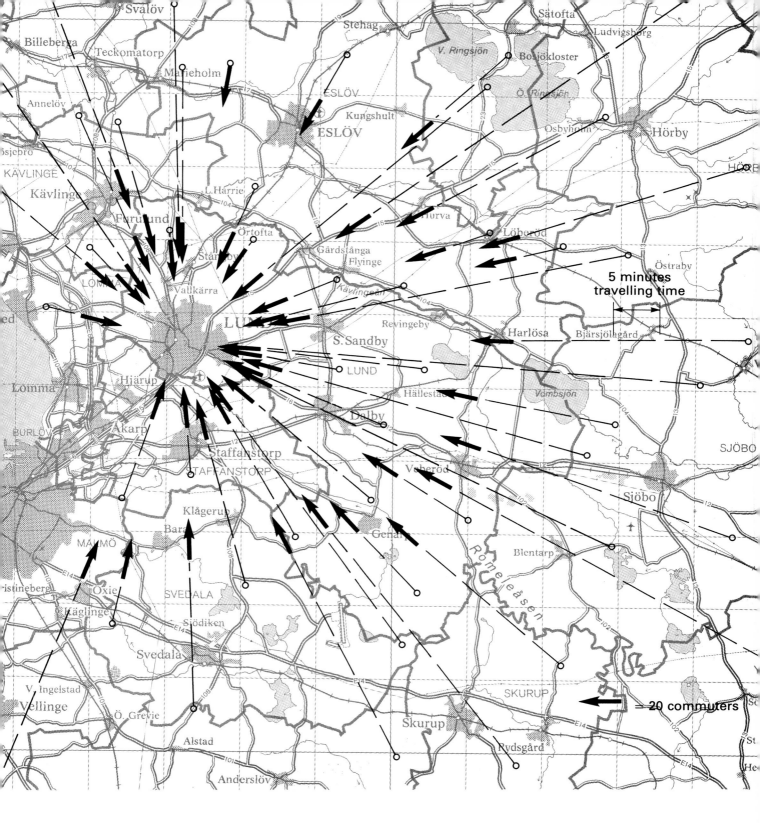

Figure 70   Commuters in motion towards their places of work in the
             morning. Each arrow represents 20 people who work in
             the city of Malmö and live near one another. The "first
             wave" starts at 8 o'clock, the second at 8.30. Each
             segment of the broken line represents 5 minutes of
             movement.

presented with the aid of such a map as in figure 70, and if the occupations and branches of industry of the mapped population are known, it is then possible to construct maps which are more realistic simulations of the actual process.

The static dot map can thus be induced to reproduce movements.

Example B): *Development of symbol maps*

The point symbols on dot maps and related types of maps are designed so as to correspond with a given population. The areas which contain this population are formed by the consolidation of smaller sub-areas. (The latter process is usually not accounted for.)

Other symbol maps are based on optionally-demarcated areas whose populations are represented by a symbol. In these cases it is necessary to present the area boundaries (the link between the setting and the actor). The borders of countries, counties or municipalities or the boundaries of statistical areas are some examples. The boundaries of statistical areas especially create difficulties. Maps which contain information such as this are rare and often difficult to reproduce. Figure 69 gives an example of a solution to this problem. The symbols represent populations and their compositions by age within the statistical areas of Lund's urban core. These symbols are centred on selected, centrally-located points. We let a number of lines radiate out from the symbol leading to the reference point for each sub-area (here: a unit of real property) whose population is included in the symbol. Taken together the rays define the statistical area (in this special case its inhabited portions) and special area boundaries do not need to be drafted.

The choice of symbol points can be made mechanically (for example the centre of gravity of the population constitutes the reference point); visually (the reference point is chosen so that the symbol is placed near the visual midpoint of the area) or by a combination of the two (the centres of gravity are determined first. Their positions are adjusted after a visual assessment.)

The radiating lines can be drafted finely or applied as rasters so that they do not become too visually dominant on the map.

The map types presented above are now being developed. The principles of their design were elaborated during the course of this work. Some reservations may be necessary: it is not inconceivable that equivalent solutions have been employed previously in other contexts unbeknown to the author. The illustrations show the first attempts to translate the elaborated principles into computer-drafted maps or — when time was insufficient — into manually-drafted prototype sketches. These prototypes need additional work. In spite of this the examples show that the traditional cartographic methods can be improved with the aid of modern tools which are already available.

2) Development of systems for cartographic analysis

Example A) *Calculations of influence.*

The impact of
fluctuating
influences on a
dynamic
population

The aim of the calculations is to estimate and present cartographically the effect of various sources of influence on a *dynamic* population. The model has been developed primarily to analyse large urbanized areas (major towns), and is especially suitable for analysis of the impact of many similar sources of influence operating simultaneously. The same model is, however, also quite suitable for applications involving an entire region with a population which rearranges itself within the territory during the course of the day.

The movements on which the model is based are the daily journeys to work in a town. It is assumed that the portion of the population who are not gainfully employed stay in the vicinity of their dwellings during the entire day. According to the model, it is the gainfully-employed who create the urban dynamics through their movements between dwelling and work.

Influences and
sources of
influence

The influences whose effects are calculated can be either negative (noise disturbances, air pollution or other emissions) or positive (access to community facilities, supply of services, etc.). It is assumed that the force of the influences can be expressed numerically.

The influences may have distinguishable sources with limited range, or they may affect the entire analysis area without any variation in intensity. The force of the influence may be constant within the entire affected area or may vary geographically, for example fade with increasing distance from the source of influence. The force of influence may vary in time or be permanent through the duration of the observation period.

The internal
dynamics of
towns

The fluctuations of the population within a town are suggested in figure 71. By way of a cross-section through the fictive town, the figure shows the density of the population present simultaneously within the different districts of the town. The solid outline shows the density of the population at night, the broken line the same during the day. The internal dynamics of the town come about through the transition between night-time and daytime situations in the town. The arrow in the lower part of figure 71 indicates the part of the town for which the highly-simplified influence calculations have been carried out. This urban model is assumed to be circular (see figures 72-75 A, C and D showing parts of this simplified model) and consists of three zones: the urban core; a zone with blocks of flats which also contain many premises for other uses (offices, industrial and commercial facilities, etc.) and an outer zone consisting solely of housing (single-family housing).

Urban structure
mapped with
the aid of
population data

In figures 72-75 A and C the town's structure is illustrated with the aid of "TT" (total population density) which consists of the total population and employment density in an area. TT indicates then how densely the basic functions of the town — housing and employment — are packed together in different urban districts. An analysis of a number of towns showed that

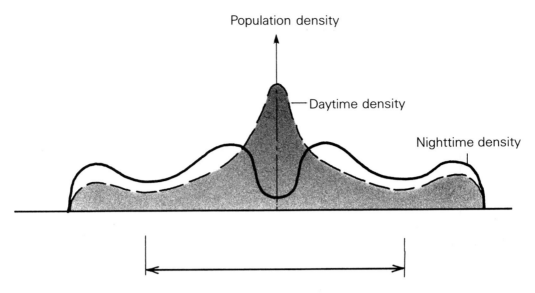

Population density

Daytime density

Nighttime density

The arrow indicates the portion of the model
which is reproduced in figures 72–76

Figure 71   Night-time and daytime population distribution in a town.
The dynamics of an urbanized area arise, among other
things, through the regrouping of the population during
these two phases. Both lines show the total number of
people per hectare. The arrow indicates the part of the
town which is treated in figures 72–76.

a three-dimensional model illustrating this factor for a town exhibits great
similarity with the physical structure of that town. Figure 71:1 shows a
cross-section through a model of this type depicting the town of Lund in
the year 1980. The numerical value of TT

$$TT = BT + ST$$

where BT = housing density, the number of permanent residents per unit
   of area

   ST = employment density, the number of employees per unit of area

TT, BT and ST are all calculated on an area basis, often using statistical
areas. The theoretical background of the method is presented in Szegö
1974.

The half cross-section in figures 72-75 A and C describes the structure of
the imaginary town (black: density of employment; vertical hatching:
housing density). A portion of the population can usually be found in or
near their dwellings — here considered equivalent. Others — the gainfully-
employed — travel back and forth between their dwellings and their places
of work. The number of persons present simultaneously in the different
districts of a town varies — even if, as in the present case, we discount

Fluctuations in
population are
calculated on
the basis of
urban structure

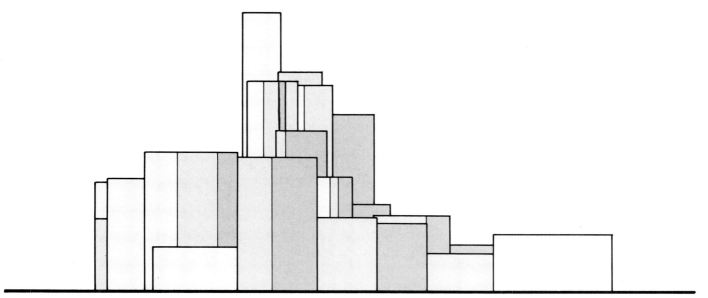

Figure 71:1   The structure of a town illustrated with the aid of
population data. The height of the three-dimensional
model shows the total dwelling and employment density
in the town of Lund, district by district in November
1980.

Figure A. The model observed from the side.
Figure B. A cross-section through the model. The cross-
             section passes through the city core.

Population density
(Inhabitants + employed/hectare)

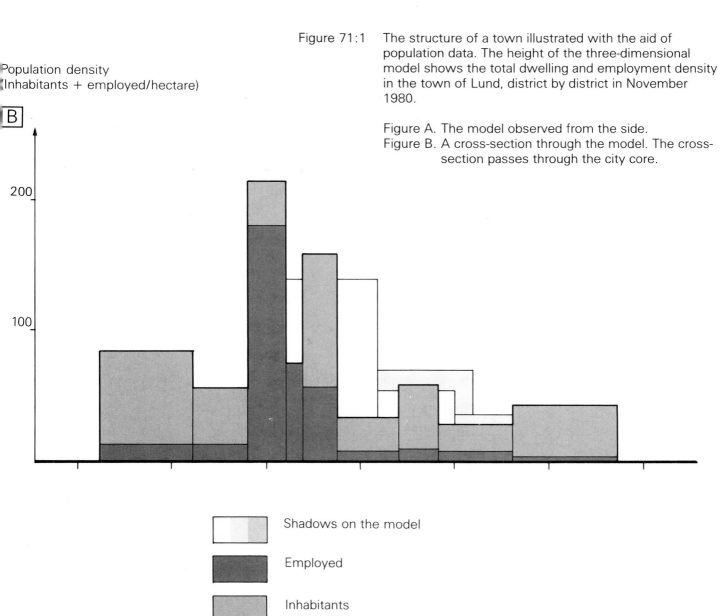

Shadows on the model

Employed

Inhabitants

occasional visits to the town centre. The variations in the density of people simultaneously present are illuminated in diagrams E and H in figures 72-75. Figure H shows how the number of people simultaneously present varies in a test area in the centre of the town. The test area is designated Y and is assumed to cover a surface area of 1 hectare. Diagram H in figure 72 first illustrates housing density — here in the sense of density of residents simultaneously present — during the night (from 0 to t_1). Between t_1 and t_2 the number of remaining residents decreases, but the places of work fill with people (see the black area), and the number of people simultaneously present remains high until the end of the working day at t_3. It then decreases until t_4 after which it remains the same as during the dawn hours.

In test area X the number of people simultaneously present remains constant during the entire 24-hour period since the number of people who leave their dwellings in the test area is identical with the number of people who come to their places of work in the same area.

When employing the model, the calculations are carried out square for square within the entire urban area.

Four typical cases are presented here.

Case 1)   The force of influence is constant within the entire town being studied $(I = 1)$, and is unaltered during the course of the observation period (see figure 72 F and I).

The term: "effect of influence"

The effect of influence IE is

$$IE = I \times TT_i$$

where I = force of influence

TT_i = the number of people simultaneously present per unit of area (residents + employees)

Since $I = 1$, IE varies in relation to the number of people simultaneously present (see figures 72 G and K).

The term "amount of influence"

The shaded area in figures G and K is proportional to the *amount* of influence received by test areas X and Y since the amount of influence = the effect of influence x its duration.

Case 2)   The force of influence is constant throughout the entire area of the town, but it varies in time (see I_1, I_2 and I_3 in figure 73 B). Example: an large volume of air pollution passes through the town. Its force is measured on six occasions. The force IE is assumed to remain constant between these occasions. In test area X where the number of people simultaneously present does not vary, IE varies in relation to the variations in the force of influence (figure G).

In area Y the current population density as well as the force of influence I vary (figures 73 H and I) which produces a complex variation of the effect of influence (figure 73 K).

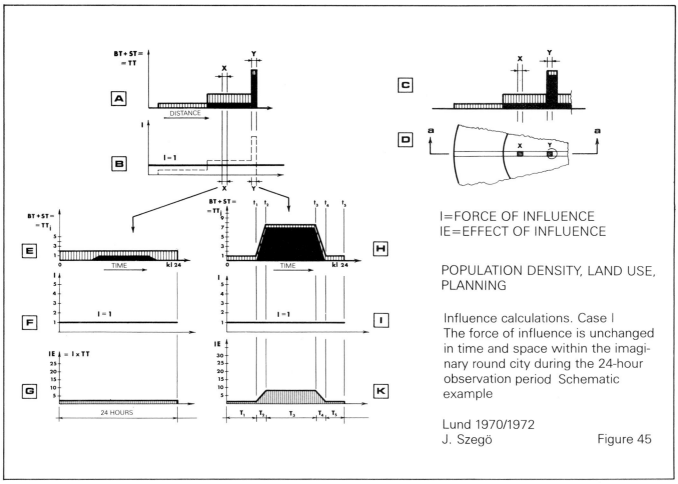

I=FORCE OF INFLUENCE
IE=EFFECT OF INFLUENCE

POPULATION DENSITY, LAND USE,
PLANNING

Influence calculations. Case I
The force of influence is unchanged
in time and space within the imaginary round city during the 24-hour
observation period Schematic
example

Lund 1970/1972
J. Szegö   Figure 45

Figure 72▲   Figure 73 ▼

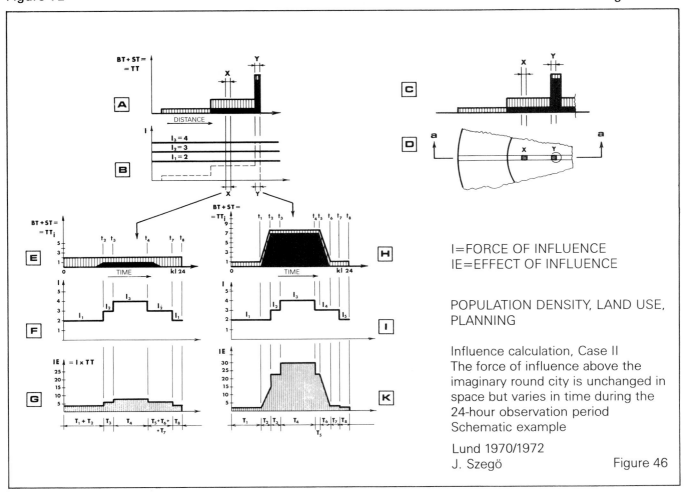

I=FORCE OF INFLUENCE
IE=EFFECT OF INFLUENCE

POPULATION DENSITY, LAND USE,
PLANNING

Influence calculation, Case II
The force of influence above the
imaginary round city is unchanged in
space but varies in time during the
24-hour observation period
Schematic example

Lund 1970/1972
J. Szegö   Figure 46

Case 3) A source of influence IK is located on the border between the outer and intermediate zones of the town (see figures 74 D and B). The force of influence diminishes linearly in all directions (see figure B). The force of influence is constant during the entire observation period in both test areas, but has a higher value in area X since this lies closer to the source IK than area Y.

The effect of influence varies in relation to the number of people simultaneously present.

Case 4) The source of influence IK is located in the same location as in case 3, and its force diminishes linearly from IK but varies as well between different intervals (figure 75).

The force of influence is greater in X than in Y. The effect of influence varies in X in relation to the fluctuations in the force of influence while in Y, variations occur both when the momentary population density changes and when the force of influence varies.

The implementation and presentation of influence calculations

The influence calculations contain two dynamic components: the distribution of the population and the fluctuation of the force of influence in time and space. Census data provide the prerequisites for reconstructing the dynamics of the distribution of the population. The gainfully-employed can be located with the aid of information on their dwellings and places of work. These locations can be indicated using the co-ordinates which describe the location of units of real property. Their movements can be approximated by assuming shortest-distance movements (see figure 70 and the section entitled "A dot map which reproduces movements").

Reconstruction of the movements of the inhabitants

The spatially-referenced population can be assigned to squares — eg. test areas X and Y. The number of people simultaneously present can be calculated for each square for both daytime and night-time situations. It is even possible to approximate transitional periods.

Population maps which "freeze" characteristic situations

The geographical distribution patterns of the population on these different characteristic occasions can be shown with the aid of existing mapping methods. Dot maps can illustrate the distribution patterns of the population; isarithmic maps its density. Grid maps can indicate the number of persons per square.

The effect of influence IE is a factor of the number of people simultaneously present within a square. If the power of influence is constant in time and space its geographical pattern corresponds with the population density. It can be displayed with the help of a grid map or visualized in the form of an isarithmic map.

Complex change

If the power of influence varies in time, a new calculation — and a new map — must be presented for each period in which the power of influence and/or the population distribution differ.

216

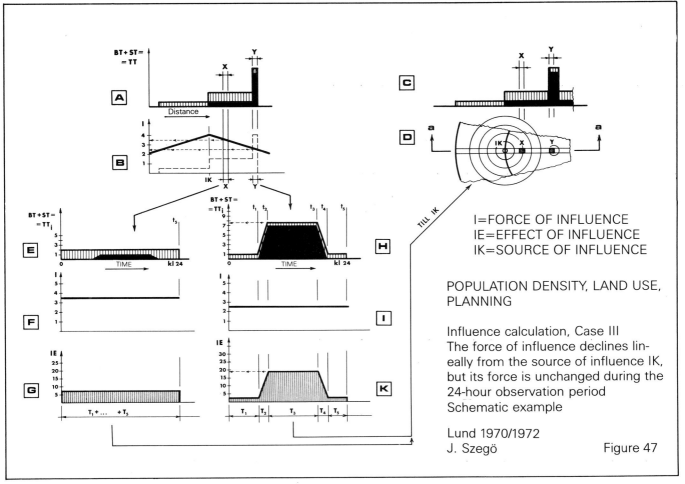

I=FORCE OF INFLUENCE
IE=EFFECT OF INFLUENCE
IK=SOURCE OF INFLUENCE

POPULATION DENSITY, LAND USE,
PLANNING

Influence calculation, Case III
The force of influence declines lin-
eally from the source of influence IK,
but its force is unchanged during the
24-hour observation period
Schematic example

Lund 1970/1972
J. Szegö   Figure 47

Figure 74 ▲

Figure 75 ▼

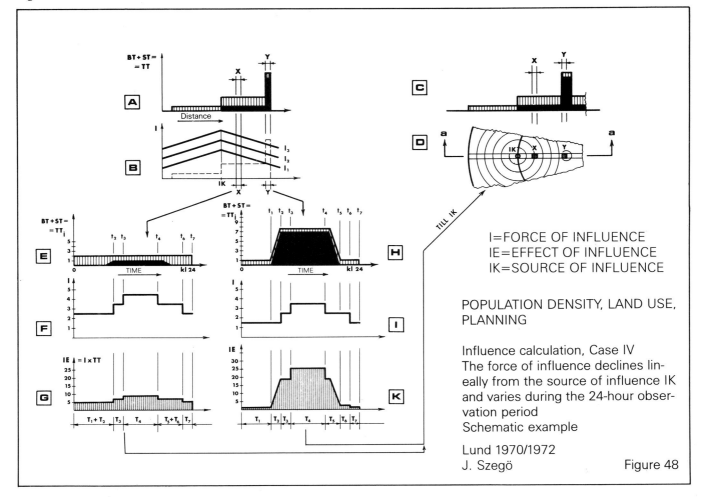

I=FORCE OF INFLUENCE
IE=EFFECT OF INFLUENCE
IK=SOURCE OF INFLUENCE

POPULATION DENSITY, LAND USE,
PLANNING

Influence calculation, Case IV
The force of influence declines lin-
eally from the source of influence IK
and varies during the 24-hour observation period
Schematic example

Lund 1970/1972
J. Szegö   Figure 48

If the power of influence varies in space — there are discernible sources of influence — the power of influence as well as the effect of influence must be calculated square by square. A special computation must be made for each period with an altered population distribution.

Even more calculations must be carried out — and even more maps drafted — when the power of influence varies in time as well as in space. However, these calculations are quite possible to implement and to present in map form using tools and methods currently available in Sweden: the technical and administrative preconditions for creating geo-coded data in registers of population, employment, etc., and for reproducing them in the form of maps without exposing the identity of the people being depicted.

Summary presentations of the effects of influence

Total effects of influence on an entire town (region) — a summary diagram

Other forms for presenting the results of the calculations can also be considered. If we sum up at regular intervals the effects of influence IE affecting each and every square, we obtain the total effect of influence IE on the entire town on these occasions. If we plot these (total) values on a diagram constructed as in figure 73 K, we obtain a summary of the fluctuations of the total effect of influence on the town. The shaded area of the diagram then presents the total amount of influence (the effect of influence x its duration) which arises in the entire town during the observation period.

Another summary presentation is shown in figure 76 H. It answers the following question. Assume that a source of influence with a power that fluctuates in time is operating within a town. Within which areas and during what periods does its power exceed a certain given or optional threshold value, I_{TR}?

Where and when is a threshold value exceeded? A four-dimensional map in three dimensions

Figure G shows the surface area of the town with its three zones and the source of influence IK located within it. The three triangles above it show the variations in the force of influence with increasing distance from the source of influence IK on three occasions and three values of I_{TR}. In figure H is shown the circular space within which the force of influence exceeds I_{TR}. The vertical axis represents time. We can see how the area of influence expands when the force of influence at the source first increases and then diminishes (without transition). Finally, figure K presents, in the form of a cross-section, how the force of influence varies in time as well as space *within* the area thus demarcated (where and when does the force of influence exceed the value I = 4.5 for example? See the black core). The principle of construction is illuminated in figures A-F.

The last solution is somewhat more demanding technically, but is fully possible to implement with the aid of tools of computerized cartography which are currently available and employing the methods of CAD/CAM.

218

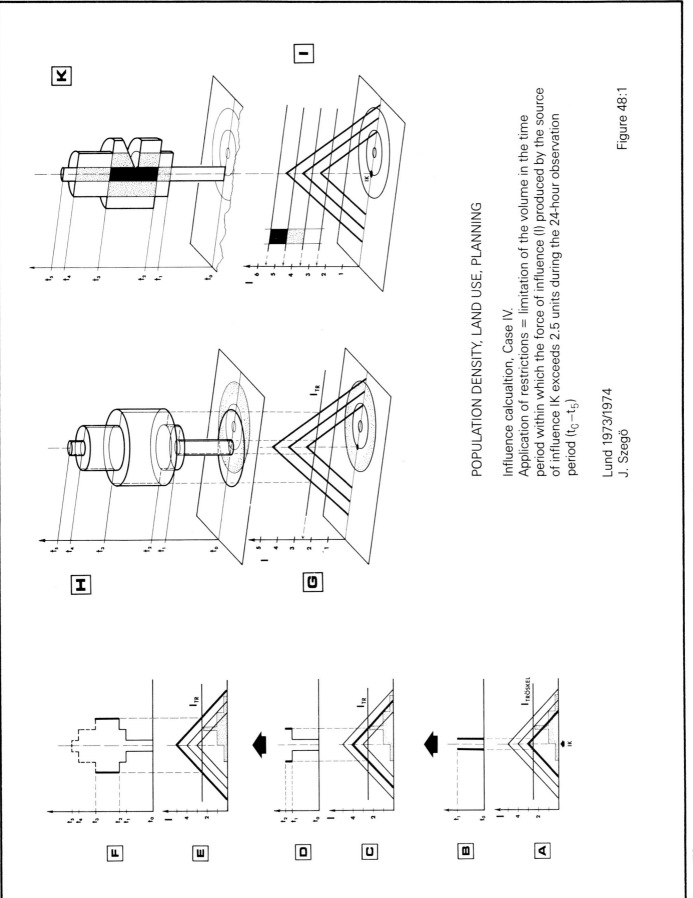

POPULATION DENSITY, LAND USE, PLANNING

Influence calcualtion, Case IV.
Application of restrictions = limitation of the volume in the time
period within which the force of influence (I) produced by the source
of influence IK exceeds 2.5 units during the 24-hour observation
period $(t_0 - t_5)$

Lund 1973/1974
J. Szegö

Figure 48:1

Figure 76

219

Example B: A system for an overview of cartographic information

Map information forms "cultural deposits". The need for an overview

Maps are continually being produced in great numbers in all corners of the globe. The production of landscape information in Sweden for the year 1979 for instance was estimated at approx. 1.5 thousand million SEK (AgLinFou 1986). The continuous production of cartographic material forms a kind of "cultural deposit" with an abundance of informational content for which it is hard to form an overall view. It is not only difficult to assess which geographic areas the maps cover, but also what kinds of information they contain. Another important aspect is the chronology of the information. It is essential to know when or during which period the informational content of a map was produced or for which periods and geographical regions a certain type of information is available.

"Information geography" and "information geology" profiles

In the first part of this book, (Wanderings in time and space) a method was outlined for analysing masses of geographical information in these terms. The method is first determines the geographical coverage of the individual maps and their time co-ordinates. Taking this as point of departure, a number of, what could be called, geographical profiles are then constructed showing the fluctuations of the volume of cartographic information along selected lines. The profiles indicate not only the total informational density along the profiles, but also from what periods these volumes of information originate. Somewhat disrespectfully, we have named them "information-geology profiles".

The need for "second level maps"

In that instance, the method under discussion was given an extremely simple form. Differences in informational density between different maps was disregarded. The time co-ordinates referred only to the median age of the maps (if a map showed conditions between 1775 and 1825 it was then considered to originate in the year 1800). The thematic differences in the cartographic material were also disregarded. The presentation was done solely in the form of profiles, not on maps etc. The method needs to be elaborated in all of these respects as well as some additional ones. It was not possible to complete this work within the framework of the project due to lack of time. However, results of the work now in progress — which are not published here — indicate that the method can well be developed into an effective means of creating "second level maps", maps of the existence and composition of cartographic information. The method is expected to satisfy a need which will become evermore acute with the increase in the volume of cartographic production.

Example C: Mapping change

In contrast to the specific character of the two previous examples (mapping influences and information) the mapping of change is general in nature. Good maps of change are among the most frequently-demanded (and least-often seen). A thorough treatment of the matter would require a separate study. The following brief observations can be made.

There are in principle three types of maps of change:

A) Maps which show existing conditions during certain, characteristic phases of development. When viewed in sequence, these maps of conditions *suggest* change. Example: the populations of the various districts of a town are presented in the form of a pie chart for each district (see figure 48). A similar map is drafted depicting conditions 10 years later, for example.

B) Maps which present the changes themselves, i.e. the dissimilarity which appears when we compare two different situations. In order for the implications of the change to appear clearly, the change can be presented against the background of either the initial situation or the final situation.

   Example: The populations of the various parts of the town of Lund were presented for the year 1965 in the form of graduated circles. Population decrease in a district up to 1969 was illustrated as a black circle sector; growth as an extra black circle sector with the same radius placed adjacent to the circle representing the 1965 population (see figure 50).

C) Maps which show the actual *process* of change. The change in population size depends — partly — on migration within a town as well as in and out-migration. Specially-designed arrow maps can illustrate this process (Borgegård 1984, see figure 76:1).

The development of good maps of change is one of the most urgent tasks in the field under discussion.

Development efforts according to III. Improving the cartographic methods of today aided by the technology of tomorrow

Higher speed can mean higher quality

Higher speed, greater accessibility and higher quality in the production of (census) maps are what we can expect when today's cartographic methods are used in conjunction with new, advanced technology. These seemingly-limited improvements may have a decisive influence on the use of census cartography in a planning context, for example. Today, map production is largely characterized by batch processing. There are often gaps of several days between the various stages of production. The concepts on which the map is based become stale before the map is finished.

Closer to the user

Maps are often produced at central production units several hundreds of kilometres from the client. Face-to-face contact between the producer and the client is, therefore, not possible. This sharply limits the opportunities for discussions. A new phase ("a loop") in the discussions is only possible after the first version is produced and its deficiencies become visible when the map arrives by post.

Contact between the production facility and the client/user can be more spontaneous if the order — i.e. the specifications of the attributes of the future map — is made by way of a terminal (after preliminary discussions). A criterion for a smoothly-operating system is, however, that the client can immediately see the approximate design and major structural features of his future map, for example on his monitor.

Ordering maps via the terminal

The next major technological advance is when the map user, with the aid of his personal computer, can produce his own map on the spot in an interactive way. Thanks to the large capacity of the personal computer, the operations which at present are carried out in the form of batch processing will probably soon be possible to implement interactively. The implications of this change are the following. In batch processing all the attributes — parameters — of the future map, for example the scale, the values represented by the map's symbols, etc., are described in advance. The consequences become evident for the client only when he sees the map produced, for example by a drafting machine. In interactive map production, the map appears on a terminal monitor. The individual attributes of the map can be changed there, and the appearance of the modified map can be monitored continually. This makes it possible to alter the governing parameters of the map until the results — which are immediately visible — satisfy the user's demands. With this type of design method, census cartography is much more likely to become an integral part of the planning process. The new technology is expected to be useful not only in the production of simpler, descriptive maps, but also of maps based on more sophisticated mathematical methods such as influence calculations.

Interactive map production via the terminal

The practical matter of drafting the maps is often the source of problems in the map production of today. The pen plotter's pen can be the most fragile link in a cartographic system. It sometimes proves quite difficult in practice to produce a draft with high technical quality of a computer-produced colour image. When it comes to photocopying, it is especially difficult in the case of urban and regional planning where the number of copies needed is often quite limited, to produce copies with good graphic quality at a reasonable cost. This applies not only to colour images but even to black-and-white ones.

Some practical problems

Advances in the printing of computer-drafted images on paper, plastic or the like (hard copy) and in photocopying technology are so rapid, however, that great improvements can soon be expected.

One of the weakest links in the chain of operations leading to the statistical map is the connection of the cartographic theme — here census data — to the map of the physical landscape where it is staged. One of the most fruitful efforts to facilitate the practical application of census cartography may, therefore, be the use of video technology and the processing of video-registered map images to adapt them to the requirements for base maps (which describe the landscape).

The above-mentioned possibilities are, however, not only areas of potential progress but also areas in which efforts are needed if the potential is to be realized.

Development efforts according to IV. New cartographic methods based on the technology of tomorrow

New technology in the field under discussion is characterized by its capacity for handling large volumes of information with a high degree of complexity in ways which are becoming increasingly simple for the operator. The input of graphic information and the output of the result — also in graphic form — can also be expected to improve steadily, and to be carried out in increasingly-varied ways involving a growing number of different media.

Both of these trends can open the door to a number of lines of development.

An enriched language of computer cartography

Direct contact between the map author — the map

The design of a map is often heavily dependent on the technical expertise of the cartographer/map author. A map author who makes no preliminary graphic sketches at all (if such a person exists) is limited to existing forerunners for elaborating his ideas. The more complete the graphic outline made by the map author, the more probable it is that the final result — which is often produced by someone other than the map author — will conform with his intentions. It is inherent in the nature of cartography that the problems of a map appear while they are being solved. The further a map author can follow the future map on the way to its final design, the greater his opportunity to penetrate the problems he has determined to present in map form. One of the major advantages of computer graphics would appear to be that it is becoming increasingly easy to create graphically-competent results — even for people who do not possess professional skills. This should tend to increase freedom of choice with regard to graphic means of expression — at least for those who master the new technology.

Innovative use of the manual air brush has created new forms of expression and furthered the spread of a new approach to historical cartography. A corresponding development may, if conditions are favourable, also take place in other areas of thematic cartography as a result of the advances in the field of computer graphics. Today's system already offers a certain amount of freedom of choice which, for example in the use of colour, is not too far behind the manual methods. The tendency towards increasing flexibility should make itself felt more and more strongly even though the technical advances are extremely unevenly distributed — dramatic improvements in certain respects, stagnation in others, unexpected obstacles for practical applications of available new technology, etc.

The new technology would seem to be particularly well-suited for depicting fading effects, illustrating the consequences of the human presence and human activities which diminish with increasing distance, dynamic proces-

223

ses, overlapping influences, etc. Even more so than for graphic design, the new technology should be of assistance for making calculations concerning the geographical distribution of such effects.

Composite models — presentation, simulation

Sophisticated presentation of complex models

The calculation of influences is an example of a complex mathematical procedure in urban and regional planning. To make the results of such calculations easy to grasp and suitable for widespread use in planning as well as in investigations and research, it is desirable that the results be presented rapidly — preferably interactively — and if possible also using sophisticated forms of expression. Three-dimensional graphics employing transparent and translucent, superimposed sheets can be effective, desirable and often necessary. On the other hand, this manner of map production may help revive interest in complex calculation models which have not enjoyed frequent use during the past 15-20 years in part due to their being costly and cumbersome.

Dynamic models

The state of a dynamic, living society varies continually during the course of a day or week, from season to season and on the longer range. The most sophisticated models can be expected to reproduce these fluctuations. It is conceivable, for example, that influence calculations can be simulated in film-like sequences. They must be able to make dynamic presentations of, for example, variations in population distribution, the fluctuating effects of the various sources of influence, areas within which certain effects are exceeded, etc. Not only should the user be able to observe these processes and perhaps see them repeated. He should also be able to "dissect" the model, to stop certain sequences, to lift out various aspects and pose specific questions about their significance. He should be able to "zoom in" certain portions of the observed area and also of its thematic content — as outlined in the section concerning the conceptual world of the planner. It is necessary in this context, however, to be prepared to analyse complex conceptual structures. For the planner to be able to make such an analysis with a reasonable amount of effort, the graphic presentation must be exceedingly distinct, and the problems must be correspondingly well organized and well presented.

Presentations with shifting approaches, levels of detail, modes of presentation

The most advanced atlases of historical events are characterized in part by their integrated use of maps, illustrations and text, in part by the fact that the contents, level of detail and cartographic language vary from map to map. These changes are accomplished in a way which enables the maps to be mutually supplementary and illuminating.

A corresponding development can hopefully take place in the field of computer cartography. It is expected that it will be possible within a foreseeable future to create individual maps with data from several diffe-rent sources: to integrate digital measurement data, map data acquired through scanning, satellite data and aerial photographic elements with digital, geo-coded information from registers. Editing and design capabilities can be expected to become steadily more advanced.

The first signs of the new technology have been visible on the heavens for awhile. Complex editing systems were presented several years ago which produce printed matter incorporating both graphic and textual elements. Similar "desk-top publishing systems" — somewhat simpler yet still highly-effective and based on personal computers — are currently enjoying great popularity.

Systems with "zooming-in" capabilities for displaying maps describing the landscape — i.e. with the ability to delve down into the observed segment of the terrain and to display it in ever-greater detail — have been presented in the professional journals (Taylor 1986). Interactive video technology and image storage on compact discs improve the prerequisites for image processing. In the English "Domesday Project" these capabilities have already been utilized to a considerable extent.

These lines of development will probably converge to create presentation systems which integrate different data sources and present the data using a combination of different output equipment (colour monitors, colour photos as "hard copy", digitally-produced printing plates and/or digitally-stored images on tape, discs or other memory media, and possibly even optical media (for example, holographic images or perhaps other, entirely new ways of projecting images).

They will hopefully make it possible for the user to observe his own material in ways as diversified as those displayed today only in the best atlases — and to document these concepts in a competent manner. When we reflect on the scope of the progress which can be expected, we realize that our ability to visualize this future situation is rather limited. Forecasts are, as a rule, only projections into the future of conditions already in existence. It is difficult for us to imagine the ideas and solutions which may crop up during the actual course of development and how they will affect future progress. The diagonal limitation of field IV in figure 65 suggests that actual developments will probably stretch beyond what we can foresee today. It would, however, seem reasonable to assume that substantial advances will be made with regard to the *tools* of computer graphics. It can be expected to become substantially easier than it is today to design individualized solutions to problems, to construct and present tailor-made graphic models adapted to current problems. In favourable instances this may lead to enrichment of the design of models as well as of the presentation of their results.

Information overviews — cartographic information analysis

Large volumes of information will be created in this way. Some of it will be of temporary value. Some will probably have to be stored. It must be possible to process the collected volumes of information as well as to gain an overview of the data. The development and spread of geographical information systems (GIS) will reinforce this need — provided that the present trends prove to be lasting. New systems must be designed which will make possible a comprehensive overview. Simple, schematic prototypes of presentations like the one described in the first part of the book (see Wanderings in time and space) must be further elaborated. Today's accelerated production of geo-data makes this type of activity appear increasingly necessary. It will possibly comprise a special branch of cartometry. Since it must be based on a thorough analysis of the nature and existence of cartographic information, a suitable name for this activity would be *cartographic information analysis*.

Traps to avoid

All of these developmental potentials also create traps which must be avoided.

A new directory technology is needed

The opportunities may be so abundant that everyone — except the creator of the system — is intimidated by the very diversity. A well-arranged presentation is necessary to open up this jungle of opportunities, preferably " an active directory" ("marked trails"). A new kind of teaching strategy, "directory technology", must be developed, adapted especially for the field of cartography. It must be based on human thought patterns rather than on the technological prerequisites. The great financial success enjoyed by user-friendly equipment today proves that this route is not unrealistic. Computer systems which are well adapted to the user attract a lot of interest today. The related questions must be studied with special consideration given to the demands placed by geographical information processing and cartographic presentation.

The technology must be so simple and easy to use that it can even be employed as a matter of course by users without technical ability. There is a tendency which is sometimes observed today for the technology itself to capture and divert the user's attention from the subject area. This is due in part to the technology's inherent fascination but also to the demands which it places on the user.

All of the development potentials outlined above begin to resemble the expectations of the 1960's. The technological prerequisites appear to be slowly catching up with the expectations. Whether or not these hopes and ideas are to be realized at last depends on several factors. Continued technical progress — though perhaps of even greater scope than appears necessary today — is an obvious requirement. Cartographic data of great

226

breadth and uniformity must be made available. It is not by chance that data standardization has been assigned high priority among related issues (see for example AgLinFoU, Autumn 1986). Substantial improvements must be made in the map images created on computer terminals and especially in printed form (hard copy). But above all, it is necessary that interest and know-how with regard to the use of geographically-oriented planning methods be revived. The new technological opportunities can actively contribute to this.

Concluding observations

On the synthesis of geographical content and cartographic form

Map design is an oscillation between ...

All cartographic design — except the purely repetitive kind which strictly imitates previous forerunners — takes place in the interaction between two poles, between two conceptual worlds. One consists of an array of conceptual elements related to the depicted environment, i.e. the observable components, physical structures and processes which take place there. The other pole is comprised of the abstract graphic world and its store of terms and symbols which the map author uses to give form to his observations of the environment.

... geographical elements and ...

The basic elements in the geographical pole are concepts such as "movement", "channel", "node", "territories", etc. The observer who views his environment defines what he sees in such terms and attempts to distinguish patterns in the interaction among them. He notes phenomena which recur in combination with one another and he suspects that they are parts of a pattern. We can call these combinations model elements. A group of such elements form model components and finally an entire model. The model elements can be very diversified in composition depending on the nature of the reproduced phenomena, but together they form three different categories of model components, namely the setting where the illustrated phenomena take place, the actors who appear there and the interaction among them: the play. (See figure 77, left side.)

... cartographic ones

The observer needs tools to formulate his thoughts and relate them to others. The cartographic pole contains an array of basic elements for this purpose: basic graphic elements — points, lines, areas and alphanumeric symbols — and fundamental rules for their co-ordinated use. Finally — and this is where the boundaries of the field become diffuse — this pole contains knowledge about the relationship between these elements of the environment and the map reader's mental map.

Patterns are sought after

The map author who observes and analyses his environment must turn to the stores of cartographic elements to formulate his thoughts. Formulating a model from scratch implies abstraction and these abstract elements are found in the world of the cartographer. When the abstract image of the environment assumes the form of graphic symbols, a picture emerges

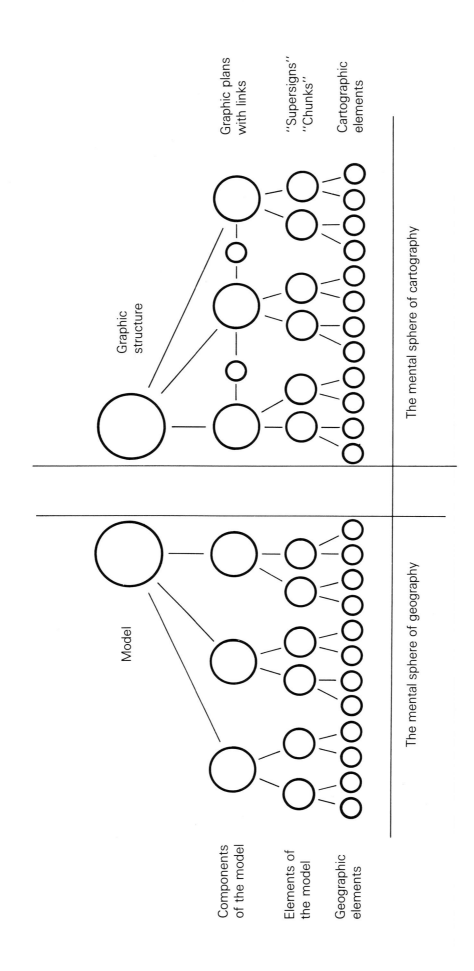

Graphic plans
with links

"Supersigns"
"Chunks"

Cartographic
elements

Graphic
structure

The mental sphere of cartography

The mental sphere of geography

Model

Components
of the model

Elements of
the model

Geographic
elements

Figure 77   Structure of and relation between the mental spheres of geography and cartography.

228

which is often chaotic, hard to grasp, yet still manageable. It is this image with which the map author labours in order to discover within it a definable and significant internal structure. In practice this can mean that the author creates maps which appear chaotic and meaningless. It is necessary to rearrange and modify the contents of the map, make excerpts from it and combine it with other elements which can imbue the map with meaning. The sign indicating that this goal has been achieved is when the map displays a perceptible, organized pattern. When this phase of the work has been completed, and the discovered pattern has been given a suitable form, a graphic structure will usually appear in which the graphic elements assume their positions according to a distinct order. They are often arranged in visual planes at carefully determined distances from one another, or they may be arranged in other, logically-motivated patterns in the visual space. What appears to characterize good cartography is that it is based on well-organized models of the environment, and consists of graphic structures which are uniformly constructed according to this conceptual model (figure 77, right side).

"Three-dimensional" map images are created ...

The land surveyor who is trained to use stereoscopic aerial photographs learns to view a pair of images with his naked eye until the illustrated terrain appears in three dimensions without the aid of any instrument. Good cartography would appear to place somewhat similar demands on its practitioners. It is a question of combining the observer's picture of the environment with the map designer's graphic construction of it, and adjusting their relationship so that a "three-dimensional image" emerges before the eyes of the observer. When this occurs, when the basic conceptual structure and the graphic form of a map are brought into a suitable, uniform relationship with one another, a kind of "three-dimensional" effect comes about: a living, comprehensible, communicative map, figure 77.

The road to such a map is not a straight one — it is a winding road that oscillates between the conceptual worlds of the observer and the designer, and is symbolized by the suggested, spiral-shaped movement in figure 78.

The convergence of two conceptual worlds

The oscillating movements may in fact be substantially more complex than this. In the first place, a frictionless transition is required between the two conceptual worlds. They should preferably exist within the mind of a single person. This is probably not very common: the world of cartography places other kinds of demands on its practitioners than does geography. Communications between the map author and the map designer may be so smooth that the intentions of the author are realized to a considerable extent. However, in the case of innovative cartographic design — the creation of new cartographic solutions based on new concepts — this kind of concerted effort is still only a poor substitute for the author's giving tangible form to his own thoughts.

If developments now underway in the field of computer graphics continue to progress so favourably, the prerequisites for cartographic design by the map author himself will be considerably improved. If the observer — the map author — is supplied with powerful yet easy-to use tools for giving shape to his thoughts, the gap which inhibits or even blocks the necessary

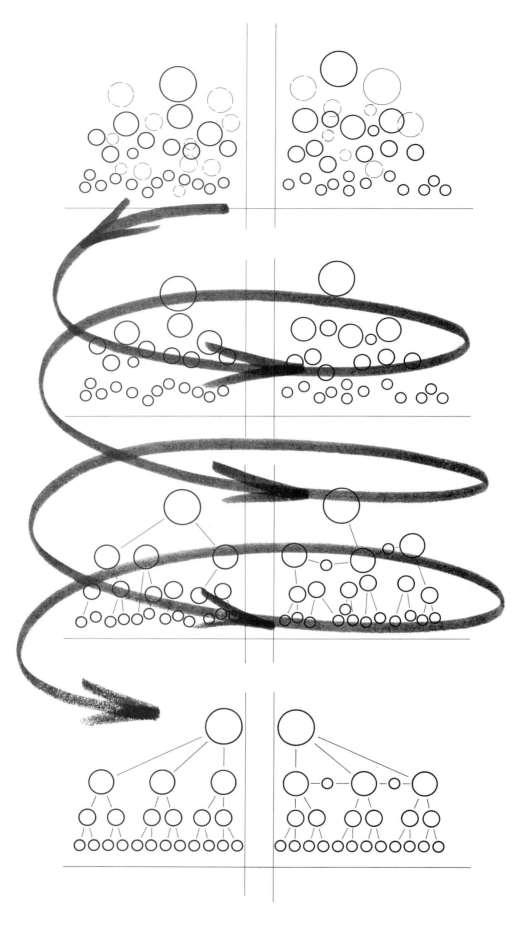

Figure 78   A geographical model is formulated with the aid of
cartographic methods and obtains its expression in a
(well-designed) map.

communication between the two conceptual worlds will disappear. This type kind of "supplemental intelligence" — long foreseen but not yet achieved — may initiate a new phase of strong, perhaps explosive development in the field.

These developments may appear threatening to the pure cartographer whose professional orientation is mainly graphic — especially if his activities are based on manual methods. This is not necessarily a real threat. In the same way as the geographically-oriented map author can gain access to the methods of cartography, the cartographer can use his ability to think in graphic terms to deal with and analyse the geographical problems reproduced on the maps. His work should then be considerably enriched.

The above discussion has only dealt with the individual map. As has been stressed time and time again in this book, a single map is only one — albeit the most important — of many means for presenting aspects of complex processes in time and space. The design of maps is — much more so than the text and even the illustrations — determined by the technical prerequisites. The rather dramatic improvements in these prerequisites expected in the near future will broaden the professional range of the cartographer/geographer. The field may, in the not-too-distant future, include means of expression which were previously reserved for various artistic activities. Maps with richly varied colours, integrated map — illustration — and text elements, animated maps, film-like sequences composed of maps, illustrations and text, graphic tools ("pointers") used for moulding the contents of maps and illustrations and advanced legends in which concepts are chiseled out — these are just a few intimations of things to come. The inspiration may come not only from the field of geography/cartography but also from different fields of artistic endeavour, and lead to the design of maps of human activities which are much more vital than the thematic maps of today. Paradoxically, developments in computer technology may lead to the creation of maps which, when it comes to spontaneity and liveliness, have more in common with the popularly-admired and beloved, hand-drawn maps of the middle-ages and the renaissance than with the strict, formalized cartography of the modern day.

However, certain conditions must be fulfilled for this to happen. Suitable cartographic data must be made available, and computers must be adapted to user needs in such a way that the technology does not impose itself between the user and his future map. An additional precondition is a revived interest in working with spatial/geographical problems, and a renewal of the skills involved in solving such problems by graphic means as well as in presenting these solutions in a creative way.

If these requirements are fulfilled — and the geographer/cartographer must assume a great deal of responsible for this — a new era will be initiated for human cartography.

Bibliography

ADAMS, K.R. (1966)
Cartography in the Psycology of Perception.
Unpublished paper
Experimental Cartography Project. Royal College of Art,
London. Refered to in ROBINSON (1982).

Ag LinFoU Arbetsgruppen för forsknings- och ut-
vecklingsråd inom landskapsinformationsområdet.
(The working party for a research and development
council in the field of landscape information.)
(Lantmäteriverket, Planeringssekretariatet) (1986)
(The Planning Secretariat of the National Land
Survey) *Program för forskning och utveckling inom området
landskapsinformation.* (Programme for Research and
Development in the Field of Landscape Information).

ALFREDSSON, BJÖRN; SALOMONSSON, OWE;
SELANDER, CHRISTER (1970)
Försök med rumslig informationssystem. Introduktion.
(Trial of a spatial information system. Introduction.)
Rapport FRIS A:1.
Centralnämnden för fastighetsdata, Utvecklingsenhe-
ten. (The Central Board for Real Estate Data, Develop-
ment Unit.)

ANTES, JAMES R.; CHANG, KANG-TSUN; MULLIS,
CHAD (1985)
The Visual Effect on Map Design: An Eye Movement
Analysis. *The American Cartographer.* Vol. 12, N.o. 2,
October 1985.

ASKA-gruppen.
Uppföljningsrapport över 1978 års försöksproduktion
av befolkningskartor i Malmöhus län. (Evaluation of
the Test Production of Population Maps in the County
of Malmöhus 1978). September 1979. Gävle/Örebro/
Malmö.

ATLAS ÖVER SVERIGE (1953-1971)
Svenska Sällskapet för Antropologi och Geografi.

BAUDOIN, AXEL (1986) Kartografiske redskaper:
symboler och visuelle variabler. (Cartographic tools:
symbols and visual variables).
Föreläsning vid *Nordisk Sommerskole i Hönefoss*, Norge,
1986. (Lecture at the *Nordic Summer School in Cartography,*
Hönefoss, Norway.)

BERGSTRÖM, LENNART AXEL; NILSSON, BENGT
Redovisningsteknik för kommunal planering. (Presentation
Methods for Municipal Planning). Statens Råd för
Byggnadsforskning, 1977. (The Swedish Board for
Building Research).

BERTIN, JAQUES (1967)
Semiologie Graphique.
Les Diagrammes — les Reseaux — les Cartes.

BESCH, W.; KNOOP, U.; PUTSCHKE, W.; WIEGAND,
H.E. ET AL (1982)
Dialektologie
Ein Handbuch zur deutchen und allgemeinen
Dialektforschung.

BOARD, CHRISTOPHER (1967)
Maps as Models.
Models in Geography. Choarley, R.J — Haggett, P (ed) p
671-725, 1967.

BOARD, CHRISTOPHER (1984)
Higher Order Map-Using. Tasks: Geographical
Lessons in Danger of Being Forgotten.
Cartographica Vol 21, No 1, Spring 1984.

BORGEGÅRD, LARS-ERIK (1984)
Ökad efterfrågan på mindre lägenheter. (Increased
demand for small flats). Tidskriften *Byggforskning*, nr 7,
1984. (Building Research magazine), no. 7.

BRINGEUS, NILS-ARVID (1976)
Människan som kulturvarelse, Lund 1976. (Man as a
Civilized Being).

BRINGEUS, NILS-ARVID (1968)
Skördegudstjänst (Thanksgiving Services).

CARLESTAM, GÖSTA (1986)
Samhällsbyggarna vid Storsjön (The Community Develop-
ers of Storsjön).

CASTNER, HENRY W. (1983)
Research Questions and Cartographic Design.
*Graphic Communication and Design in Contemporary Carto-
graphy,* (ed. D.F.R. Taylor).

A CENSUS ATLAS OF SWEDEN
(Atlas till Folk- och bostadsräkningen) by Janos Szegö.
Published by Statistics Sweden, Central Board for Real
Estates Data, Swedish Council for Building Research
and The University of Lund.

DARBY, H.C., och FULLARD, HAROLD (ed.) (1970)
The New Cambridge History Atlas.
Maps: Georg Philips Ltd.

DOBSON, MICHAEL W. (1977)
Eye Movement Parameters and Map Reading.
The American Cartographer, Vol 4, No 1, 1977, pp 39-58.

EDLUND, L-E,; FRIES, S. (ed)
Diabas — Datamaskinell dialektgeografi och dialektometri,
(Diabas — Computerized Dialect Geography and
Dialectometry). Umeå 1986.

EASTMAN, J. RONALD (1985)
Graphic organisation and memory structures for map
learning.
Cartographica, Vol 22, No 1, 1985, pp 1-20.

FOLVING, STEN (1986)
Elementaere grupperings/klassifikationsmetoder.
Kartometriske begrepp. (Elementary grouping/classifi-
cation methods).
Föreläsningar hållna vid *Nordisk Sommarkurs i Kartografi,*
Hönefoss, Norge, 1986. (Lecture held at the *Nordic
Summer Shcool in Cartography,* Hönefoss, Norway).

FRASER TAYLOR; D.R. (Ed) (1983)
*Graphic Communication and Design in Contemporary Carto-
graphy.* Progress in Contemporary Cartography.

GILBERT, MARTIN (1966)
Recent History Atlas.
Cartographer: FLOWER, JOHN

GILBERT, MARTIN (1968)
British History Atlas.
Cartographer: BANKS, ARTHUR

GILBERT, MARTIN (1968)
American History Atlas.
Cartographer: BANKS, ARTHUR

GILBERT, MARTIN (1978)
Imperial Russian History Atlas.
Cartographer: BANKS, ARTHUR

GILMARTIN, PATRICIA P. (1986)
Maps, Mental Imagery and Gender in the Recall of
Geographical Information.
The American Cartographer, Vol 13, No 4, 1986, pp 335-344.

GOULD, PETER; WHITE, RODNEY (1986)
Mental Maps. 2nd edition.

GRAVES, M.E. (1951)
The Art of Colour and Design.

HAGGET, PETER (1965)
Location Analysis in Human Geography.

HANSSON, ÅKE (1986)
Europeiska förebilder i fråga om dialektometrisk
metod. *DIABAS* nr 1. Umeå Universitet, Umeå.
(European precursors with regard to dialectometrical
method. *DIABAS* no. 1, The University of Umeå,
Umeå).

HARVEY, P.D.A. (1980)
The History of Topographical Maps.
Symboles, Pictures, Surveys.

HEAD, GRANT, C. (1984)
The map as a natural language. *Cartographica,* vol 21, nr
1, Spring 1984, pp 1-32. *New Insights in Cartographic
Communication.* Christoper Board, ed.

HEYDEN, A.A.M.; SCULLARD, H.H. (1969)
Atlas of the Classical World.

HODGE, FRANCIS (1971)
Play Directing Analysis, Communication and Style.

HOLMBERG, STIG C. (1985)
*Some remarks on computer supported cartographic information
systems.* The Royal Institute of Technologi Dept of
Geodesi Stockholm.

HÄGERSTRAND, TORSTEN (1955)
Statistiska primäruppgifter, flygkartering och "datapro-
cessing maskiner". (Statistical primary data, aerial
mapping and computers). *Svensk Geografisk Årsbok.* (The
Swedish Geographical Yearbook).

HÄGERSTRAND, TORSTEN (1957)
Migration and Area. *Migration in Sweden. A Symposium.*
Lunds Studies in Geography. Serie B, nr 13.

HÄGERSTRAND, TORSTEN (1962)
Geographic Measurement of Migration. *Entretiens Ade
Monaco en Sciencies Humaines.* Monaco 1962.

HÄGERSTRAND, TORSTEN (1974)
Tidsgeografisk beskrivning. Syfte och postulat. (Time-
geographical descriptions. Purpose and postulate).
Svensk Geografisk Årsbok 1974. Årgång 50. (The Swedish
Geographical Yearbook, vol. 50).

HÄGERSTRAND, TORSTEN (1985)
Den geografiska traditionens kärnområde. (The core of
the geographical tradition). Geografiska Notiser nr 3,
1985, sid 3-7. (Geographical News, no. 3, pp. 3-7).

HÄGERSTRAND, T – CARLSTEIN, T, – LENNTORP;
B – MÅRTENSSON, S
Individers dygnsbanor i några hushållstyper. (The
daily paths of individuals in some types of households).
Urbaniseringsprocessen, nr 18, 1968. (The Urbanization
Process, no. 18).

HÖGRELIUS, JAN (1983)
Massor av fakta men liten kunskap — den stora
teorilösheten i statistik och planering. (Volumes of fact
but little knowledge — the great lack of theory in
statistics and planning).
Tidskriften *Reko,* nr 4, 1983. (REKO magazine, no. 4).

IGN INSEÉ (1980)
Institut Geographique National. *Population Francaise.*

IMHOF, EDUARD (1972)
Thematische Kartographie.

INTERNATIONAL CARTOGRAPHIC ASSOCIATION
(1984)
Basic Cartography for Students and Technicians.
Vol 1, 1984.

JENKS, GEORG F. (1973)
Visual Integration in Thematic Mapping: Fact or
Fiction? *International Yearbook of Cartography* XIII.

KEATS, J.S. (1973)
Cartographic Design and Production.

KEATS, J.S. (1982)
Understanding Maps.

KINDER, HERMANN; HILGEMANN, WERNER (1964
resp 1966).
dtv-Atlas zur Weltgeschichte, vol I-II, Munchen 1964; 1966.
The Penguin Atlas of World History I-II (1974; 1978).
Cartography: BUKOR, HARALD och BUKOR,
RUTH

LeGUIN, URSULA, K. (1975)
A Wizard of Earthsea.

LEVAN, NILS (1969)
Om pendling mellan bostad och arbetsplast. (On Commuting between Dwelling and Place of Work). Meddelanden från Lunds Universitets Geografiska Inst. Avh XXXVIII. (Report from the Geographical Institution at the University of Lund. Doctoral thesis XXXVIII).

LeGOFF, JACUES – NORA, PIERRE (1974, Stockholm 1978) OD-ÉN, BIRGITTA (urval och inledning)
Att skriva historia. (Writing history).

LENNTORP, BO (1976)
Paths in Space-Time Environments. A Time-geographic Study of Movement Possibilities of Individuals. Meddelanden från Lunds Universitets Geografiska Institution. Avhandlingar LXXXIV.

LIDMAN, SVEN m fl (1981)
50 sekler — Världshistorien i ord och bild. Stockholm 1981, 395 sidor. (50 Centuries — The History of the World in Words and Pictures. Stockholm, 395 pp.)

LIDMAN, SVEN (1981)
Berätta med bilder. (Tell it with pictures).

LYNCH, KEVIN (1969)
The Image of the City.

LIDSTRÖM, SVEN (1986)
Muntlig kommunikation beträffande utveckling inom datorkartografins tekniska förutsättningar. (Verbal information concerning the development of the technological prerequisites of computer cartography).

LMV, SSAG, SCB (1986)
Förslag till ny svensk nationalatlas. (Proposal for a New Swedish National Atlas). LMV-rapport 1986:12.

MACEACHREN, ALAN M (1986)
A Linear View of the World: Strip Maps as a Unique Form of Cartographic Representation. *The American Cartographer.* Vol 13, No 1, 1986, pp 7-25.

McEVEDY, Colin (1961)
The Penguin Atlas of Medieval History. Maps: WOODCOCK, J.

McEVEDY, Colin (1967)
The Penguin Atlas of Ancient History. Maps: WOODCOCK, J.

McEVEDY, Colin (1972)
The Penguin Atlas of Modern History (to 1815). (Maps lettered): ATANASOFF, IVAN.

McEVEDY, Colin (1980)
The Penguin Atlas of African History.

McNEILL, William (1967)
A World History.

McEVEDY, Colin; JONES, Richard (1978)
Atlas of World Population History.

MONMONIER, MARK STEPHEN (1981)
Trends in Atlas Development. *Cartographica.* Vol 18, No 2, 1981, pp 187-211.

MONMONIER, MARK STEPHEN (1985)
Technological Transition in Cartography. University of Wisconsin Press, Madison, 1985.

MORRISON, JOEL L (1978)
Towards a Functional Definition of the Science of Cartography with Emphasis on Map Reading. *The American Cartographer,* Oct 1978.

MORRISON, JOEL L (1984)
Applied Cartographic Communication: Map Symbolisation for Atlases. *New Insights in Cartographic. Communication;* BOARD, Ch. (ed). *Cartographica* 1984.

MUEHRCKE, PHILLIP (1981)
Maps in Geography. *Cartographica.* Vol 18, No 2, Summer 1981. Geographical Perspectives on the New Cartography, Guelke, L. (ed).

MUEHRCKE, PHILLIP (1982)
An Integrated Approach to Map Design and Production. *The American Cartographer.* Vol 9, No 2, 1982, pp 109-122.

MUELLER, JEAN-CLAUDE (1985)
Mental Maps at Global Scale. *Cartographica.* Vol 22, No 4, 1985, pp 51-59.

MÅRTENSSON, SOLVEIG (1979)
On the Formation of Biographies in Space-Time Environments. Meddelanden från Lunds Universitet. Avhandlingar LXXXIV. (Report from the University of Lund. Doctoral thesis LXXXIV.

NORDBECK, STIG – RYSTEDT, BENGT (1972)
Computer Cartography, Lund 1972.

NORDBECK, STIG – RYSTEDT, BENGT (1970)
Isarithmic maps and the continuity of reference interval functions. *Geografiska Annaler.* (The Geographical Annals). B 2.

NORDBERG, MICHAEL
Asiens Historia till 1914. Stockholm 1979.

NORDSTRÖM, OLOF (1970)
Redovisning av statistiska data i utvecklingsländer. (Presentation of statistical data in developing countries). *Svensk Geografisk Årsbok* 46, 1970. (The Swedish Geo graphical Yearbook. vol. 46).

OLSSON, ANNALIISA; SELANDER, CHRISTER (1971)
A Spatial Information System. A Pilot Study: Dot Maps by Computers. *FRIS* C:2, May 1971. Central Board for Real Estate Data. Development Department.

OLSSON, STIG
Muntlig kommunikation beträffande kartografisk metodik. (Verbal information concerning cartographic methods).

OMMER, ROSEMARY, E. – WOOD, CLIFFORD, E.
Data, Concept and Translation to Graphics. *Cartographica.* Vol 22, No 2.

OPPEN, WILLIAM A., (1978)
The Riel Rebellion: A Cartographic History. *Cartographica.* Monograph nr 21-22/1978.

PALM, CHRISTER (1986)
Behandling och arkivering av kartografiskt material. Taktila kartor (Handling and storage of cartographic materials. Tactile maps). Föreläsningar hållna vid Nordiska Sommarskolan i Kartografi. Hönefoss, Norge, 1986. (Lecture held at the *Nordic Summer School in Cartography,* Hönefoss, Norway.

235

PEOPLE IN BRITAIN
A Census Atlas
Census Research Unit Dept. of Geography. Univ. of
Durham.

PETCHENIK, BARBARA BARTZ (1977)
Cartography and the Making of an Historical Atlas: A
Memory.
The American Cartographer. Vol 4, No 1, 1977 pp 11-28.

PETCHENIK, BARBARA BARTZ (1983)
A Map Maker's Perspective on Map Design Research
1950-1980. *Graphic communication and Design in Contemporary Cartography,* pp 37-67.

PETCHENIK, BARBARA BARTZ (1985)
The Natural History of the Atlas.
Cartographica. Vol 22, No 3, Autumn 1985.

PETERY, ZOLTAN (1972)
Studier i svensk regional planering. (Studies in Swedish
Regional Planning). Meddelanden från Lunds Univer-
sitets Geografiska Institution. Avhandlingar LXVIII.
(Report from the Geographical Institutionen at the
University of Lund. Doctoral thesis LXVIII).

POST, J.B. (1973)
An Atlas of Fantasy.

PROVAKATIS, TEOCHARIS (1980)
Monastry of Arkadi. Athen, 1980.

RAISZ, ERWIN (1948)
General Cartography.

RATAJSKI, LECH
The Research Structure of Theoretical Cartography.
International Yearbook of Cartography XIII. 1973.

REITE, ARILD (1986)
Kartverkets lösningar m.h.p. EDB-assistent kartografi
(The Survey Department's solutions regarding compu-
ter-assisted cartography). Föreläsning vid *Nordisk
Sommarskola i Kartografi,* Hönefoss, Norge. (Lecture at
the *Nordic Summer School in Cartography,* Hönefoss, Norway).

REGNÉLL, HANS (1982)
*Att Beskriva och Förklara. Vad det kan innebära i olika
forskningsområden.* Lund 1982. (To Describe and Explain.
What This Can Mean in Different Fields of Research).

RHIND, D.W (1986)
Remote sensing, digital mapping and geographical
informations systems: the creation of national policy in
the UK. *Environment and Planning C: Government and
policy,* 1986, 4, 91.

RIMBERT, S. (1986)
From Map Reading to Map Making. Lecture given at
Scandinavian Summer Scool of Cartography. Hönefoss 1986.

ROBINSON, ARTHUR H. (1952)
The Look of Maps. An Examination of Cartographic Design.
University of Wisconsin 1952.

ROBINSON, ARTHUR H. (1977)
Research in Cartographic Design. *The American Cartographer.* Vol 4, No 2, 1977, pp 163-169.

ROBINSON, ARTHUR H. (1982)
A Program of Research to Aid Cartographic Design.
The American Cartographer. Vol 9, No 1, april 1982, pp
25-29.

ROBINSON, ARTHUR – SALE, RANDALL D.
– MORRISON, JOEL L.
Elements of Cartography. 4e. 1978.

RYSTEDT, BENGT (1977)
The Swedish Land Data Bank. A Multipurpose
Information System. Page 19-48 in Computer Cartography in Sweden. *Cartographica.* Monograph nr
20/1977. Supplement to Canadian Cartographer. Vol 14
1977. Ed D.F.R. Taylor – B. Rystedt – O. Wastesson.

SCOTT, R.G. (1951)
Design Fundamentals.

SIEKIERSKA, EWA (1984)
Towards an Elektronic Atlas. *Cartographica.* Auto-Carto
Six, Selected papers. Vol 21, No 2-3, 1984.

SPENCER; J.E – THOMAS, W.L. (1969)
Cultural Geography – an Evolutionary Approach.

SPIESS, ERNEST (1986)
Symbol Use; Class Intervals in Thematic Cartography.
Föreläsningar vid *Nordisk Sommarskola i Kartografi,*
Hönefoss, Norge, 1986.

SVENSKA SLLSKAPET FÖR ANTROPOLOGI OCH
GEOGRAFI (1953-1971)
Atlas över Sverige.

STRACHEY, BARBARA (1981)
Journeys of Frodo. An Atlas of J.R.R. Tolkiens's The Lord
of the Ring.

SZEGÖ, JANOS (1969)
Befolkning och bostäder i Lund. En grafisk presentation.
(Population and Housing in Lund. A Graphic Presentation). Stadsarkitektkontoret i Lund. (The City Architect's Office, Lund).

SZEGÖ, JANOS (1972)
*Studenter i Lund 1970. En kompletterande undersökning till
Folk- och bostadsräkningen 1979.* (Students in Lund 1970. A
Supplemental Study for the Census of Population and
Housing 1979). Stadsarkitektkontoret i Lund. (The
City Achitect's Office, Lund).

SZEGÖ, JANOS (1974)
*Befolkningstäthet, markanvändning, planering. Total be-
folkningstäthet som centralt element i en modell för beskrivning,
analys och planering av städers aktivitetsmönster.* (Population
Density, Land Use, Planning. Total Population Density
as a Central Element in a Model for Describing,
Analysing and Planning the Activity Pattern of Towns).
Meddelande från Lunds Universitets Geografiska
Institution. Avhandlingar nr 73 1974. Volym 1-2.
(Report from the Geographical Institution of the
University of Lund. Doctoral thesis no. 73. Vol. 1-2).

SZEGÖ, JANOS (1978)
Fastighetskoordinater i kommunal planering. (Property
Co-ordinates in Municipal Planning). Centralnämnden
för fastighetsdata, Gävle. (The Central Board for Real
Estate Data, Gävle).

SZEGÖ, JANOS (1980)
Kartor till FoB -80.
Skissbok nr 2. Förslag till problemstrukturering.
Skissbok nr 3. Utkast till kartförteckning. (Maps to the 1980
Census of Housing and Population. Sketch Pad no. 2.
Proposal for Structuring the Problems. Sketch Pad no.
3. Outline Proposal for Map Catalogue).

SZEGÖ, JANOS (1982)
Befolkningskartor som planeringsunderlag.
Praktikfall: Trafikförsörjningsplan för Hultsfred. (Population Maps as Basis for Planning. Practical Example: Transportation Plan for Hultsfred).

SZEGÖ, JANOS (1984)
Atlas till Folk- och bostadsräkningen.
A Census Atlas of Sweden.
Sveriges Officiella Statistik. (The Official Statistics of Sweden).

TAYLOR, D.F.R. (1985)
The Educational Challenges of a New Cartography.
Cartographica. Vol 22, No 4, Winter 1985.

TAYLOR, BRUCE A. (1986)
Atlas Doesn't Shrug. *Computer Graphics World,* oktober 1986.

THE TIMES ATLAS OF WORLD HISTORY
Barraclough, G. ed. (1978)

TELEMAN, ULF (1982)
Ordens och bildernas språk. (The Language of Words and Pictures). Lund 1982.

TÖRNQVIST, GUNNAR (1963)
Studier i industrilokalisering. (Studies in the Location of Industries). Meddelanden från Geografiska Institutionen vid Stocholms Universitet nr 153. (Report from the Geographical Institution at the University of Lund, no. 153).

TÖRNQVIST, GUNNAR (1978)
Om fragment och sammanhang i regional forskning. (On fragments and context in regional research). I samlingsvolymen *"Att forma regional framtid".* (Shaping Regional Futures).

TÖRNQVIST, GUNNAR (1979)
On fragmentation and Coherence in Regional Research. Lunds Studies in Geography, Ser. B, Nr 45.

WALLIN, ERIK (1977)
Budgeting Human Time. Paper presented at *the Institute of British Geographers Annual Conference,* Newcastle upon Tyne.

WASTENSSON, LEIF (1986)
Geografiämnet i fokus genom ny svensk nationalatlas. (The subject of geography in focus through a new Swedish national atlas). *Svensk Geografisk Årsbok,* årgång 62. (The Swedish Geographical Yearbook, vol. 62).

WESTERMANNS ATLAS ZUR WELTGESCHICHTE (1958)
Atlas till världshistorien. (The Atlas of World History). Svenska kartor: Generalstabens Litografiska Anstalt. Övriga kartor: Georg Westerman, Braunschweig. (Swedish maps: Generalstabens Litografiska Anstalt. Other maps: George Westerman, Braunschweig).

WIKFORS, ÖRJAN (1981)
Information för resurshushållning. Plan nr 3-4, 1981. (Information for resources management).

WONG, K.Y. (1979)
Maps in Minds: an Empirical Study. *Environment and Planning* A, 1979, vol 11.

WÄRNERYD, OLOF (1981)
Att se det stora i det lilla. (To see the big in the small). *Svensk Geografisk Årsbok* nr 57. (The Swedish Geographical Yearbook, vol. 57).

YOELI, PINHAS (1984)
Cartographic Contouring with computer and Plotter. *The American Cartographer.* vol 11, No 2, 1984.

YOELI, PINHAS (1982)
Cartographic Drawing with computers.
Nottingham, England.

ÖBERG, STURE (1976)
Methods of Describing Physical Access to Supply Points. Lunds Studies in Geography. Ser B, No 43.